Owls
of the World

Great Horned Owl *Bubo virginianus* from a series of
engravings published in London by G. Kearsley in 1808.

Owls
of the World

their evolution, structure and ecology

Revised Edition

Edited by John A. Burton

Illustrated by John Rignall

PHILIP BURTON
MICHAEL EVERETT
MICHAEL FOGDEN
HOWARD GINN
DAVID GLUE
COLIN HARRISON
G.P. HEKSTRA
HEIMO MIKKOLA
RONALD MURTON
IAN PRESTT
JOHN SPARKS
BERNARD STONEHOUSE
REGINALD WAGSTAFFE
C.A. WALKER
W. VAN DER WEIJDEN

Peter Lowe

EDITOR'S NOTE

In this book we have attempted to write about and to illustrate every known species of owl. The type of information available about owls varies widely. A few of the common species have been well studied but many others are still largely unknown. The explanation for this is quite simple: not only are most species nocturnal, but most also live in forests, particularly in tropical forests where observation is difficult.

Each chapter has been written by a different author and inevitably there are differences of approach and style. Generally, we have aimed at an ecological rather than a taxonomic approach. We have illustrated as many owls as possible with colour photographs; many, however, have rarely or never been photographed, and these have been specially painted by John Rignall. Although it has not been possible to reproduce these to scale, we have tried to give some sense of size differences.

Some genera are undergoing extensive re-evaluations and experts do not always agree on which birds are full species and which subspecies or races. In cases where species separation is made principally by voice or genetic analysis, or where too few examples are available for an accurate representation to be made, we have not attempted an illustration.

John A. Burton

The Publisher gratefully acknowledges the advice and assistance given by many people in producing this book. Particular thanks are due to:
C. W. Benson, Robert Burton, Michael and Patricia Fogden, Graham Hirons, Dr G. F. Mees and the Rijksmuseum van Natuurlijke Historie, Leiden, the Netherlands, The Academy of Natural Science, Philadelphia, USA, The British Museum (Natural History), Tring, England, the Koninklijk Museum voor Midden-Afrika, Tervuren, Belgium and the Institut vor Taxonomische Zoölogie, Zoölogisch Museum, Amsterdam.

PUBLISHER'S NOTE TO THE THIRD EDITION

Since this book was first produced in 1973 a considerable amount of new information has become available on some genera. New species of owls have been described and there have been taxonomic re-evaluations, often now using DNA and egg-white protein analysis. Knowledge of the prehistory of owls is also increasing. In this third edition, the text has been fully revised and the illustrations updated to include newly separated species, and to correct errors. Revised distribution maps reflect the destruction of habitats in many areas.

We are grateful to Professor K. H. Voous for revising the chapters on What makes an Owl, Hawk Owls and Little, Pygmy and Elf Owls; to Peter Hayman for checking Fishing Owls, Eagle Owls and the Snowy Owl; to Dr David Hollands for his comments on Australasian species of *Ninox*; to Dr Claus König for information on *Glaucidium* species; to Ian Newton for revising the late Ronald Murton's chapter on Conservation and to Michael Everett of the Royal Society for the Protection of Birds.

British Library Cataloguing in Publication Data
Owls of the world—3rd ed.
  I. Owls
  I. Burton, John Andrew
  598.9'7 QL696.S8

ISBN 0 85654 657 7
Printed in Italy

Contents

7 Preface

9 Introduction
BERNARD STONEHOUSE

PART I

14 Owls and humans
JOHN SPARKS

23 The origins of owls
C.A. WALKER

29 What makes an owl
PHILIP BURTON

PART II

36 Barn and Bay Owls
Tyto, Phodilus
MICHAEL EVERETT, IAN PRESTT
AND REGINALD WAGSTAFFE

51 Fishing Owls, Eagle Owls
and the Snowy Owl
Ketupa, Scotopelia, Bubo, Nyctea
MICHAEL FOGDEN

84 Scops and Screech Owls
Otus, Ptilopsis, Lophostrix
G.P. HEKSTRA

108 Wood Owls
Pulsatrix, Ciccaba, Strix, Asio
HEIMO MIKKOLA

141 Hawk Owls
Ninox, Sceloglaux, Uroglaux, Nesasio, Surnia
COLIN HARRISON

159 Little, Pygmy and Elf Owls
*Athene, Speotyto, Micrathene, Aegolius,
Glaucidium, Xenoglaux, Pseudoscops*
HOWARD GINN

182 Conservation
RONALD MURTON

189 Owl Pellets
DAVID GLUE

193 Owl voices
WOUTER VAN DER WEIJDEN
AND MICHAEL EVERETT

PART III

198 Check list of species
200 Glossary
201 Books for further reading
203 Index

Preface

It seems incredible that nearly 20 years have passed since Peter Conder wrote the Preface to the first edition of 'Owls of the World'. He drew attention to man's fascination with owls, something we can trace back to Ancient Greece and beyond. That fascination remains: if anything, it is greater now than it has ever been, especially among ornithologists. This has led to many new discoveries about owl distribution and owl biology, to revisions of some of our ideas about owl taxonomy and, inevitably, to more and more unanswered questions.

Nobody reading this new and thoroughly revised edition can avoid noticing the changes that new scientific study has brought, but also that our knowledge and understanding of many species is still incomplete. A great deal is known about European and North American owls, some of the African species and some of those from Australasia, but our knowledge of most of the remainder—especially tropical forest species and those confined to remote, small islands—ranges from poor to practically nil. I hope that this book will encourage more research—the opportunities for further studies and new discoveries are enormous.

One purpose of this book is to point the way towards a better understanding of owls as predators. Unfortunately, in many of the developed countries at least, there is a long history of misunderstanding and prejudice which has led to a great deal of unjustified persecution. Owls may never have been involved in the sort of hysteria that surrounds creatures like wolves and sharks, but like any predators which are thought to impinge on man's interests they have often been treated as vermin and have suffered accordingly. Helping to change this attitude is one role of any major book on birds of prey.

Fortunately, while misunderstandings persist, direct persecution is not the problem it used to be. Some owls face much greater difficulties, related to the way in which we use the world we share with them. The Barn Owl, traditionally the 'farmer's friend', is an accidental victim of agricultural progress: with careful planning, and the goodwill towards the bird which undoubtedly exists, this is a problem which can be overcome. The Spotted Owl of western North America, on the other hand, is severely threatened by greedy over-exploitation of its old forest habitat by logging; it has, in fact, become symbolic of a conservation battle with implications which reach far beyond the fate of a single species.

This book will help us all to understand more about how owls—and other creatures—relate to their environment and how important it is for us to use that environment wisely. For years to come it will also serve as a standard work of reference, until, as will surely happen, enough gaps in our knowledge have been filled to justify the next revision.

Ian Prestt
President
Royal Society for the Protection of Birds

Introduction

Like penguins or pelicans, owls are easy birds to identify. With few exceptions they look like nothing but owls, and the most inexperienced ornithologist among us knows very well when he is looking at one. Their distinctive appearance—huge head, large, forward-looking eyes, concentrated expressions, chunky body and sober habit—has made us notice them, and owls have insinuated themselves to an extraordinary degree into human affairs. Children the world over meet them in legends and storybooks, humanized and endowed with solemn wisdom—pompous like archetypal headmasters, but on the whole benign. Without owls, advertisers would have to find a new symbol for sound scholarly judgement, and horn-rimmed executives a new professional image.

Small birds, too, react strongly to owls, though their response is inborn, not taught: on sighting an owl, many Passerine birds break off whatever they are doing to 'mob' the bird, making aerial attacks with an elaborate display of alarm and concern. These displays alert the community to the presence of the owl, effectively robbing it of any chance of surprising them. What is there about owls that fascinates humans and small birds alike?

Superficially, owls as a group show several striking qualities which distinguish them from other birds. Many are adaptations to night hunting. Where most birds are strongly diurnal, owls are specialized in hunting in poor evening light and at night. Not all are nocturnal: some hunt by day and by night. But about two-thirds of the 140 or more species of owls are busiest in late evening and during the dark hours, when they become the nocturnal counterpart of eagles, harriers and falcons.

Their prey includes small birds, which as diurnal foragers are ill-adapted for poor light, and at a disadvantage after sunset. A few species hunt actively on the wing, taking moths and other small creatures in flight. This is not a role for which most owls are especially well adapted: far better at catching nocturnal insects on the wing are frogmouths and nightjars (Caprimulgiformes) which are among their closest kin. Some owls are highly skilled fishermen, catching fish in their talons from the surface of rivers; others hunt crabs on shores and river shallows. But most quarter the ground in silent flight, or scan it from a convenient perch, waiting—often listening intently—for ground-living insects and small mammals.

Birds which hunt mainly in poor light or darkness need excellent, specialized eyesight capable of using every scrap of light to the best advantage. The huge owl eyes set forward in the skull to provide overlapping binocular vision have, like expensive cameras, a combination of qualities which render them unusually efficient in dull light. When they are wide open, the owl's eyes are alert and perceptive, especially at night when the circular curtains of irides are drawn back and the dark pupils distended. Half-hooded by heavy eyelids during the day, they remain watchful and efficient, like the eyes of sleepy invigilators. When disturbed in the day, owls see well in daylight, and are also able to adjust remarkably rapidly to the change from day to night conditions.

The eyeballs, shaped like tapering cylinders to provide the largest possible expanse of retina, lack even the small mobility of most birds' eyes; they cannot rotate up, down or sideways. Alerted to some object or movement in its foreground, an owl cannot swivel its eyes like a mammal. Instead it turns its whole head, mounted on unusually flexible bearings, and stares directly with a curiously human intensity. Contrasting with the sideways glance of most birds, this conveys an air of concentrated attention. Owls often spoil this effect by bobbing the head up and down or craning sideways at an alarming angle, behaviour which probably helps them to judge distance.

Many species of owls have flexible tufts of feathers above the eyes, usually held obliquely or vertically, which look like ears or eccentric eyebrows, but are in fact neither. Their movements, under the control of scalp muscles, alter the outline of the head and add a range of expression to the face, which may be an important aid to identification and communication between individual birds at close quarters. Whether owls use their ear tufts and expressions to convey information about their emotional state, as other birds use crests and vivid patches of feathers, is not known. Owls certainly express themselves vocally during their nightly activity. Throughout the world they have an extraordinary repertoire of shrieks, hoots and caterwaulings, in a range of frequencies which carry far on the night air. These announce their presence and the existence of occupied territories; like the songs of blackbirds and the drumming of snipe they convey to wanderers of the same species that the area is occupied. Calls are completely diagnostic of species, and owls are as likely to recognize other individuals by voice as by sight during their travels in the dark. Apart from territorial calls, owls have an additional vocabulary of softer conversational calls for use at short range between partners and between parent and offspring.

Like other birds, owls have dense, soft plumage which makes them look much bigger than they are and helps to keep them warm during long periods of inactivity between hunting forays. Apart from facial discs and ear tufts, they have few decorations—unadorned by crests or curliques, their plumage is usually a delicate, drab colour, matching their background by day and blending readily with the darkness of night. Some are colourful indeed as the portraits in this book show, but there is a collective sobriety about their appearance. In most species the plumage is unusually soft, lacking the hard sheen of many birds' feathers, and the leading quills on the wings have a soft, serrated edge. These qualities,

combined with lightness and large wing area, help owls to move silently through the air—to hear other sounds while they are in flight, and to avoid giving alarm to their prey. Small birds which mob owls seem to respond especially to their shape, colour and texture. Tests with models have shown that to a songbird owlness is a chunky, rounded shape without neck or protrusions, matt in texture and drab in colour, sitting upright on a perch.

Apart from their eyes, owls have other superlative aids for night hunting. Where vision fails, hearing grows in importance, and many of the truly nocturnal owls have ears of extraordinary efficiency. The saucer-shaped discs of feathers surrounding the eyes of most nocturnal species, which look as though they should be concerned with sight, are in fact reflectors. Their rear surfaces, lifting slightly from the face by muscular action, help to deflect sound into the vast openings of the ears which lie beneath. In several species with especially acute hearing, the ear openings are placed asymmetrically on the skull, one higher than the other, and guarded by feathered flaps of skin which probably serve as additional sound deflectors. Barn Owls, Tawny Owls and other night-hunting species hear sounds well below the threshold of human hearing. They are especially sensitive to sounds with a component of high frequencies—the squeals of small rodents, the rustle of dry leaves—and the asymmetry of their head helps them to locate the source of the sound with precision. Centres of the brain associated with hearing are correspondingly well developed, containing more cells and linkages than are found in auditory centres of less gifted species.

With this enviable apparatus of sight and hearing, packed neatly and unobtrusively in a moderately oversized skull, night hunting owls scan the ground from their perch or sweeping flight. Ears and eyes together detect and locate each source of sound, and the experienced bird swoops precisely to strike with its talons. Under experimental conditions Barn Owls have shown their ability to strike mouse-sized prey successfully in complete darkness—a combination of sensory and muscular skills.

Owls occupy all kinds of habitats, though many prefer woodland or forest edge. A few, like the Arctic Snowy Owl and some desert-living species, live in situations where it is impossible for trees to grow at all. Woodland species nest in trees, roost in them during the day, and use them as convenient bases for their hunting sorties at night. Many small owls of old, well-established forests are hole-nesters, often taking over cavities previously occupied by woodpeckers or other species. Newly planted woodlands with few old trees generally lack suitable holes to attract them but foresters who provide nest-boxes find that owls take readily to them, and help their hosts by keeping down stocks of woodland rodents. Larger owls nest untidily in open sites, often in the abandoned nest of a raptor or corvid high in the treetops. Owls of desert, taiga and tundra nest on open ground or in low vegetation; species of tropical deserts tend to live underground taking over abandoned rodent burrows to escape the heat of the sun.

Whether nesting in the open or deep in cavities, owls are not houseproud and do not include homebuilding among their skills. Some add lining material to existing nests, providing at least a minimum of protection for their eggs and young. The eggs are white and undecorated; most are rounded, some almost spherical, and clutches of two, three or four are characteristic. Burrowing Owls and other ground-nesting species tend to lay more, and clutches of ten to thirteen have been recorded when food is abundant. Chicks wear a thick down of grey, brown, or white, warm and serviceable but characteristically drab. Incubation and care of young tends to be the responsibility of females, while the males—which are usually smaller—forage and bring food home to the family group.

Many but not all species of owls adopt a family planning measure common to other groups of predatory birds. Eggs laid at intervals of two or three days hatch asynchronously at similar intervals, because incubation begins with the first egg laid, providing a brood in which the oldest may be over a week in advance of the youngest. When food is plentiful, all survive: when it is scarce, competition between nestlings is biased heavily in favour of the one or two oldest chicks, which survive at the expense of the others. Investing the available food in this way ensures that one or two well nourished chicks, rather than three or four starvelings, are launched to face the rigours of the following winter, and increases the chance that one at least will survive to maturity.

Like other birds, owls have light, flimsy bones which make poor fossils, and the record of their evolution is meagre. The oldest owl remains so far discovered appear in Palaeocene rocks of Colorado, United States, probably dating from about sixty million years ago. Fossils from the mid and late Tertiary are more plentiful, and include recognizable ancestors of living genera. In time the history of the group will probably be traced back into the late Cretaceous. However, at present it seems likely that the major diversification of owls and their spread across the world occurred during the early to middle Tertiary.

This was the time when the recently established families of modern mammals were beginning to diversify, and many new forms of small mammal were occupying new niches in newly established grasslands and forests. Both the diurnal and the nocturnal predators of small mammals would be seizing opportunities to exploit these new food reserves; hence the development and diversification of the owl pattern of living.

The fossil record tells us little about ancestral links between owls and other groups of birds. Bones of the earliest owls are good owl bones, but not halfway stages between owls and some other ancestral groups, and nothing in the later record suggests that other groups of birds have arisen from diverging from the mainstream of owl evolution. Similarities of way of life, and basic anatomy have suggested to bird taxonomists for well over a century that owls are mostly closely related to diurnal birds of prey, especially to hawks and falcons. Some taxonomists placed owls and hawks together in the same order. Others ascribed them to separate orders but grouped them closely under the general title of 'raptors'. Today there is general agreement that owls merit an order of their own (Strigiformes), hawks, falcons and vultures another (Falconiformes), and there is perhaps less certainty that the two orders as a whole are closely linked.

Recent opinion based on a new taxonomic indicator—the distribution of proteins in egg white—confirms that owls form a closely knit group and suggests that their closest kin are the Caprimulgiformes—the oilbirds of the Caribbean (which eat fruit and live in caves) and the nocturnal, insect-feeding potoos, nightjars and frogmouths which are highly adapted for catching their food on the wing, and show many superficial and anatomical similarities to owls. Egg-white proteins also support small anatomical characters in suggesting affinities between barn owls and true falcons—two slightly maverick families of their respective orders which have often been linked also on minor points of anatomical similarity. Until further evidence is forthcoming we can only say that the owls are most clearly akin to the Caprimulgiformes and show affinities also with the Falconiformes—especially with the true falcons themselves.

Within their order Strigiformes living owls fall readily into two clear-cut groups—the barn owls (Tytonidae) and the others (Strigidae). The most obvious character distinguishing the two is the shape of the face; barn owls have a heart-shaped face, strigid owls a round or oval face without a prominent dip in the upper border between the eyes. The barn owl's tail usually ends in a shallow V, its second and third toes are roughly equal in length, the claw in the middle toe has a comb-like serrated edge and the wishbone and breastbone are fixed together for strength. Strigid owls have a round tail, second toe shorter than the third, no comb on the middle claw, and separate wishbone and keel. Apart from some further small but constant differences in feathering and skeletal structure, barn owls and strigid owls are very similar. More than one author has suggested that classifying them in separate families over-emphasizes the differences between them, and that the two should be no more than subdivisions of a single family. Two further families of extinct owls, known only from fossil remains, have also been described.

The Tytonid owls include thirteen species of barn owl (genus *Tyto*) and two of bay owls (*Phodilus*). *Tyto alba*, the Common Barn Owl, is one of the world's most widespread species, appearing on every inhabited continent. A skilled hunter of rodents, for hundreds, even thousands of years, it has profited from living in rural areas close to man. Clearing forest and cultivating the land, combined with wasteful methods of sowing, reaping and storing grain, encouraged the development of large local populations of rats and mice. As its name implies, the Barn Owl found farm buildings an acceptable alternative to trees and cliffs for roosting.

Recent changes in agricultural practice—including use of chemical insecticides and dressings, have upset this happy relationship and decimated populations of Common Barn Owls in civilized countries: less civilized communities continue to enjoy the company and help of these engaging birds. Other species of barn owls are found in Africa, on islands in the Indian Ocean and East Indies, and in Australasia. Bay owls are an anomalous pair of species respectively from Central Africa and the Oriental region, which have puzzled several generations of taxonomists. Included by most in the Tytonidae, they have also been linked with *Asio* (the long-eared and short-eared strigid owls) and, by a recent reviewer even ascribed to a family of their own.

The very much larger family of strigid owls includes about 130 species, of wide-ranging habitats and ways of life. There is no general agreement as to how the two dozen genera should be grouped. Traditionally they are divided into two subfamilies, mainly according to the complexity of their ear flaps. Owls of the subfamily Buboninae including screech, scops, eagle, fishing, pygmy, hawk and burrowing owls, among many others, in general have relatively simple external ears; those of the subfamily Striginae, including Tawny, Long-eared, Short-eared, and Tengmalm's Owls, have larger, more complex ear apertures, with correspondingly elaborate flaps. Though the justification for this division is in doubt, the traditional subfamilies tend to be retained for want of a better arrangement.

In some owl genera, the division into species is open to different interpretations. Some authors accept a considerable degree of variation within a species, naming geographically separated populations which are capable of interbreeding as subspecies or races of the main type. Others consider the same regional variations sufficiently important to justify classifying the birds as fully separated species in their own right.

Large or small, diurnal or nocturnal, pursuing fish, flesh or fowl in their various professional ways, owls have practised their skills as avian master-predators with little regard for the presence of man. Throughout their long co-existence the world has always been broad enough to contain both ancient birds and modern man without enmity—without even rivalry, for their paths have seldom crossed. Owls first caught man's imagination simply by being owls—wide-eyed birds of the night. Then they caught his interest, as creatures endowed with unusual skills and adaptations to support their way of life. Now they must command his attention, his respect, and his protection; like so many other animals of outstanding quality, they stand in twin jeopardy from his ruthless destruction of habitat and his mindless spreading of poisons across their world.

PART I

OWLS AND HUMANS
John Sparks

THE ORIGINS OF OWLS
C. A. Walker

WHAT MAKES AN OWL
Philip Burton

CHAPTER ONE

Owls and humans

These are they which ye shall have in abomination among fowls; they shall not be eaten...the eagle, and the owl, and the nighthawk, and the cuckow...And the little owl, and the cormorant, and the great owl.

This quotation, from Leviticus Chapter 11, verses 13—17, must be one of the first recorded natural history lessons: these birds were judged unwholesome, not for superstitious reasons but because of their preference for feeding on carrion and choosing to inhabit derelict and desolate places.

The paths of humans and owls had, however, crossed long before the Jewish law was formulated. The pictorial legacy of the Palaeolithic people of Europe includes representations of owls. At Trois Frères, in France, the unmistakable outline of a pair of Snowy Owls and their chicks is etched into a rock face. The artist lived at a time when the Arctic climate extended farther south than today, and rendered much of France suitable as a breeding ground for these large white owls. Snowy Owls were not only considered as birds worthy of an artist's attention, but also appealed to the palate: the presence of their scraped bones on Neolithic dwelling sites proves that many a plump owlet was taken for the pot, as Snowy Owls are today by Eskimos.

From very early days to the present, owls and humans have had a continuous relationship, and owls are prominent in myth, superstition and folklore. Myths and superstitions are often based upon the animal's real habits which, by association, become linked with happy or fearful events. Or they may be founded upon the fact that we see animals as projections of ourselves. Furthermore, we envy their qualities which would enhance our own performance in certain situations—in battle for instance, or in the dark. The evidence suggests that owls have generated strong passions in us. Though we cannot feel indifferent to them, our emotions are clearly ambivalent. On one side, to see or hear an owl is an omen of bad news; a message of doom and gloom. On the other, owls are wise old birds, and enough toy owls are sold over the counters every year to support the view that we also look on owls with a certain amount of affection.

What evidence is there of a love-fear relationship between us and these predatory birds, and what facets of the owl's appearance and character arouse such powerful feelings in us? Normally the answers to such questions would be mere conjecture, but fortunately a British television survey into the public's attitudes towards wildlife programmes provides some very revealing information about owls. Over 300

A cave painting at Balu-Uru, in northern Australia demonstrates that owls have fascinated humans for thousands of years. The 'owl-man' probably represents one of the half-human spirits that Aborigines believed existed at the creation of the world. In other parts of Australia owls were thought to guard the souls of women—a belief that gave them a measure of protection.

people above the age of 15 were carefully and methodically interviewed about their animal likes and dislikes. In the list of favourite animals, headed by dolphins, owls came a long way down, at twenty-seventh. Penguins, 'tropical birds', flamingos, pelicans, robins, swallows and ostriches were all judged to be more appealing than owls. One-third of the people would have made a point of watching a television programme about owls; one-sixth would have avoided being exposed to them on their television screens. Owls were clearly not in the same class as penguins, the universal favourite, but were much more favourably considered than vultures. Ambivalence towards owls was clearly reflected in the way the panel described these birds. The consensus was that owls were *cruel* as opposed to *kind*, *strong* as opposed to *weak*, *not cuddly* as opposed to *cuddly*, and *unapproachable* as opposed to *approachable*. These could all be said to be characteristics causing us to dislike owls. However, owls were also thought to be *clever*, *sad*, *fascinating*, and—surprisingly—*beautiful*. In view of the balance between likeable and dislikeable features, it was interesting that when given a choice between the terms *frightening* and *non-frightening*, 39 per cent of the people found them frightening, 35 per cent did not, and 26 per cent preferred to view owls as neither. This modern survey confirms the owl as a Jekyll and Hyde character, worthy of our respect for its cleverness and beauty but at the same time evil and sinister.

Why do we hold these conflicting views? It is not difficult to see why we should find owls unedifying. They are killers, superbly adapted for finding prey and despatching it quickly and efficiently. With a few notable exceptions, predators have never been popular with us, although in certain cases we have through sympathetic magical rites attempted to acquire their strength and ferocity. It is no accident for instance that armies such as the Romans and the Germans have marched behind eagle-adorned banners. Whatever else we may feel for them, we have no love for eagles; and yet they are not so very different from owls. An owl, too, is equipped with cruel talons, and has a large beak curved like a meat hook. However, because of their design for nocturnal hunting, they also present us with signals to which we react favourably, if unconsciously. It is a truism that, for an animal, the way to our hearts is to look as human as possible, and owls display so many

anthropomorphic characteristics, while at the same time managing to hide the tools of their killing trade, that we cannot help seeing them as endearing caricatures of ourselves.

An owl has enormous eyes set at the front of its head to enhance visual acuity and provide stereoscopic vision. These are set in cheek-like facial discs. The head is broad like ours to accommodate widely spaced and highly developed ears. The beak is all but hidden by feathers; what little of it shows, projects just where we would expect a nose. A vertical body posture adds to the 'human' illusion, and the soft, billowing plumage produces an attractive shape while hiding murderous talons. Ear tufts on some species, a voice of human quality and eyes that blink with upper eyelids, reinforce the human image.

It should come as no surprise that we think of owls as learned. The truth is, of course, that owls are no more or less intelligent than other predatory birds. However, looking like us, they have been credited with some of our own cleverness. Owls appear to be highly perceptive, their large eyes seeming to penetrate even darkness. This may be responsible for the association between owls and deities; the best known of these is between the Little Owl (*Athene noctua*) and the Greek goddess of wisdom, Pallas Athene. The origin of Athene is obscure. She may have evolved from a pre-Hellenic rock goddess from Anatolia and the owl, as a crevice inhabitant, may have become linked with her. Lilith, the goddess of death, is depicted with two lions and owls on a Sumerian tablet dating back to 2300—2000 BC. Whatever her history, Athene

Left: A coin from ancient Greece shows the Little Owl *Athene noctua*, the sacred owl of Athens, traditionally linked with the city's patron goddess Athene, goddess of wisdom.

Anthropomorphic owls are common in children's literature in many parts of the world. Usually they are endowed with wisdom: the owl that set sail with the pussy-cat in Edward Lear's song was perhaps a less sober bird.

became associated with the sacred owl of Athens, which now bears her name. Little Owls were also shown on the city's coins.

The tradition of the wise old owl appears later, in the legends of King Arthur, where Merlin is described as having an owl perched on his shoulder. Owls generally became widely accepted as symbols of learning and scholarship and, as in the Middle Ages knowledge was largely vested in the clergy and alchemists, the owl became the companion of the wise. In the thirteenth century allegory *The Owl and the Nightingale*, owls represented the clergy. The myth has persisted and has been reinforced by another of the owl's features: its stony reticence when observed during the daytime. Someone who says nothing must surely be contemplating deeply. Are not scholars given to long bouts of silence?

> A wise old owl sat in an oak,
> The more he saw the less he spoke,
> The less he spoke, the more he heard,
> Why can't we all be like that wise old bird.
>
> *Anon*

Nursery tales, cartoon films, advertisements of all kinds still project the scholar owl—sometimes wearing a mortar board and gown, usually sporting spectacles, often holding a book. Perhaps the most famous of the wise old owls of the nursery is 'Wol' created by A.A. Milne to solve the problems of Pooh, Piglet and Eeyore.

Owls have very large eyes, the irides of which are often bright yellow or orange. They are probably the most conspicuous and compelling eyes in the world. The sudden exposure of roundels has a startling effect on animals and has formed the basis of many defence displays by insects. We can also be frightened by powerful eye patterns and owls have been employed for intimidation, on the basis that what can startle us can also be used to scare our real and imaginary enemies. The Carthaginians are said to have been routed in 310 BC by Agathokles, who released owls which settled on the helmets and shields of his men. Their self-confidence was thereby increased. Representations of owls were used by the Romans to combat the 'evil eye'. In many places throughout the world, owls have been used to counteract demonic powers or to ward off evil spirits. The Ainu peoples of Japan, for example, made wooden models of Eagle Owls during famines and nailed them to their houses in the hope of bringing better fortunes. At such time, conditions could only improve, so the owls frequently proved to be powerful magic! Storms and lightning have also been combated with owls' carcasses.

Many of the myths and superstitions that concern owls stem from the fact that many of these birds are crepuscular or nocturnal. Their relatively large eyes are adaptations for collecting as much light as possible in the dim night world. To us, night is full of mysteries. When the glare of the sun is replaced at best by the silver glow of the moon, vision on which we so much depend is of relatively little use. Where our eyes cannot penetrate, we think strange things may be lurking; and the noises and voices we hear could be the sounds of a whole gamut of sinister underground spooks and demons. Furthermore the night is dark and, by association, like the grave and death. It is therefore little wonder that our nocturnal fears and fantasies are heaped on the shoulders of the owl. Apart from the fact that they are night birds, owls fly on silenced pinions—moving through the dim landscape like ghosts, without a rustle or a whisper. Their voices have a mournful human quality and Barn Owls can produce screams worthy of the tortured souls in hell. Churchyards and derelict ruins often tend to provide roosting and hunting grounds for Barn and Tawny Owls, and the sight and sound of these birds in such places has done nothing to allay traditional fears. Pliny the Elder wrote of the owl '...when it appears [it] foretells nothing but evil, and if auspices which import the public weal are being taken at the time, is more to be dreaded than any other bird...whenever it shows itself in cities or at all by daylight, it prognosticates dire misfortunes.'

The relationship between owls and death is widespread. To the Chinese, owls snatched away souls, and their calls were referred to as 'digging the grave'. In some parts of the world, it was believed that the soul became united with an owl after death. In southern Australia, for example, tribal life was much bound up with animals, but men were especially represented by bats, and women by owls. Since no one knew exactly which owl guarded a particular soul, all owls were effectively protected—'if my sister Mary's life is an owl, then the owl is my sister and Mary is an owl'. The Kirwa Indians believed that, after dying, their medicine men became owls. Owls themselves were less lucky: they were reincarnated as crickets.

Owls are universally acknowledged messengers

Right: With cats and occasionally dogs, owls were recognized as witches' 'familiar spirits', given them by the devil to help them carry out their evil deeds.

Below right: With their silent flight and eerie calls, owls have become universal messengers of ill-tidings. The Barn Owl's preference for using churchyards and deserted ruins as roosting places has only added to its supernatural reputation.

of ill tidings. To hear the hoot of an owl is to know of an imminent death. If the cry is dull and indistinct, a near neighbour will die, if clear and distinct, then a person far away. Spenser referred to the owl as 'Death's dreadful messenger'—a superstition still adhered to in many rural areas. In Sicily, Scops Owls are especially feared. Should one call near to the house of a sick man, he will die three days later. If there are no ailing people around, then it announces that someone will be struck down with tonsil trouble.

Poets and playwrights have used the image of wailing owls to arouse emotions of foreboding in their readers and audiences. The murder of Julius Caesar was preceded by screeching owls:

> And yesterday the bird of night did sit
> Even at noonday, upon the market place,
> Hooting and shrieking.
>
> *Julius Caesar*

And the ambitious Lady Macbeth, listening and waiting while her husband murders his king, exclaims:

> Hark!—Peace! It was the owl that shriek'd,
> The fatal bellman which gives the stern'st goodnight.
>
> *Macbeth*

One verse, clearly about the Tawny Owl, combines natural and unnatural history:

> Te whit, te whoo, te whit, to whit.
> Thy note, that forth so freely rolls,
> With shrill command the mouse controls,
> And sings a dirge for dying souls,
> Te whit, te whoo, te whit, to whit.
>
> *Anon*

Even today the calls of Tawny Owls are used by

radio, television and film producers when they wish to add a hint of evil and mischief, a suggestion of supernatural forces at work.

Whether rich or poor, weak or powerful, no one could escape from the owl's prophetic course. The fate of Julius Caesar has already been referred to. Agrippa's death was precipitated by an owl. Having fallen into disfavour with Tiberius Caesar, he was arrested at Capreae and was tied to a tree in which an Eagle Owl was sitting. A German augur, who was present, prophesied that he would be released and would become king of the Jews—adding however that when he saw that owl again his death would be near. And so it was; for when sitting on his throne in state at Caesarea, he looked upwards and saw an owl perched on one of the cords which ran across the theatre. Recognizing the portent of ill, he fell back smitten with disease, and in five days was dead. A variation of this belief was found in Ethiopia. When the Ethiopians wished to pronounce sentence of death on a criminal, they carried the condemned prisoner to a table on which an owl was painted. Seeing it the guilty man was expected to do the honourable thing and kill himself.

Death, particularly an untimely one, is the ultimate in bad luck. There are, however, other misfortunes which owls are said to foretell. In Wales, the loss of virginity is foretold by the hooting of owls. An owl presiding at one's birth is generally thought to be an evil sign. In France, the shrieking of an owl indicates to a pregnant woman that she will shortly produce a girl and not a son to till the fields.

At various times the word 'owl' has been incorporated into our language as slang. Now obsolete, the meanings were inspired by the bird's nocturnal habits. Thus a harlot could be referred to as an owl in the nineteenth century. If she had been engaged in *owling* (i.e. smuggling sheep or wool from England to France), she might have to *walk by owl light* (i.e. in fear from being arrested). As a result of her calling, she would have regularly had *to owl* (to sit up at night), and should any of her clients refuse to pay then it would have been reasonable for her to have *taken the owl* (to have become angry). Should love have intervened and kindled her enthusiasm for a more permanent relationship, then she would have had to set about *turning a night owl into a homing pigeon*.

The association between owls and witchcraft probably stems from the bird's way of life, particularly its mysterious ability to find its way about in the dark. Owls also figured regularly in black magic recipes—in *Macbeth* a lizard's leg and owlet's wing were part of the witches' bubbling hell-broth.

It is easy to see how, through sympathetic magic, the eating of owls' eyes could help one to see in the dark or restore one's eyesight. An English version of this Indian treatment required the eating of owls' eggs charred and powdered. Cherokee Indians bathed their children's eyes in water containing owls' feathers so that they would be able to keep awake all night. There is also a Yorkshire belief that owl soup will help to cure whooping cough. This is based on the idea that these birds hoot and whoop so much without coming to any harm that a broth made from their bodies should cure the disease. Other recipes are less easy to understand. If the heart and right foot of an owl are laid on a sleeping person, then he will confess all. Feathers placed beneath a pillow can produce a peaceful slumber. Soup made from owls' eggs while the moon is waning can cure epilepsy or, in many parts of Europe, is said to be a sure remedy for drunkenness. To give a child an owl's egg would by the same token ensure that he would never become a drunkard. There are many variations on this belief.

Owls roosting by daytime are often bedevilled by persistent mobbing attacks of smaller birds. It is a common response to certain predators that pose some degree of threat. Presumably this behaviour has survival value to the mobbers by drawing everyone's attention to the whereabouts of the killer. For many centuries, hunters have made use of the innate reaction of other birds to owls. By tethering an owl, otherwise wary species can be lured within the range of guns, nets or snares. Eagle Owls have always been a favourite decoy, and countless thousands or millions of crows, jays, and magpies have died as a result of meeting a far more devious enemy than the one on which their attention has been rivetted. There is a report of 120 jays being caught during a single day. Smaller birds were once lured for the pot by the strategic placing of cleft sticks or perches smeared with sticky bird lime around the owl. A woodcut in Petrus von Crescens' *Opus ruralium* (1493) shows this method very clearly and testifies to the antiquity of the practice. Sometimes a portable hide was used, bedecked with perches and owl. The operator sat inside

Right: Chinese bronze wine vessel, eleventh or twelfth century BC.

'Owl and full moon', a Japanese brush painting by Isen-In Hogen Fude, 1775-1825.

and, by calling, could tempt flocks of song birds close enough to see the owl. The method was so profitable that the sticky perches would often have to be cleared several times during each sitting. The basic method is still used today in Italy to lure migrating song birds to the ground. Once there they are trapped or shot. More often than not, living owls have given way to stylized rotating models equipped with supernormal eyes and flashing plates—a substitute which is just as effective and deadly.

Owls have been used to entice birds in other kinds of hunting. An Eagle Owl, tethered to a fox's brush to make it more conspicuous, was an indispensable part of the team for hunting buoyant-winged kites. While these fine birds of prey were busy mobbing the owl at low altitude, speedy-winged Peregrine or Lanner Falcons were loosed. Their aim was to ground the kite, which was afterwards released. Sometimes, however, the hawks or falcons did not return to the fist and the falconers, always eager to make good their losses, took the opportunity to snare Goshawks which also came to parry at the jessed and tethered owl. Today the technique has been brought up to date by bird photographers interested in snapping hosts of angry, mobbing birds which are aroused by a stuffed owl. In North America, the bird-catching techniques of the Middle Ages have come in useful for capturing birds of prey for ringing (banding). A Great Horned Owl tethered near a nest has been successfully employed for catching Hen Harriers (marsh hawks). As the parents swoop onto the trespassing owl, they collide with nets strategically placed round it. Even Ospreys have been caught by this technique, using a captive Great Horned Owl, on a floating timber platform.

Many species of owl are rodent eaters, and so should be among the farmer's best friends. In Europe the creation of meadows and pastures, and the growing of cereals, have favoured the spread of Barn Owls at the expense of the woodland-living Tawny Owl. The remains of Barn Owls have certainly been found on the site of the Iron Age lake village of Glastonbury in Somerset, which flourished in pre-Roman times. Rats, mice and voles which lived off the rich pickings from grain farmers must have formed a healthy supply of food for Barn Owls, and ramshackle buildings provided the roosting and nesting sites. The very name testifies to the close association between farmer and owl, and some barns even had built-in nest-boxes. In the Netherlands, the Friesland farmers have for a long time encouraged these silent white hunters of the hated rats and mice, by providing them with access into the lofts and roof spaces. Some of the large farmhouses so characteristic of the Friesland landscape often show a decorative complex called an 'owl board' (*oeleboerd*) on the front of the roof ridge, with a round opening in the centre—'the owl hole' (*oelegat*).

In the British Isles, changes in agricultural practice, the cleaning up of farm buildings and country churches, and the introduction of poisonous pesticides have decimated the Barn Owl population, despite its total protection by law. The Tawny Owl, which suffered a decline in the eighteenth and nineteenth centuries, due to the contraction of woodland and the indiscriminating campaign of extermination carried out by gamekeepers, is now the most common bird of prey in the British Isles, with a population estimated at one hundred thousand pairs. An adaptable species, it has come to populate even towns and cities, where it thrives by snatching small birds from their roosts rather than by catching rodents. A survey carried out in London revealed that no less than 48 pairs were living within 20 miles of St Paul's cathedral. A pair of Barn Owls was once found nesting in a tower of the Smithsonian Institution building in Washington. Alexander Sprunt records that the 200 pellets collected from the nest contained 454 mammal skulls—225 meadow mice, 179 house mice, 20 rats and 20 shrews, 'an amazing collection for a pair of owls living in the heart of America's capital city'.

Because of their nature and habits, owls have undoubtedly aroused dread in us and have therefore spawned more superstitions than any other family of birds. Despite this, we have retained a place in our hearts for them. We have enlisted them as allies against the powers of evil, and, on a more mundane level, protected them for rodent catching around the sheaves and hayricks. It is consequently satisfying to recall that, in spite of habitat destruction and pesticides, not all owls have fared badly, and some are even making a good living in our own city strongholds. Nevertheless, when the territorial hooting of Tawny Owls stirs us in our snug suburban bedrooms, it is difficult to suppress that spinal shiver and to exclude all superstitions from the mind.

CHAPTER TWO

The origins of owls

Palaeornithology remains one of the most neglected of natural history subjects. There are two main reasons for this: firstly, bird bones are extremely difficult to identify, and secondly the study of fossil vertebrates has been closely associated with evolution from primitive forms to higher mammals, birds being regarded only as an interesting diversion from the main line. The majority of scientific workers now agree that birds evolved from one group of dinosaurs (Theropoda) possibly during the Jurassic Period. Unfortunately, as so often happens, the fossil record is incomplete and one cannot trace all the steps between birds and their reptilian ancestors.

Opinions differ as to the nature of the 'pre-avis'. Some say it was a tree-dwelling reptile which began flight by gliding from one branch to another; others claim that it was a running, leaping, terrestrial animal which gradually increased the length of its leaps by the use of elongated forelimbs. Both sides have put forward good arguments and the truth is probably to be found somewhere between the two.

Compared with fish, reptiles and mammals, birds are poorly represented as fossils, partly because bird bones are thin-walled, hollow, very fragile and easily destroyed by predators or scavengers. Often they are so badly damaged during the process of fossilization that they cannot be identified. The best medium for preservation of fossils is probably silt, which forms a matrix that preserves fine details of bones so necessary for critical analysis. Rather a high proportion of the best avian fossil material comes from large aquatic or semi-aquatic birds—the kinds which stood the

best chance of having at least part of their skeleton preserved.

In evaluating the record of fossil birds, it is important to understand the conditions under which the palaeornithologist distinguished a particular species. In most cases fossil species are known not from whole skeletons but from a few dis-articulated bones. Even today the two living owl families (Strigidae and Tytonidae) are not always clearly defined osteologically, and it is obviously very difficult to place extinct species within these families on the evidence of an odd bone. When a whole fossil bird is available it is easy to see the difficulties involved. The bird may have lived during the time when birds were still experimenting with the numerous ecological niches open to them and may show characteristics now associated with several different modern families; the skull may be like one family, the pelvis or tibiotarsus like another. If the bones become separated then they may easily be described as belonging to different species— even to different orders. However, naming a species on the basis of a solitary bone is often justified, if only because it can provide a guide for subsequent workers.

Some of the confusion which still surrounds the relationships of ancient birds has been caused by the conservatism of some of the earlier scientists. Bird bones themselves are conservative and in most cases if there is any slight consistent variation it usually indicates at least a new species. The earlier workers often noted these differences but, either because modern bird bones were insufficiently known, or because they wanted to show the relationships of their fossil birds, they more often than not placed them within extant genera. At the other extreme, some workers have felt that if a specimen comes from a different geological age it must automatically be a different species and as a result some forms have been described with little reference to their distinguishing characters.

OWLS AS FOSSILS

In 1971 Brodkorb published the fourth volume of his *Catalogue of Fossil Birds* in which he lists some 41 extinct species of owl, 5 of which belong to the Protostrigidae, 25 to the Strigidae and 11 to the Tytonidae. Much of the up-to-date information in this chapter is extracted from this work.

In geological terms birds are relative newcomers to the earth's fauna. *Archaeopteryx lithographica*, the first accepted bird, appeared in the Upper Jurassic, but it is not possible to say how soon after this owls evolved. The first reliable records of owls date from the Palaeogene (the Palaeocene, Eocene and Oligocene Periods). Three distinct strigiform families (Protostrigidae, Strigidae and Ogygoptygidae) are known to have existed during this time, and it is reasonable to assume that the order must have evolved much earlier, in the latter half of the Mesozoic Era. It is impossible to draw any evolutionary lines from Mesozoic birds to the earliest owls. *Archaeopteryx* was so primitive that it retained many of the characters (teeth and long, bony tail) normally associated with reptiles, and if the feather impressions had not been preserved it would almost certainly have been described as a lightly built dinosaur. The remaining Mesozoic forms all appear to be birds normally found in or around an aquatic environment, and none of these seems to be related in any way to owls. Although it is still not clear from which group the owls evolved, it is generally thought that the Strigiformes and Caprimulgiformes (nightjars and frogmouths) are in some way related. Unfortunately, the fossil record of the nightjars is very poor, so it does not help us in our search for owl ancestors.

MESOZOIC ERA
Cretaceous Period (135 to 65 million years ago)

During this Period the environment consisted of large seas, lakes and deltas with deserts, coal-forming swamps and occasional glaciers. The evidence of the flora suggests that a mild climate was widespread. In the very early stages, the vegetation was very much like that of the Jurassic and included cycads, ferns and conifers, but towards the end the flowering plants became a dominant part of the flora. The land fauna was still dominated by the great 'dinosaurs' which were to become extinct before the Period ended.

As yet no fossil owl has been described from the Cretaceous, but it was probably towards the end of this Period, when the last of the dinosaurs were dying out, that the first primitive owls evolved.

Right: Scientific names are usually made up of two parts. The first indicates the genus and the second the species. Authors' names appearing within brackets show that the species were placed in the wrong genera in the original descriptions, and have been subsequently corrected, e.g. *Eostrix mimica* (Wetmore) was originally described as *Protostrix mimica* Wetmore.

An artist's reconstruction of an extinct owl in the family Protostrigidae, from the Eocene Period of North America.

CAENOZOIC ERA

Palaeocene and Eocene Periods
(65 to 40 million years ago)

The first ten million years of the Eocene are now referred to as the Palaeocene, but for convenience they will be dealt with here as part of the Eocene. Geographically, the Palaeocene and Eocene were Periods of great change, with considerable volcanic activity and geological unrest. Tropical and temperate conditions were more widespread than they are today. Southern England and parts of France were covered with sub-tropical forests, and temperate plants grew in what is now the Arctic. Mammals were evolving and spreading, and the ancestors of many modern forms were recognizable. The radiation of birds into this complex variety of modern types also took place at this time; all but ten of the recognized orders are represented in the record by the end of the Eocene. Of the once-dominant reptiles only a small fragment—crocodiles, turtles, snakes, and lizards—remained alive and active.

Only one owl (*Ogygoptynx wetmorei*), which is placed in its own extinct family (Ogygoptygidae), has so far been described from Palaeocene deposits. Two tarsometatarsi from the phosphorite deposits of Cernay (France), however, are awaiting description. These leg bones are large, and must have belonged to an owl of the same proportions as the eagle owl (*Bubo bubo*). At present, there are fifteen species of owls described from Eocene deposits. They are placed in eight genera which, in turn, are incorporated into three families (Protostrigidae, Tytonidae and Sophiornithidae). Except for the Tyntonidae, the other two families became extinct before the end of the Oligocene. Until recently, the Tytonidae was

Table I Fossil owls from the Palaeocene, Eocene and Oligocene Periods (collectively known as the Palaeogene)

OGYGOPTYGIDAE

Ogygoptynx wetmorei RICH & BOHASKA	Middle Palaeocene	Colorado, U.S.A.

PROTOSTRIGIDAE

Eostrix marinelli MARTIN & BLACK	Lower Eocene	Wyoming, U.S.A.
Eostrix mimica (WETMORE)	Lower Eocene	Wyoming, U.S.A.
Minerva antiqua (SHUFELDT)	Middle-Upper Eocene	Wyoming and California, U.S.A.
Minerva leposteus (MARSH)	Middle Eocene	Wyoming, U.S.A.
Minerva saurodosis (WETMORE)	Middle Eocene	Wyoming, U.S.A.
Minerva californiensis (HOWARD)	Middle Eocene	California, U.S.A.
Oligostrix rupelensis FISCHER	Oligocene	Germany

TYTONIDAE

Necrobyas harpax MILNE-EDWARDS	Lower Oligocene	Quercy, France
Necrobyas rossignoli MILNE-EDWARDS	Upper Eocene	Quercy, France
Necrobyas edwardsi GAILLARD	Upper Oligocene	Quercy, France
Necrobyas medius MOURER-CHAUVIRÉ	Middle Eocene-Upper Oligocene	Quercy, France
Necrobyas minimus MOURER-CHAUVIRÉ	Oligocene	Quercy, France
'Necrobyas' vincenti HARRISON	Lower Eocene	Kent, England
Nocturnavis incerta (MILNE-EDWARDS)	Upper Eocene	Quercy, France
Palaeobyas cracrafti MOURER-CHAUVIRÉ	Middle Eocene-Lower Oligocene	Quercy, France
Palaeotyto cadurcensis MOURER-CHAUVIRÉ	Middle Eocene-Lower Oligocene	Quercy, France
Selenornis henrici (MILNE-EDWARDS)	Middle Eocene-Lower Oligocene	Quercy, France
Palaeoglaux perrierensis MOURER-CHAUVIRÉ	Upper Eocene	Quercy, France

SOPHIORNITHIDAE

Sophiornis quercynus MOURER-CHAUVIRÉ	Middle Eocene-Upper Oligocene	Quercy, France

FAMILY UNCERTAIN

Strigogyps dubius GAILLARD	Upper Eocene	Quercy, France

thought to have evolved after the Strigidae, but this hypothesis is now regarded as incorrect. In fact, the genera described from the Eocene Period, and originally placed within the Strigidae, have now been transferred to the Tytonidae. As a result, the first example which can be placed in the Strigidae family does not occur until the Lower Miocene. Unfortunately, the phosphorite deposits of Quercy were once thought to be one age and in consequence some collectors took little note of the exact horizon from where some specimens were found. These deposits are now known to range from Middle Eocene to Lower Oligocene times, and thus the precise age of five species remains in doubt. (See Table I.)

Oligocene Period (40 to 25 million years ago)

Disturbances in the earth's crust continued during the Oligocene and started the formation of great mountain ranges, including the Alps. Uplift caused some former marine basins to be cut off from the sea, turning them into brackish lagoons or freshwater lakes. Europe was at one stage joined to Asia (which was still linked to North America). Temperate conditions were widespread, though certain continents had cooler areas, and grasslands increased at the expense of forested regions. About one quarter of the present-day families of birds were represented.

The Protostrigidae are only known from one specimen (*Oligostrix rupelensis*) in the Oligocene, although when a critical analysis has been carried out, some of the genera from the Quercy deposits may be found to have closer links with this family than their present arrangement indicates.

Miocene Period (25 to 12 million years ago)

During the Miocene Period movements of the earth's crust continued, and the upheaval of the Alps and Himalayas was completed. Asia became finally joined to Europe and for a short time was still connected to North America. The climate became cooler, and temperate floras replaced the sub-tropical ones; grassy plains spread even further as the forests retreated. Most of the mammals of this Period belonged to families which have persisted to the present day; they included elephants, rhinoceroses, pigs and antlered deer. Birds followed the same pattern, and over a third of them are sufficiently close to living species to be placed in the same genera.

Until Mourer-Chauviré's recent reappraisal of the pre-Miocene owls from France, it was thought that the first known example of the family Tytonidae occurred at this Period. Her findings, however, have shown this family to have a greater geological antiquity by realizing that the various species, previously placed within the Strigidae owls, would be more appropriately included in the Tytonidae. In consequence, no owl

Table II Fossil owls from the Miocene Period

STRIGIDAE

'Bubo' poirreiri MILNE-EDWARDS	Lower Miocene	France
Otus wintershofensis BALLMANN	Middle Miocene	Germany
Otus cf. senegalensis	Middle Miocene	Kenya
Strix dakota MILLER	Lower Miocene	South Dakota, U.S.A.
Strix brevis BALLMANN	Middle Miocene	Germany

TYTONIDAE

Prosybris antiqua (MILNE-EDWARDS)	Lower Miocene	France
Tyto ignota (PARIS)	Middle Miocene	France
Tyto cf. alba	Middle Miocene	Tunisia
Tyto sanctialbani (LYDEKKER)	Upper Middle Miocene	France
Tyto edwardsi (ENNOUCHI)	Upper Middle Miocene	France
Tyto robusta (BALLMANN)	Upper Miocene	Italy
Tyto gigantea (BALLMANN)	Upper Miocene	Italy
Necrobyas arvernensis (MILNE-EDWARDS)	Lower Miocene	France

Table III Fossil owls from the Pliocene Period

STRIGIDAE

Bubo florianae KRETZOI	Lower Pliocene	Hungary
Speotyto megalopeza FORD	Upper Pliocene and Lower Pleistocene	Kansas & Idaho, U.S.A.
Asio pigmaeus SEREBROVSKY	Lower Pliocene	Ukraine
Asio brevipes FORD AND MURRAY	Upper Pliocene-?Lower Pleistocene	Idaho, U.S.A.

TYTONIDAE

Lechusa stirtoni MILLER	Middle Pliocene	California, U.S.A.
Tyto balearica MOURER-CHAUVIRÉ ET AL.	Plio-Pleistocene	Balearic Is.

belonging to a genus placed in the Strigidae family has yet been recorded before this Period. In the same study, it was realized that *Paratyto arvernensis* should be reclassified as the last example of the genus *Necrobyas*. It is probable that the species placed in extant genera (*Bubo, Otus, Strix,* and *Tyto*) are the first true examples of their genus. (Table II.)

Pliocene Period (12 to 3 million years ago)

The Pliocene Period was one of greater stability, though the land continued to rise. Continents and oceans were assuming their present-day form, and towards the end of the Period ice-caps began to develop in the northern hemisphere. The climate was cooler than the preceding Periods, but not as cool as those prevailing today. The mammal fauna was less varied than in the Miocene, but more diverse than at present. The first man-like apes were to be found in South Africa, while elephant, wild horses (*Hipparion*) and deer of many different types roamed the grasslands and forests respectively. Three-quarters of the avifauna described from this time have been assigned to living genera.

Owls are known from seven Pliocene localities, four in North America and three in Europe. Bubo and Asio are represented, also the genus Lechusa (now extinct). Speotyto megalopeza, related to the modern Burrowing Owl, has been recovered from the Hagerman lake deposits of Idaho which some authorities believe to be early Pleistocene in age, so Speotyto megalopeza could range from Upper Pliocene to Lower Pleistocene. (Table III.)

QUATERNARY ERA

Pleistocene Period (3 million to 10,000 years ago)

The Pleistocene Period is sometimes referred to as the Great Ice Age because of the ice-sheets and glaciers which spread across the northern continents. Many people believe that Arctic conditions prevailed throughout the world at this time, but in fact many parts of the earth were never affected by glaciation. Even the areas affected by the ice had alternating cold and warm conditions. There were also important land movements and volcanic activity in Africa and the Middle East and changes of sea level.

The record of fossil birds is much more extensive than for earlier Periods, with about fifty species of owls, all belonging to extant genera having been recognized from Quaternary deposits in many parts of the world. They include 17 extinct species (10 Strigidae and 7 Tytonidae), 12 of which having been discovered on islands. Some of these island forms show a marked inclination towards gigantism. (See Table IV.)

Holocene Period (10,000 years ago to the present)

Cave deposits often provide conditions suitable for preserving the remains of dead animals. As many species of owls habitually roost in such places, their skeletal remains are commonly found there. At the same time the owl's habit of producing pellets, containing the indigestible remains of their last meal, especially bones, has greatly added to our knowledge of the small fauna of the time.

Next page: Table IV. In the Quaternary Era fossils of modern species appear, together with more extinct species belonging to modern genera.

Table IV Fossil owls from the Quaternary Era (Pleistocene-Holocene)

STRIGIDAE/EXTINCT

Bubo binagadensis BURCHAK-ABRAMOVICH	Middle Upper Pleistocene	Azerbaijan
Bubo insularis MOURER-CHAUVIRÉ & WEESEI	Upper Pleistocene	Crete
Bubo sincliari MILLER	Upper Pleistocene	California, U.S.A.
Bubo leguati ROTHSCHILD	Quaternary	Rodriguez Is.
Athene cretensis WEESIE	Upper Pleistocene	Crete
Athene murivora (MILNE-EDWARDS)	Quaternary	Rodriguez Is.
Gymnoglaux sp.	Upper Pleistocene	Cuba
Ornimegalonyx acevedoi ARREDONDO	Upper Pleistocene	Cuba
Ornimegalonyx minor ARREDONDO	Upper Pleistocene	Cuba
Ornimegalonyx gigas ARREDONDO	Upper Pleistocene	Cuba
Ornigmegalonyx oteroi ARREDONDO	Upper Pleistocene	Cuba
Pulsatrix arrendoi BRODKORB	Upper Pleistocene	Cuba
Asio priscus HOWARD	Upper Pleistocene	California, U.S.A.
Strix brea HOWARD	Upper Pleistocene	California, U.S.A.

Neospecies (still living) of Strigidae

Otus scops	Europe, Asia and Middle East
Otus flammeolus	Central and North America
Otus asio	Central and North America
Otus trichopsis	Mexico
Otus nudipes	West Indies
Bubo virginianus	Central and North America
Bubo bubo	Europe, Asia and Middle East
Bubo africanus	Sardinia
Ketupa zeylonensis	India and Crete
Nyctea scandiaca	Europe and Asia
Surnia ulula	Europe and North America
Glaucidium passerinum	Europe
Glaucidium siju	Cuba
Glaucidium gnoma	Central and North America
Glaucidium brasilianum	Central and South America
Ninox novaeseelandiae	New Zealand and New Caledonia
Sceloglaux albifacies	New Zealand (may now be extinct)
Athene cunicularia	Bahamas, North and South America, W. Indies
Athene noctua	Europe, Asia and Middle East
Ciccaba virgata	Mexico
Strix aluco	Europe
Strix occidentalis	Central and North America
Strix varia	Central and North America
Strix uralensis	Europe
Strix nebulosa	Romania
Asio otus	Europe, Asia, North and Central America
Asio stygius	Dominican Republic and Brazil
Asio flammeus	Europe, Asia, North and Central America
Asio (Rhinoptynx) clamator	Venezuela
Aegolius funereus	Europe and North America
Aegolius acadicus	North America

TYTONIDAE/EXTINCT

Tyto noeli ARREDONDO	Upper Pleistocene	Cuba
Tyto riveroi ARREDONDO	Upper Pleistocene	Cuba

Neospecies of Tytonidae

Tyto ostologa WETMORE	Upper Pleistocene	Haiti
Tyto pollens WETMORE	Upper Pleistocene	Bahamas
Tyto cavatica WETMORE	Quaternary	Puerto Rico
Tyto melitensis (LYDEKKER)	Upper Pleistocene	Malta
Tyto sauzieri (NEWTON & GADOW)	Quaternary	Mauritius
Tyto? letocarti BALOUET & OLSEN	Holocene	New Caledonia
Tyto punctactissima	Holocene	Galapagos

Neospecies (still living) of Tytonidae

Tyto alba	Europe, Middle East, Australasia, West Indies, and The Americas
Tyto cf. novaehollandiae	Australia

CHAPTER THREE

What makes an owl

To operate efficiently as nocturnal predators, owls have evolved extensive modifications; their distinctive appearance is largely a consequence of these. This is obvious above all in the anatomy of the head. The large forward facing eyes, surrounded by broad facial feather discs, give owls a semi-human appearance, in which lies much of their appeal to man but these features are primarily an indication of the great refinement of the senses of sight and, particularly, hearing, essential for hunting in the dark. It seems appropriate, therefore, to begin this account of owl anatomy by dealing with the structure of eyes and ears.

Sight is of vital importance to all birds; this is reflected in the relatively enormous size of the eyes, which take up a huge amount of space in the head; in most birds the two eyes are separated only by a thin bony sheet in the mid-line of the skull. The eyeballs of some large hawks and owls are in fact, bigger than our own. Underlying this seemingly disproportionate size is a basic design limitation in the structure of eyes. This limitation is imposed by the light-sensitive cells of the retina, the rear part of the inner eye on which the image is thrown. The resolution of the eye—that is, its capacity to discern detail—depends on the number of retinal cells over which the image is spread, a greater number giving more detailed perception. Since the size of these cells is roughly constant, it follows that a larger eye will generally provide higher resolution than a smaller one of the same basic shape. This limitation is a particularly acute problem for owls, since their eyes are also modified for extreme sensitivity under poor lighting conditions and, in many respects, adaptations for high sensitivity run counter to those for high resolution.

The light-sensitive cells of the retina are of two types, named, from their shapes, rods and cones. The rods are more sensitive to low light, but they achieve this sensitivity partly by functioning in small groups, each group stimulating only a single nerve cell, whereas cones generally each have their own nerve cell to conduct their response to the brain. The result of this is that image details falling on a group of rods are merged and lost, whereas, had they fallen on cones, they might have been separately perceived. Cones are thought to conduct responses to different colours to the brain centres and as colours are not obvious under conditions of low light intensity, cones play a restricted role in light perception by nocturnal owls.

A retina with many rods, as found in the eyes of owls and other nocturnal animals, has thus sacrificed some of its capacity for resolution. Many nocturnal animals also possess a reflecting layer—the tapetum—inside the eye, to use the light which enters more fully, in fact twice. However, the presence of such a layer in the eyes of owls has yet to be conclusively shown, though the eyes of some (but not all) species strongly reflect the light of a torch directed upon it in the dark.

A further adaptation to low light intensities is to bring the lens and retina closer together, so that the image itself is less dispersed and consequently brighter. In consequence it is also smaller, and hence spread over fewer retinal cells, thus further worsening the capacity for resolution.

ANATOMY OF A TYPICAL OWL

Owls show a number of adaptations which enable them to operate with outstanding efficiency as nocturnal predators. Large forward-facing eyes give them a considerable degree of binocular vision; wide skulls and asymmetrical ear openings in the more specialized species are thought to help in pinpointing the source of sound more accurately; softened flight feathers make silent flight possible, while bill and claws are obviously suited to their predatory way of life.

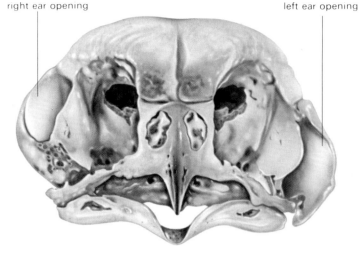

right ear opening   left ear opening

Skull of Tengmalm's Owl *Aegolius funereus* showing the asymmetrical ear openings, most obvious in this species.

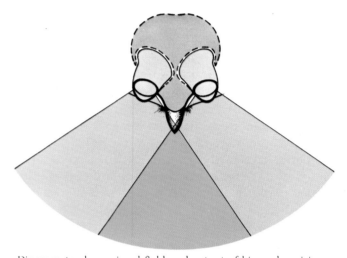

Diagram to show visual field and extent of binocular vision in an average owl.

The wing of a Tawny Owl *Strix aluco*. The enlarged detail shows the softened edges of the flight feathers—an aid to silent flight.

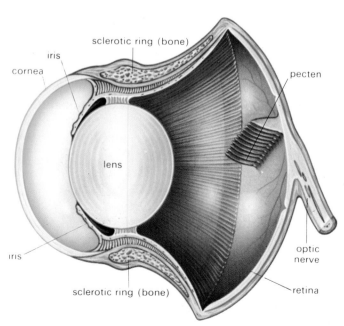

sclerotic ring (bone)
iris
cornea
pecten
lens
iris
optic nerve
sclerotic ring (bone)
retina

Cross-section of the eye of an Eagle Owl.

Right: Tawny Owl *Strix aluco*. The skeleton of a Tawny Owl is actually considerably smaller than its soft, loose feathers make it appear. Found mainly in deciduous woodland and among scattered groups of trees, it has rather shorter wings than owls of more open country. An owl's eyes are forward facing, and the bird must turn its whole head to look sideways. Its exceptionally long and flexible neck enables it to turn its head a full 180 degrees.

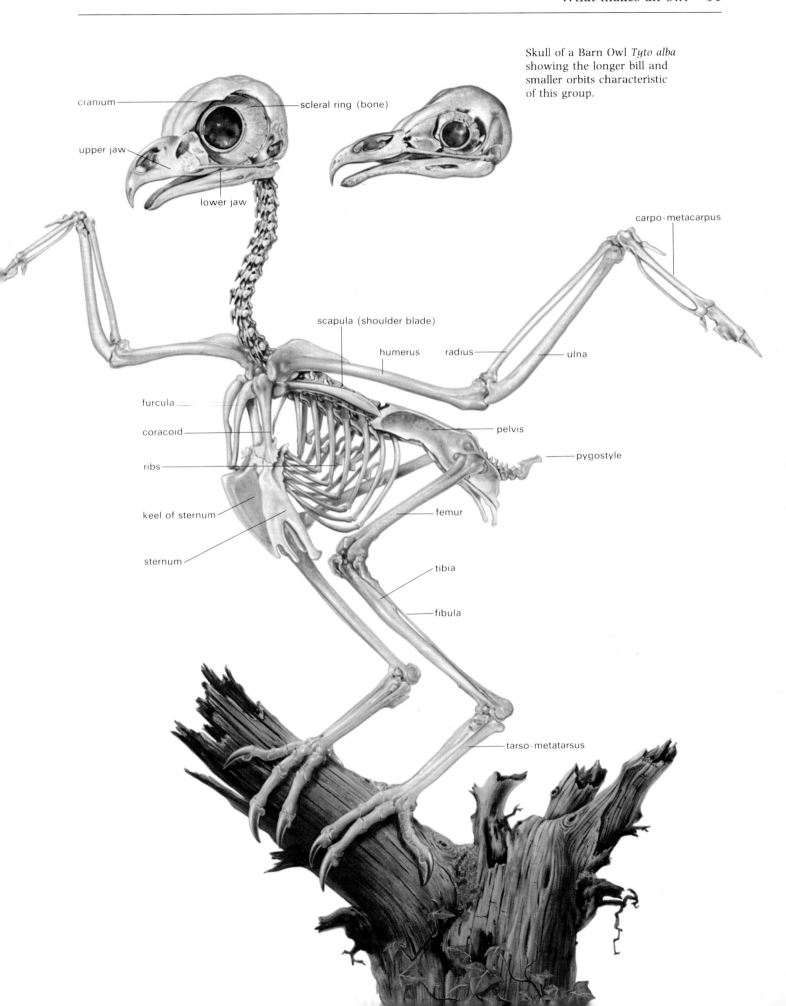

Skull of a Barn Owl *Tyto alba* showing the longer bill and smaller orbits characteristic of this group.

cranium

scleral ring (bone)

upper jaw

lower jaw

carpo-metacarpus

scapula (shoulder blade)

humerus — radius — ulna

furcula

coracoid

pelvis

ribs

pygostyle

keel of sternum

femur

sternum

tibia

fibula

tarso-metatarsus

Enlarging the eyes to the maximum has helped
owls to overcome these disadvantages, but to do
this they have had to accept a sacrifice in field of
view, so that, although the image is spread over
an adequate area of retina for purposes of
resolution, it covers a smaller proportion of the
owl's surroundings than in other birds. This has
led to the evolution of the 'tubular' eye, with a
relatively abbreviated retina, and a huge, highly
convex lens. As in all birds, the eyeball is
protected by a ring of small bony plates (scleral
ossicles), and in owls these form a long bony tube
which is one of the most striking features of a
prepared skull specimen. In many hawks the eye
is superficially similar, but lengthening has taken
place without any proportionate enlargement of
the lens, or reduction of retinal area. The object
in their case is to spread the image over as many
retinal cells as possible, to give maximum
resolution.

The forward-facing arrangement of the eyes of
owls is partly a means of accommodating them in
the head, but also makes possible a considerable
degree of binocular vision—that is, vision in
which both eyes view the same scene from
slightly different aspects, an aid to depth
perception. The total visual field in owls is some
110° of which about 60° to 70° is overlapping;
man in comparison sees a total field of 180°, of
which about 140° is covered by both eyes. These
figures may be compared with, for example, a
total field of about 340° in a homing pigeon, of
which only 24° is covered by both eyes.
Compensating for their rather narrow field of
view, owls have an exceptional ability to rotate
the head. Even a diurnal bird of prey can turn the
head through about 180°, and, in owls, this
figure reaches 270°. Many owls are able to hunt
in daylight, and none are helpless during the day.
This is made possible by an exceptional range of
aperture—pupil size—controlled by the iris.

Statements that the sight of owls is up to one
hundred times more sensitive to low light levels
than the average sight of man are exaggerated.
About two and a half times is closer to the truth,
but this is an indication of the great sensitivity of
the sight of most humans, rather than any lack of
sensitivity of the sight of owls. The sensitivity of
the sight of both owls and man is close to the
theoretical limit. Individual differences in vision
capability in darkness is probably greater in man
than in owls, as owls lacking optional capabilities
will not readily survive in nature.

Spotted Eagle Owl *Bubo africanus*. Though specially
constructed to see well in poor light, owl eyes are also useful
in daylight, for they have an exceptional range of pupil size,
controlled by the iris. In bright sunlight the inner eye is
further protected by a movable, opaque nictitating
membrane, or 'third eyelid'.

Right: Claws of the Eagle Owl *Bubo bubo* (top), Brown Fish
Owl (*Ketupa zeylonensis*) (far right) and Snowy Owl *Nyctea
scandiaca* (lower right). Most owls have fairly short legs,
though terrestrial species such as the Burrowing Owl *Speotyto
cunicularia* are exceptions. Legs and toes are usually
feathered: the Snowy Owl's abundant covering is an extreme
example, providing useful insulation against the cold Arctic
climate. The Brown Fish Owl's scaly, bare legs are an
adaptation which enables it to grasp fish in the water.

Owls supplement their vision with hearing of
equal refinement, and it has been demonstrated
that a Barn Owl can capture living prey in the
total absence of light. This is made possible by
adaptations in ear structure which have modified
the skull as profoundly as those of the eyes. The
most obvious of these adaptations is the sheer size
of the ear openings. Instead of fairly small round
openings, as in most birds, some owls have long
vertical slits, nearly as deep as the head itself. The
facial discs, so characteristic of owls, are an
indication of their presence, for the edges of the
discs are fringed by stiff, short feathers bordering
the openings, and carried upon flaps, front and

back, which can move to control the direction of best sound reception for the ear opening. This control enables owls to scan different parts of their environment for sounds in the same way that many mammals can move their external ears. (The 'ear tufts' which many species possess, are, in fact, nothing to do with the sense of hearing and do not even indicate the position of the outer ear openings.)

The skulls of owls are proportionately much wider than those of most birds. This is partly a consequence of their large eyes and the possibility of binocular vision, but it also helps them in the essential ability of locating the direction of a

sound. This is because a sound made to one side will be perceived by one ear fractionally before the other; the tiny time difference, some 0.00003 seconds, is sufficient to be perceived and to indicate on which side the sound source lies. The sound will also be louder in the ear nearer the sound source, at least for sounds with wavelength equivalent to or shorter than the width of the head. Another factor, which is clearly important in many species, though not fully understood, is the asymmetry of the structure and size of the ear flaps and the asymmetrical placing of the ear openings in the most specialized owl species. Mostly the right hand opening is higher, and it is thought that this exaggerates the effect of displacement of the sound to one side or the other, permitting more rapid readjustment. The inner ear of owls is also large, and the auditory region of the brain is provided with many more nerve cells than in other birds of comparable size. The range of frequencies which they can detect is, if anything, more limited than our own, particularly at the lower end of the scale. Nevertheless, the region of maximum sensitivity is relatively high in most species, and ideal for locating the high pitched squeaks of rodents. For the Tawny Owl, the region of greatest sensitivity lies between 3000 and 6000 cycles per second. In the Great Horned Owl, as in ourselves, it is around 1000 cycles.

Not all owls have ears as highly developed as this. In general, eagle owls, including the Great Horned Owl, and scops owls have relatively small openings, with little or no asymmetry, while large openings and asymmetry are marked in *Strix*, *Asio* and a few others. However, recent studies have shown that, in regard to size, the ear flaps are best developed in northern species, and smallest in tropical forms. This may be connected with the fact that northern nights are more silent, and in winter very much longer than those of tropical areas, with their chorus of frogs and cicadas.

Keen hearing would be almost useless if the owl itself made a great deal of confusing noise, to say nothing of the warning this would give to potential prey. Owls have consequently evolved the ability to fly in nearly complete silence. This faculty results in part from the structure of the feathers, which have markedly softened edges compared with those of other birds. In addition, owls have a low wing loading, that is to say, they are light in relation to their wing area. This gives them a buoyant, effortless flight, which eliminates much of the need for noisy flapping. The usual descent of an owl to its prey is, in fact, a glide.

In most other features of their anatomy, owls show obvious adaptations for a predatory way of life, many of them paralleling those of diurnal birds of prey. The hooked bill, with a soft cere at the base, around the nostrils, is common to both owls and hawks, but in owls the bill is more sharply deflected downwards—a modification to reduce obstruction of the already limited visual field. The claws are extremely long and sharp in both groups, but in owls the outer toe is reversible, and can be pointed backwards alongside the hind toe—a faculty which only the Osprey possesses among diurnal birds of prey. The legs and toes are feathered, to various degrees, as in many hawks and eagles—a protection against possible bites from prey. An exception to this is shown by the fishing owls, which catch their prey, fish, in the water; they have bare legs and feet with rough spiny soles, as in the Osprey and other fishing species. Most owls have fairly short legs, like mammal-eating hawks, but unlike the hawks of the genus *Accipiter*, which prey on small birds. An exception is the Burrowing Owl (*Speotyto cunicularia*) of South America, whose terrestrial habits have led to a noticeable increase in leg length. Barn owls also have long legs and can run remarkably fast. Unlike diurnal birds of prey, owls have no crop, and their intestines are provided with long caeca (blind ending tubes), an unusual feature among carnivores.

As a group, owls show much more uniformity of structure than the diurnal birds of prey. This is partly because their primary adaptations to nocturnal life have restricted their capacity to exploit daytime niches; thus, carrion feeding owls are unknown, and bird-catching adaptations are much less in evidence. There are no soaring forms, and no real equivalent of the falcons— probably the Hawk Owl (*Surnia ulula*), with its pointed wings and long tail, is the nearest approach, but the hunting methods of the Long-eared Owl by night and those of the Short-eared Owl at any time of night or day resemble those of the harriers to some extent. Wings are in general rounded amongst the owls, shorter in forest forms which have to manoeuvre between trees, and relatively longer in open country and migratory species. The size range of owls, though considerable, is less than that shown by the hawks and falcons. The largest are some eagle owls (*Bubo*), reaching 710 mm in length, and the smallest are the Least Pygmy Owl (*Glaucidium minutissimum*), 120 to 140 mm long, and the Elf Owl (*Micrathene whitneyi*), which weighs less (e.g. 40 g). Anatomically, the most distinctive owls are the barn owls, usually separated as a family (Tytonidae) from the remainder, the Typical owls (Strigidae). The barn owls are distinguished by their smaller orbits, different structure of the outer ear slits (which are longer than in any other owl), and rather longer skulls; in life, the distinctive feature of the head is the heart-shaped rather than round facial disc. They are distinguished also by their inner toes, which equal the middle in length. The claw of the middle toe is provided with serrations, absent in Typical owls.

The anatomy of owls provides little clear cut evidence about their relationships, but there are some suggestive similarities to the Caprimulgiformes (nightjars and others) e.g. in the curious form of the intestinal caeca, which have swollen ends in both groups, a feature not seen in other orders. The Caprimulgiformes are linked to the owls by other evidence as well, and seem very likely to be their closest relatives. It is of interest that both groups are more or less nocturnal, although the Caprimulgiformes have specialized more in the capture of insects, especially on the wing, never using their feet to capture prey. They include a curious family, the Aegothelidae, known as owlet nightjars. These are surprisingly owl-like in many features of their structure and habits, and seem to fill a niche rather like that of *Glaucidium* owls.

PART II

BARN AND BAY OWLS
*Michael Everett, Ian Prestt
and Reginald Wagstaffe*

FISHING OWLS, EAGLE OWLS AND
THE SNOWY OWL
Michael Fogden

SCOPS AND SCREECH OWLS
G. P. Hekstra

WOOD OWLS
Heimo Mikkola

HAWK OWLS
Colin Harrison

LITTLE, PYGMY AND ELF OWLS
Howard Ginn

CONSERVATION
Ronald Murton

OWL PELLETS
David Glue

OWL VOICES
Wouter van der Weijden and Michael Everett

CHAPTER FOUR

Barn and Bay Owls

Tyto, Phodilus

The fifteen species described in this chapter belong to the family Tytonidae, a group of owls which, because of a series of small differences, particularly in bone structure, are classified separately from the Strigidae or Typical owls. All but two species are included in the subfamily Tytoninae and the genus *Tyto*. They are commonly known as barn owls, although two which live in open grassland are popularly known as grass owls.

Barn and grass owls are typified by heart-shaped faces, a lack of ear tufts, long slender legs covered with narrow feathers, bristled feet and a comb-like middle claw. With the notable exception of the two Australian sooty owls, all species have relatively small eyes; the eyes are uniformly dark in all species. The outer ear openings are relatively small and asymmetrically placed, the left usually being higher on the skull than the right, and are covered by a large flap (the operculum). In total length the different species range from about 270 to 530 mm.

The remaining two species are placed in the subfamily Phodilinae and the genus *Phodilus*: they are commonly called bay owls. They are similar to barn owls in many respects, but are smaller (230 to 330 mm), have facial discs which are incomplete above the eye, lack ear flaps and have much more rounded wings. In contrast to the strongly hooked bills of barn owls, those of the bay owls are weak and compressed.

An outstanding feature of the distribution of the barn and bay owls is the very wide world range of one species, the Barn Owl (*Tyto alba*), which

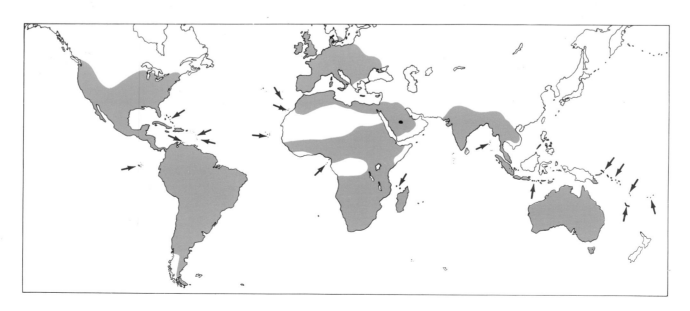

European farmers recognize the Barn Owl *Tyto alba* (330 to 430 mm) as an important predator of rats and mice and often build special 'owl doors' into their barns to encourage the birds to use them as roosts and nest-sites. This individual belongs to the dark-breasted race *T. a. guttata* of Scandinavia and central and eastern Europe.

Map: *Tyto alba*: open habitats including moors, cultivated grassland, desert and parkland.

includes the Americas, Europe, much of Africa, Arabia, India, South-east Asia and Australia, as well as many of the islands associated with these regions. Although it is often described as cosmopolitan, this is slightly misleading since, apart from in parts of Europe and the Americas, it is mainly a bird of tropical and sub-tropical regions and is essentially restricted to a band 40° on either side of the Equator. Scottish Barn Owls are the most northerly in the world; the southernmost outpost is Tierra del Fuego. The greatest number of species of the Tytoninae occurs in the Australasian region. One bay owl is oriental, occurring in South-east Asia, and the other African.

No fewer than six owls—mainly island birds with very restricted distributions—appear in the list of 1029 species threatened on a world scale drawn up by the International Council for Bird Preservation. These are the Madagascar Red Owl, the Taliabu (or Sula Islands Barn) Owl, the Minahassa (Barn) Owl, the Lesser Masked Owl, the Golden (or New Britain Barn) Owl and the Itombwe (or Congo or Tanzanian Bay) Owl. Almost nothing is known about any of these birds.

The Barn Owl (*Tyto alba*) must be one of the best known and most studied owls in the world. Not surprisingly, its pattern of distribution has given rise to many local races—somewhere between 35 and 40, although the relationships between some of these are unclear and in some cases subspeciation is still a matter of debate. The fossil record suggests that the *Tyto* line is an ancient one, with several species extant during the Miocene period, over 12 million years ago, and it also seems likely that the history of *Tyto alba* itself is a very old one. Its wide distribution is not believed to be of recent origin. Whether the species originated in the western or the eastern hemisphere, however, remains a matter of speculation.

The extreme sizes of the races vary from about 330 to 430 mm (overall length), with the largest in the Americas and the smallest races nearer to the Equator. There is also a good deal of colour variation, from birds with pure white underparts to those of a deep reddish-brown. As a general rule, the birds with the palest upperparts (some appear almost as white above as below) tend to occur in the Australian, Mediterranean and Middle Eastern regions.

In addition to its natural range, the Barn Owl

occurs as an introduced bird in the Seychelles, on Lord Howe Island (between Australia and New Zealand)—where two quite separate races are involved—and in Hawaii. Some native island races have turned to feeding on colonial seabirds and, although they take other birds too, this has happened with the introduced Seychelles Barn Owls: they have had no impact on the large rat populations in the sugar-cane plantations, the control of which was the reason for the birds' introduction in the first place. Attempts are now being made to eradicate the owls.

The white-breasted nominate race *Tyto a. alba* has been studied in considerable detail and these studies form the basis for much of the remainder of this account. It was first described in 1769 from specimens collected in Italy, but is now known to breed from the British Isles to the Channel Islands, western France, Spain, Portugal, Italy and other Mediterranean countries.

With its relatively large size and mainly white appearance, the Barn Owl is an easy bird to identify. It is about 350 mm long, with a wingspan of around 900 mm and a shortish tail. The upperparts are orange-buff, rather variable in tone and beautifully marked with black, grey and white, while the face and underparts are white, the latter often with a pale buff tinge at the sides of the breast and sometimes with sparse, fine dark spots. The sexes are very similar, but females have a tendency to be slightly larger and darker and are often more obviously spotted below. The bill is pale yellow and the claws black. Apparently reliable reports of Barn Owls glowing in the dark are possibly explained by luminous bacteria, from decayed wood, adhering to the plumage.

The Barn Owl's long wings and buoyant flight are adaptations to hunting in open habitats such as heaths, moor edges, deserts, cultivated land, grasslands, wetland margins and open parkland. When feeding young, or in hard winter weather, it will hunt during the day, but as a rule hunting is undertaken from around dusk (late afternoon in winter) to dawn. It roosts in dark places in ruins, churches, barns and outbuildings, in hollow trees or in holes and crevices in cliffs, quarries and walls. In spite of its pale coloration, a Barn Owl can be surprisingly hard to spot as it stands bolt upright and motionless in a dark corner.

Often its presence is first indicated by droppings on walls or beams, or by the blackish, firm pellets (glossy when fresh) which accumulate under favourite perches. Barn Owls normally roost singly or in pairs, but small groups roosting together have also been recorded. Roosting sites may also be used for nesting or be close to the place eventually selected for breeding. When disturbed from a roost, a Barn Owl will often only fly a short distance before alighting again and, as with most other owls abroad during the day, is very likely to be mobbed by small birds.

Barn Owls are active hunters, foraging on the wing and probably covering many kilometres during a single night. They often follow regular routes, particularly along hedgerows, the edges of ditches and watercourses, road verges and woodland margins, always showing a preference for areas with rough grass or other fairly short vegetation where small mammals are likely to be most abundant. When hunting, an owl will rarely rise much above a few metres, except when passing over hedges, walls, trees or other obstacles, and it flaps and glides in a manner which looks haphazard but which, in reality, is buoyant and beautifully controlled. Abrupt twists and turns are frequent, as are short spells of rather clumsy-looking hovering. Prey is taken in the talons after a swift pounce or a shallow dive and, if necessary, may be killed by crushing with the bill. Barn Owls also employ the watch, wait and pounce tactics common to many other owls and birds of prey, hunting from fence-posts, walls and other low vantage points. They are also adept at pursuing and capturing prey on foot over short distances.

It is now generally believed that the Barn Owl's visual acuity is fairly poor and that a hunting bird relies far more on its phenomenal hearing than on its eyesight. The asymmetrical ears give the bird a remarkable ability to locate sound with great precision: laboratory experiments have shown that Barn Owls can both locate and capture live prey in conditions of complete darkness. They can, quite literally, hunt by ear alone. Their silent flight enables them both to hear the movements and calls of their prey and to approach within striking distance without themselves being heard.

Unless it is too large, the prey is swallowed whole, either on the spot or a very short distance from the point of capture. If it is feeding young, an owl will take the prey directly to the nest-site, flying close to the ground with the prey carried in its talons. The undigested portions, such as bones, fur and feathers, are regurgitated in the form of pellets. The pellets, produced at a rate of about 2 per 24 hours, are very resistant to decay, last for many years and accumulate in considerable quantities at breeding sites: valuable data on prey can be obtained through pellet analysis.

Over most of its range, the Barn Owl's principal food is rodents and other very small mammals, with the main species varying according to locality and habitat. Voles and mice predominate in many places, with shrews and rats often featuring as secondary or alternative prey. On a world scale, the variety of small mammal species recorded as Barn Owl prey is enormous. Small

birds, such as sparrows snatched at the roost or flushed from bushes by the owl, can also form an important if generally small part of the diet, or may be of particular seasonal importance; again, the list of species involved worldwide is huge and, as noted earlier, includes even colonial seabirds in some island Barn Owl populations—in such cases, though, usually as major consituents of the diet. Other assorted prey includes lizards, small snakes, frogs, toads and large insects—any of which may assume considerable importance to owls living in, for example, arid regions around the Mediterranean. Even fish may be eaten at times: a Barn Owl has actually been seen plunging into a pool rather like a small Osprey!

Above all, the Barn Owl is essentially a fairly specialized or 'restricted' small mammal feeder,

Barn Owls have taken to nesting in barns, churches, ruins and other buildings, wherever they are available, in preference to hollow trees, rock crevices and other natural sites.

not as restricted perhaps as some of the *Asio* owls, but on the other hand not as versatile or adaptable as, say, a Tawny Owl (*Strix aluco*). As such, its numbers and breeding performance over large parts of its range are governed by the cyclic population fluctuations of voles and mice.

Breeding starts early in the year and may continue into late summer. In Britain, it is at its height in May but young have been recorded in every month except January. Displays include much shrieking, flying over the territory, noisy aerial chases, occasional (but probably largely accidental) wing-clapping and presentation of food by the male. Tongue-clicking, bill-fencing and mutual preening with cheek-rubbing are all important ingredients in the behaviour of paired birds.

No nest is built, although the often large accumulations of pellets at a site may form a compact surround for the eggs. Common sites are on beams, ledges and floors in lofts and buildings and the floors of assorted crevices and hollows; artificial sites in boxes and baskets will also be used. Nests in holes in trees are common in many areas. When first laid, the eggs are pure white, with no gloss, but they soon become stained and dirty. They are more elliptical than those of most owls, with average dimensions of 40 x 32 mm. A clutch is normally 4—7 eggs, but may be as small as 2 or as large as 14. The eggs are laid at 2 or 3 day intervals and incubation, by the female only, begins with the first egg. Hatching occurs at 33 days. Throughout incubation, and while the owlets are small, the male provides for the family, but later both adults share in feeding the young. Newly hatched owlets are clothed in a short grey first down, more plentiful on the upperparts than beneath, which is gradually replaced by a second, longer white down which persists until the juvenile plumage is complete. If disturbed at the nest-site the young are usually docile and can be handled with ease, while the parent birds quickly fly to safety. On occasions, however, the adult birds will take up a distinctive defensive posture. The bird crouches, or even becomes almost prone, with its wings widely spread. The head may be swung from side to side while the bird hisses and snaps its bill. Both parent and nestling owls can make an audible 'snap' with their bills, together with hissing and snoring noises. The young leave the nest after 9 to 12 weeks, by which time they are virtually indistinguishable from their parents, apart from lingering wisps of down.

From its protracted breeding season, its varying clutch sizes, the asynchronous hatching of the young and its fluctuating breeding output, it is clear that the Barn Owl is geared to a variable food supply. This in turn is habitat related and it is habitat that almost certainly lies at the root of the big declines in Barn Owl populations which have occurred in some countries. In Britain, where the population has declined by well over half since the 1930s, the main cause is probably most closely associated with changes in agricultural land use, particularly the rise in intensive arable farming in some areas, which has led to the loss of much prey-rich habitat. This has been exacerbated by other factors, such as poisoning by pesticides (notably aldrin, dieldrin and heptachlor) in the 1960s, severe winter weather with prolonged periods of snow lying (Barn Owls are highly vulnerable in these conditions) and the loss of nest-sites through the disappearance of hedgerow trees and the modernization or replacement of old barns and outbuildings. Saving what habitat remains and urging farmers and landowners to create more, plus the careful protection of the remaining owls and their breeding sites, all backed by more research into Barn Owl ecology, could offer the best chance of arresting and reversing the decline: the release of captive-bred birds, a popular technique, is unlikely to make much difference unless the environmental problems are solved first.

Until comparatively recently, the Ashy-faced Owl *T. glaucops* from Hispaniola (West Indies) was regarded as a race of *T. alba*, but it has been afforded full species status following the discovery that this small, dark bird is breeding sympatrically with much larger, whiter Barn Owls on the island. The intriguing suggestion has been made that *T. glaucops* may be more closely related to extinct West Indian *Tyto* owls than to *T. alba*.

Although most current authors list the two grass owls as separate but very closely related species, opinion on this treatment is by no means unanimous. They are regarded as two species here, with the cautionary note that further studies may reverse this at any time. A suitable compromise seems to be to regard the African Grass Owl *T. capensis* and the Eastern Grass Owl *T. longimembris* as forming a superspecies, with the two forms occupying a total range which is considerably wider than that of any other barn owl except *T. alba*.

Though superficially similar to the Barn Owl, the Grass Owl *Tyto capensis* (380 to 420 mm) is easily distinguished by its much darker chocolate brown back. The Eastern Grass Owl, which looks very similar to the African bird, is now treated as a separate species, *T. longimembris*. Grass Owls differ from Barn Owls in having longer, almost unfeathered legs which are presumably better suited to their more terrestrial life in grassland habitats.

Map: *Tyto capensis*: grassland.

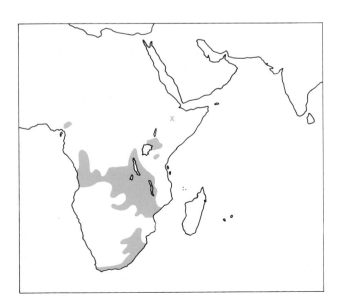

The African Grass Owl is widely distributed in parts of central and south-eastern Africa, but is scarce or local in some regions. It has been recorded a few times from Cameroon at the north-western extremity of its range and at least once from Ethiopia, beyond its normal north-eastern limits. Up to four subspecies have been suggested. As many as six or even eight races have been described for the Eastern Grass Owl, which is found from India into Burma and parts of Indo-China (where its distribution is only sketchily known), in southernmost China and Taiwan, southwards through the Philippines to Sulawesi and (probably) the Lesser Sundas, in south-eastern New Guinea, in parts of Australia and, at the extreme south-eastern end of its range, in New Caledonia and Fiji.

Both Grass Owls are similar in appearance, with only detail differences in plumage, although the African Grass Owl is much the darker of the two above. They are somewhat larger than *Tyto alba*, noticeably long-winged and short-tailed, and sooty brown (African) or dark brown (Eastern) above, with white faces and underparts; the underparts may also be pale brownish in the African species. The tarsus is noticeably long and

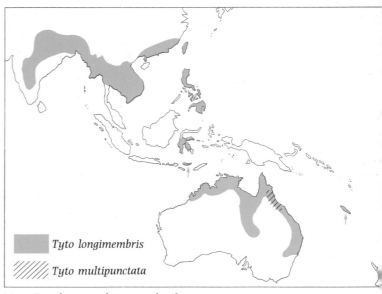

Map: *Tyto longimembris*: grassland.
T. multipunctata: rainforest, north-east Australia.

Right: The Lesser Sooty Owl *Tyto multipunctata* (320 to 350 mm), photographed in north-east Queensland. Slightly smaller and paler than Sooty Owls from other areas, these birds have recently been named as a separate species.

Below: The Eastern Grass Owl *Tyto longimembris* (380 to 420 mm). This female is outside her nest tunnel, which is well concealed among the long grass. Inside the tunnel, four owlets were waiting to be fed.

slender, and largely unfeathered, presumably an adaptation to both species' often terrestrial lifestyle: both are adept at hunting on foot as well as from the slow quartering flight that is typical of many *Tyto* owls.

They are principally birds of open grasslands, frequently in wet or at least moist situations. The African Grass Owl lays its eggs in long grass, building no nest but often using trampled vegetation as a platform. This may be linked to 'runs' through the vegetation. Four conspicuously white eggs are usually laid, but up to 6 have been recorded. Rodents and shrews are the main prey in Africa, especially the Natal Multimammate Rat *Mastomy natalensis*, the Vlei Rat *Otomys irroratus* and the Angoni Vlei Rat *O. angoniensis* in one series of studies, while in Australia the recorded prey of the Eastern Grass Owl includes the Yellow-footed Antenichus *Antechinus flavipes*, the Common Planigale *Planigale maculatas*, the Australian Swamp Rat *Rattus lutreolus* and the Sugar Glider *Petaurus breviceps*. Both species also take some small to medium-small ground-living birds and a variety of insects.

The Sooty Owl *T. tenebricosa* is confined to forests in New Guinea and pockets of rainforest and wet eucalypt forest in south-eastern Australia. Midway between these two widely separated populations, in extensive rainforest in the Atherton area of north-eastern Australia, there is another population of sooty owls, formerly regarded as *T. tenebricosa* but now treated as a distinct species, the Lesser Sooty Owl *T. multipunctata*. Sooty Owls are very distinctive, very dark-coloured barn owls, with white spots on the upperparts, grey faces and grey and white underparts; Lesser Sooty Owls are slightly smaller, somewhat paler and more liberally marked with white above and with mainly whitish faces. Both species have exceptionally large dark eyes. The weird, tremulous call of the Sooty Owl has been likened to the whistle of a falling bomb, the neighing of a horse or the singing of a boiling kettle! Lessers apparently have similar but noticeably higher-pitched voices.

Both species nest in holes in forest trees. Sooty Owls have territories which may be as large as 200—800 hectares, or even more, but Lessers seem to occupy much smaller ranges and thus to exist at greater densities. Terrestrial mammals such as rodents and bandicoots are taken by both species in Australia, plus some possums and gliders (arboreal mammals) and birds. Where

The Sooty Owl *Tyto tenebricosa* (330 to 380 mm) is the most distinctive member of the genus but is probably one of the least known, for it is confined to dense forests and is seldom seen.

Right: The Australian Masked Owl *Tyto novaehollandiae* (490 to 530 mm) is the largest member of the genus. This individual is in full threat display, snapping its bill and making itself appear as large and formidable as possible. Specimens from Buru and Tanimbar are now treated as a separate species, the Lesser Masked Owl *T. sororcula*.

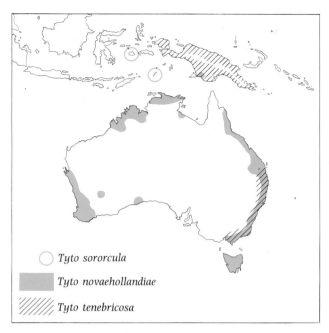

Tyto sororcula: lowland forest, Tanimbar and Buru.
T. novaehollandiae: forest and scattered woodland near open country.
T. tenebricosa: forest, New Guinea, rainforest and wet eucalypt forest, south-east Australia.

forest habitat has been cleared, the owls also hunt open areas, including road verges; this accords well with observations in the uplands of New Guinea, where Sooty Owls feed on rats and bandicoots in alpine grassland and on rats, small forest marsupials, various other mammals and some birds in adjacent sub-alpine forest.

The Lesser Masked Owl *T. sororcula* is known only from three specimens from Indonesian islands, two from Tanimbar and one from Buru: it has not been seen in the wild, but is presumed to occur in lowland forest there. Until quite recently, these specimens were treated as representing two races of the Masked Owl *T. novaehollandiae*, a similar but larger bird found in Australia and Tasmania and one fairly small region of southern New Guinea. Its Australian range is essentially around the coastal fringe, apparently not more than 300 km inland, but is still imperfectly known. The Masked Owl's stronghold is in the Tasmanian region; elsewhere it is generally scarce and has probably declined in, or disappeared from, many areas. The general pattern of decline has been linked to the progressive disappearance of native mammals since the European settlement of Australia.

Only one specimen of The Taliabu Owl
Tyto nigrobrunnea (270 to 330 mm)
has been collected and so far nothing is
known of its life or ecology.

The Masked Owl is the largest of all the barn owls, generally much darker than *T. alba* and with a characteristic dark margin to the face from which the bird takes its English name. Four subspecies of this rather variable bird are generally recognized, with the Tasmanian owl *T. n. castanops* being the darkest of all and also showing a chestnut face. Both the Tasmanian *castanops* and the small, dark race *manusi* (isolated on Manus Island in the Bismarck Archipelago) have been put forward by some authorities as candidate species in their own right, but pending further research it seems best to retain them as races of *T. novaehollandiae*.

The Masked Owl is essentially a bird of woodland and eucalypt forest where it requires clearings and extensive forest edge for hunting. In Australia, the main prey species are rodents (both native and introduced), bandicoots, gliders, possums and rabbits, plus some bats and birds. The Masked Owl's pellets are particularly large, sometimes up to 90 mm long. The bird nests in holes and hollows in trees, often fairly high, and lays 2 to 4 white eggs.

The Sulawesi Owl *T. rosenbergii* is confined to the island of that name (formerly Celebes), where it occurs from sea level up to 1100 m in woodland, grasslands and also cultivated areas near human settlements. Little appears to be known of its ecology, but it presumably resembles that of other *Tyto* owls found in similar habitats. It is a fairly large species (410 to 510 mm in length), grey-brown above with obvious white spots. Some authorities consider it to be very closely related to *T. alba*, others to *T. novaehollandiae*, but there is at present general agreement that it merits full specific status.

The Sulawesi Owl apparently overlaps to some extent with the Minahassa Owl *T. inexpectata* on the long, narrow Minahassa Peninsula in the north of Sulawesi. The Minahassa Owl appears to be a rare resident of forested hill country, but is known from only eleven specimens, all but one of them taken in the northern part of the peninsula in areas between 250 and 1500 m above sea level. The Taliabu Owl *T. nigrobrunnea*, dark above with tiny white spots and with a rufous facial disc and golden-brown underparts spotted and vermiculated with black, is known only from a single specimen collected on Taliabu in the Sula Islands. It may be a race of *T. inexpectata*, but is virtually a wholly unknown bird.

The barn owls have speciated to a greater extent in Australasia than anywhere else in the world. Two of the thirteen species of *Tyto*—the Sulawesi Barn Owl *Tyto rosenbergii* (410 to 510 mm) and, below, the Minahassa Barn Owl *Tyto inexpectata* (270 to 330 mm)—are confined to the island of Sulawesi and six other species are confined to the Australasian region.

Sulawesi Barn Owl
Tyto rosenbergii

Minahassa Barn Owl
Tyto inexpectata

Tyto inexpectata: confined to northern peninsula of Sulawesi, forested hills.
T. nigrobrunnea: Taliabu, Sula Islands.
Tyto rosenbergii: woodland, grassland, cultivated areas, Sulawesi.

//////	*Tyto inexpectata*
	Tyto nigrobrunnea
▓▓	*Tyto rosenbergii*

The Golden Owl *Tyto aurantia* (270 to 330 mm) is another island species, confined to New Britain in the Bismarck Archipelago. Below: The Madagascar Red Owl *Tyto soumagnei* (about 270 mm) is an isolated and largely unknown rainforest species, recorded only once in the last fifty years.

The little-known Golden Owl *T. aurantia* is endemic to the island of New Britain in Papua New Guinea. It is a handsome barn owl, golden buff (darker above) and beautifully mottled with blackish-brown; it is known to occur in lowlands and primary forest in the mountains up to 1830 m, and to eat small rodents. Although it is included in the ICBP list of the world's most threatened birds, and described there as 'rare', the latest published work on the birds of Papua New Guinea suggests that it is not uncommon locally.

Golden Owl
Tyto aurantia

Madagascar Red Owl
Tyto soumagnei

Map: *Tyto aurantia*: lowlands and primary forest to 1830 m, New Britain.

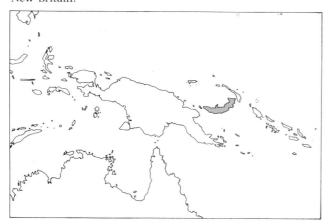

Map: *Tyto soumagnei*: rainforest, Madagascar.

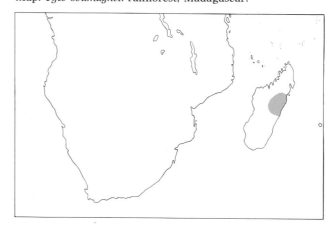

Surprisingly little is known about the Bay Owl *Phodilus badius*, a bird which looks very like some of the *Tyto* owls in general appearance but has differently shaped facial discs, with erectile feathers above the eyes, and short, rather rounded wings. The upperparts are a rich chestnut and gold, spotted with black and white, and the underparts creamy with sparse black spots. There is quite considerable variation in size, with birds from the western end of the range up to 330 mm in total length and those from the eastern end only 230—280 mm.

The limits of its western distribution are still unclear, especially in north-eastern India; its occurrence in Nepal is doubtful (contrary to earlier statements), it is rare in Sikkim and its status in Bhutan is uncertain. It is believed, however, to be generally distributed in the appropriate habitats over large parts of South-east Asia south to Sumatra, Borneo, Java and Bali; two of the five subspecies which have been described are known from single Indonesian islands—*P. b. parvus* from Belitung off south-east Borneo and *P. b. arixuthus* from the north Natunas, off north-west Borneo. The most isolated population (*P. b. assimilis*) is that in Sri Lanka.

Though superficially similar and related to the barn owls, the Oriental Bay Owl *Phodilus badius* (230 to 330 mm) is sufficiently distinct to be placed in a separate subfamily. It is a thoroughly nocturnal forest species but little else is known of its ecology and behaviour.

Map: *Phodilus badius*: forest, often near water.

In the past the Madagascar Red Owl *T. soumagnei* was erroneously regarded as a 'grass owl'. A distinctive, light reddish-brown bird, it is only known from about a dozen specimens and a few sight records and, apart from a record in 1973, has not been seen since 1934. It is evidently a rare bird, inhabiting humid rainforest in east-central Madagascar, but with three of the specimens from locations outside heavily forested areas. Nothing is known of its habits in the wild.

Two points are obvious from this account of the *Tyto* owls—that very little is known about half of them, and that their taxonomy is still far from clear: as a group, they require much further research, especially in the Australasian region where the most forms occur.

The Philippines have been included in previous accounts of this bird's distribution, but in fact there is only a single record from the 1920s.

Bay owls are essentially strictly nocturnal forest-dwellers, ranging from lowlands to hill country, although records from Malaysia also mention partially cleared country and plantations. Their short-winged form shows that they are adapted to hunting within forests or other close cover, where they prey on a variety of small mammals and birds, lizards, frogs and insects. Nests have been found in holes and hollows in trees (also used as daytime roosts); 3 or 4 white oval eggs are laid and asynchronous hatching appears to be the rule. One call is a soft hoot, but the owls are very noisy in the breeding season, with many other vocalizations.

The Itombwe Owl *P. prigoginei* was unknown until a specimen was collected at 2430 m in the Itombwe Mountains of eastern Zaire, close to Lake Tanganyika, in 1951. Since then, there has been a 1970s sight record of what was almost certainly this species from a tea estate in nearby Burundi, with another report from elsewhere in 1989. This bird has smaller, weaker feet and a smaller, even more compressed bill than *P. badius*—suggesting that it may feed more on small lizards, amphibians and insects—but so far nothing is known of its ecology. It is a darker, more richly patterned bird than the Bay Owl, with a longer tail; detailed comparisons with *P. badius* show that on plumage, size, proportions and structure it is clearly a separate species and not, as has been suggested, an isolated race of the Bay Owl.

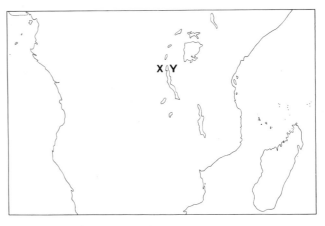

Phodilus prigoginei: mountains of eastern Zaire (X), tea estate, Burundi (Y).

The Itombwe Owl *Phodilus prigoginei* (230 to 330 mm) is known from only a single specimen from eastern Zaire (from which this illustration is reconstructed) and one or two sightings in nearby parts of east-central Africa.

CHAPTER FIVE

Fishing Owls, Eagle Owls and the Snowy Owl

Ketupa, Scotopelia, Bubo, Nyctea

The little known fish owls in the genus *Ketupa* are a group of four large, powerful species that between them range over much of Asia. Together with the three African fishing owls in the genus *Scotopelia*, they can be regarded as the nocturnal counterparts of the Osprey and fish eagles.

In the past, the Asian fish owls were sometimes included together with eagle owls in the genus *Bubo*, but nowadays they are usually regarded as warranting separate status, mainly because they have specializations for feeding on fish. Nevertheless, they strongly resemble eagle owls in appearance, having similar prominent ear tufts, colouring, size and heavy build. In fact, they are often mistaken for eagle owls, although they differ in three main respects. Firstly, their feet are devoid of feathers and adapted for gripping slippery fish; secondly, they have even less prominent facial discs, presumably because their sense of hearing is a relatively unimportant aid in locating fish; thirdly, they lack soft plumage and silent flight, no doubt because their prey, being under water, is unable to hear them no matter how much noise they make in their approach.

ASIAN FISH OWLS

The four Asian fish owls live in a wide range of environments, from hot, humid, equatorial forests to cold, boreal forests close to the Arctic Circle, but nevertheless they have similar basic ecological requirements. All four species live by lakes, rivers and streams with well-wooded banks, and feed mainly on relatively large fish and other aquatic animals. They would almost certainly compete if they lived together in the same area, but this is largely avoided by there being little overlap in their distribution.

The range of Blakiston's Fish Owl (*K. blakistoni*) is completely exclusive, for it is separated by about 800 km from the nearest definitely known population of another *Ketupa* species. It lives in wooded river valleys and, despite the fact that its range is so far to the north, it is apparently resident throughout the year. This species is rare everywhere, perhaps because it is dependent on streams and rivers which are sufficiently fast-flowing to remain partially unfrozen throughout the winter. According to the ICBP, Blakiston's Fish Owl is considered threatened in the USSR, with a total population estimated at 300—400. In Japan around 50 were located in 1984 while in China there was no recent data.

The ranges of the Brown Fish Owl (*K. zeylonensis*), Malaysian Fish Owl (*K. ketupa*) and Tawny Fish Owl (*K. flavipes*) are also largely exclusive. The Brown Fish Owl has a tropical distribution, and is replaced by the Malaysian Fish Owl in the high rainfall, equatorial region of southern Indo-China and Malaysia. Both species are common throughout most of their range, although the Brown Fish Owl is rare in the arid areas to the west of India. Both species are most numerous along sluggish streams and rivers meandering through forest or woodland, but occupy a wide range of other waterside habitats, including mangrove swamps, beach forests by the seashore, and even clumps of large trees by flooded rice-fields, fish-ponds and reservoirs. The Tawny Fish Owl has a mainly montane distribution in the Himalayas and the mountains of southern China and Indo-China. Much less catholic in its choice of habitats than the other species, it is more or less confined to precipitous mountain streams flowing through dense forest. It appears to be rather rare throughout its range, or at any rate it has rarely been recorded.

The ranges of the Brown, Malaysian and Tawny Fish Owls overlap to some extent in parts of Indo-China. There is little information about their ecology in this region, but what there is suggests that they segregate into different habitats. In Burma, for example, the Malaysian

Fish Owl is more or less confined to coastal regions and the courses of the larger rivers, particularly the Irrawaddy delta, while the Brown Fish Owl occurs mainly along the wooded rivers and streams of the interior. It is also notable that both species are absent from mountain streams in Indo-China, where their place is taken by the Tawny Fish Owl, though both occur at higher altitudes elsewhere in their range. The Malaysian Fish Owl, for example, occurs to at least 1300 m in Borneo, and the Brown Fish Owl to 2000 m in Ceylon. Much more ecological information is needed, but it appears probable that the different

fish owls seldom come into contact with each other, even when the edges of their ranges overlap. Here, the evidence suggests that the different species share out the available habitats, or occur at different altitudes, each being more restricted in areas where it overlaps with other species than in areas that it occupies exclusively.

Like most owls, the fish owls are strongly territorial and tend to be evenly spaced in suitable habitats. Travelling along small rivers in the

Blakiston's Fish Owl *Ketupa blakistoni* (510 to 610 mm) is an inhabitant of eastern Siberia and north-eastern China and the only fish owl to have fully feathered legs. Apparently it has the habit of wading in shallow water hunting for crayfish.

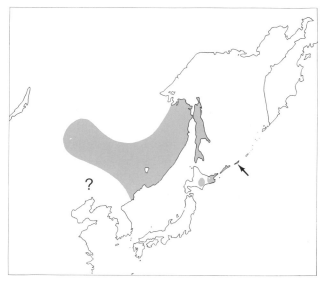

Ketupa blakistoni: wooded river valleys.

interior of Borneo, for example, it is normal to see or disturb a pair of Malaysian Fish Owls at regular intervals of 1 to 2 km. In one especially favoured area I saw nine pairs in less than 7 km of river. Fish owls usually roost in waterside trees with dense foliage, mangoes being particularly popular in tropical areas. Sometimes a pair roost together, but more often they roost in separate trees a short distance apart. They occasionally emerge from their roosts in the late afternoon, and this has earned them the reputation of being semi-diurnal. In fact, they rarely hunt before dusk, and are hardly more diurnal than eagle owls or other species that are generally regarded as thoroughly nocturnal. I have watched Malaysian and Brown Fish Owls hunting on numerous occasions, but only once before dusk, and then on a dark stormy evening.

Fish owls usually hunt from a tree-stump, dead branch or some other vantage point overlooking the water's edge. They usually catch their prey in the same way as a fish eagle, by swooping at it, and snatching it from the surface of the water with their talons. However, Blakiston's Fish Owl often simply drops from a perch onto its prey and has also sometimes been known to plunge into the water like an Osprey. The feet of fish owls are beautifully adapted to grip a wriggling, slippery, loose-scaled fish. They are devoid of feathers and covered below by numerous sharp-edged, spiky scales, while their claws are long and curved with a sharp, lower cutting edge. In fact, they are very like the feet of fish eagles and the Osprey.

The Tawny Fish Owl *Ketupa flavipes* (480 to 510 mm) has unfeathered feet covered in spiny scales, and sharp claws, superbly adapted for gripping fish. Although fish forms the main part of their diet, Tawny Fish Owls also take other prey. Crabs, crayfish and frogs can be caught in the shallows but mammals, birds, snakes and insects have also been recorded.

Ketupa flavipes: mountain streams in dense forest.

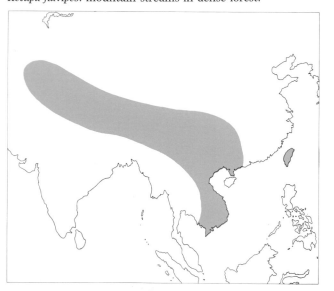

The Malaysian Fish Owl *Ketupa ketupa* (380 to 430 mm) is a common species over most of its range. Like other fish-eating owls, it watches for its prey from a perch at the water's edge, then swoops to snatch it from the surface of the water, in much the same way as a fish eagle. This individual was photographed in Sumatra.

Map: *Ketupa ketupa*: streams and rivers through forest and woodland; also mangrove and beach forests, clumps of trees near rice-fields, fish ponds or reservoirs.

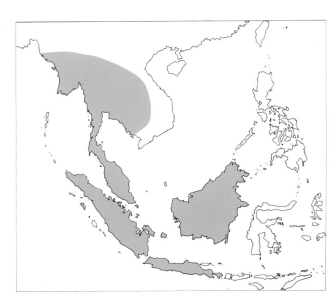

However, although fish owls have a diet that consists primarily of fish, they will take almost any other prey that comes their way, including small mammals, birds, snakes, frogs, crayfish, crabs and sometimes insects. The mammals recorded in their diet include a small porcupine, and birds include species up to the size of junglefowl and pheasants. They also scavenge to some extent; the Brown Fish Owl, for example, has been recorded feeding on the carcass of a crocodile. Fish owls are sometimes seen wading in shallow water. Often they are merely bathing, but not infrequently they are hunting for crayfish, crabs and other easily caught aquatic animals. Blakiston's Fish Owl is said to hunt regularly in this manner, and the Malaysian Fish Owl certainly does so occasionally, but such behaviour may be mainly incidental to bathing.

Blakiston's Fish Owls commence breeding as early as February, often while there is still snow on the ground. They nest in holes in large dead trees but have recently taken to breeding in nest-boxes in parts of Japan where few natural suitable nest-sites remain. The clutch is usually of 1 to 2 eggs, all the incubation being done by the female, and taking 35 to 37 days. The young leave the

Ketupa zeylonensis:
streams and rivers through forest and woodland.

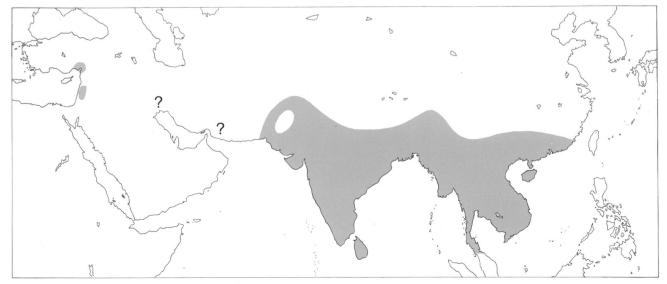

The Brown Fish Owl *Ketupa zeylonensis* (480 to 510 mm) is the most widely distributed of the four species of Asian fish owls which replace each other over a large part of the continent. Pairs call noisily to each other in the breeding season, which falls between November and May, the dry season in much of their range.

nest up to 50 days later, but are often fed by the parents for a further year. The other three species use a variety of nest-sites, including holes in trees and river-banks, ledges in cliffs and ruins, hollows in the forks of trees, and the old nests of crows and eagles. Clutch-sizes of from 1 to 3 eggs have been recorded for the Brown Fish Owl, of 1 egg for the Malaysian Fish Owl and of 1 to 2 eggs for the Tawny Fish Owl. The Brown Fish Owl appears to breed between November and May throughout its range. In India and northern Indo-China this is the dry season, which suggests that the breeding season might be timed to coincide with the period when river levels are low, the water clear, and fish therefore easy to catch. Unfortunately, the same period is wet in the Middle East and a more satisfactory explanation obviously needs to be found. There are breeding records for the Tawny Fish Owl from the Himalayas in the dry season, but they are too few to be very significant. The Malaysian Fish Owl breeds between December and May in Malaya and Borneo. It is the wettest time of the year in this region, but other times are only less wet, not dry. Obviously, much more information will have to be accumulated before the breeding seasonality of fish owls can be properly explained.

Like most owls, the fish owls are particularly noisy before breeding, and pairs sometimes indulge in bouts of duetting which continue for many minutes. They have a great variety of hooting and mewing calls which are probably distinctive, though descriptions in the literature are confusingly similar. The voice of the small Malaysian Fish Owl is perhaps the most easily recognized, for it is higher-pitched and more musical than the voices of the larger species.

Identification of the Asian fish owls is likely to be a problem only in the parts of Indo-China where the ranges of Brown, Malaysian and Tawny Fish Owls overlap. These three species are, in fact, fairly easily distinguished. The Brown Fish Owl is large, about 480 to 510 mm long, and has fine, wavy, horizontal barring on its underparts; the Tawny Fish Owl is also large, but lacks horizontal barring on its underparts and is a very rich rufous colour; while the Malaysian Fish Owl has neither horizontal barring nor rich rufous colouring, and is relatively small, about 380 to 430 mm long.

It remains to consider the relationship between the Brown Fish Owl and Blakiston's Fish Owl, for some authorities prefer to regard them as a single species. The two resemble each other, and differ from the Tawny and Malaysian Fish Owls, in having fine, wavy, horizontal barring on their underparts. However, both species are very variable, and it is difficult to point to any differences that strongly suggest that they are really distinct. It is true that Blakiston's Fish Owl is generally pale in colour, and slightly larger than the Brown Fish Owl, but these are differences that might be expected in view of its northerly distribution and, in any case, they are no greater than the differences between widespread populations of the Brown Fish Owl. Examples of the latter are very pale and buff in the arid areas of Palestine, but a richer yellow brown in the humid forested areas of India and Indo-China. It is also true that Blakiston's Fish Owl differs from the Brown Fish Owl, as well as from the other two species, in having completely feathered tarsi, but again this difference could well be correlated with its northerly distribution. To support this idea there is the fact that the Brown and Malaysian Fish Owls, which have tropical and equatorial distributions, resemble each other in having completely naked tarsi, while the Tawny Fish Owl, which lives further to the north and at higher altitudes than the two latter species, is intermediate and has tarsi that are feathered to about half way down.

This dispute can be resolved only when more is known about the status of fish owls in eastern China. The Brown Fish Owl is known to occur in Kwangsi and Kwangtung Provinces in the south, and Blakiston's Fish Owl in Hopei Province in the north, but it is not known for certain whether fish owls occur at all in the intervening area. If they do not, then it is entirely a matter of taste whether Blakiston's Fish Owl is regarded as a separate species or not. On the other hand, if there are intervening populations that intergrade with the Brown Fish Owl in the south, and Blakiston's Fish Owl in the north, then all the populations must be regarded as a single species.

AFRICAN FISHING OWLS

The three African fishing owls in the genus *Scotopelia* resemble their Asian counterparts in being large and powerful, and in having similar specializations for feeding on fish; otherwise they are quite different in general appearance. They lack ear tufts, and have loose feathering on their heads which gives them a characteristic shaggy,

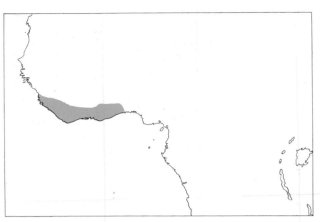

Scotopelia ussheri: rainforest.

maned look. However, in spite of their superficial dissimilarity, it is thought that the two groups have evolved from the same parent stock, and not independently on the two continents. Obviously, they must have been isolated from each other for a long time to be so different in appearance.

Even less is known about African fishing owls than about Asian species. The least poorly known is Pel's Fishing Owl (*S. peli*), which is sparsely distributed throughout most of Africa south of the Sahara. It is a huge, magnificent species, a rich orange-rufous in colour, and one of the most spectacular of all the owls. It lives by rivers, lakes and marshes with forested banks, but is just as at home in riverine forest strips in desert regions as it is by rivers flowing through the great forests of Zaire. Along the Levubu River in the Kruger National Park of South Africa it reaches densities of up to one pair per 2 or 3 km of river, and may be equally common in many parts of Africa. The other two species are more rare and much less widely distributed. The Vermiculated Fishing Owl (*S. bouvieri*) is found mainly in riverine forest strips adjacent to the great block of continuous Zaire forest, but occurs neither within the continuous forest area, nor far away from the forest edge. The Rufous Fishing Owl (*S. ussheri*) is known only from a handful of records from the

Like other fish-eating owls, the Rufous Fishing Owl *Scotopelia ussheri* (460 to 510 mm) of West Africa has a very strong compressed bill and unfeathered legs and feet. It has been seen or collected on very few occasions and little is known about its behaviour. This photograph, taken in Liberia, clearly shows that its eyes are dark brown, not yellow as was previously thought.

rainforest region between Sierra Leone and Ghana. It appears to be at risk from both habitat destruction and pollution.

African fishing owls are occasionally seen in the open in the late afternoon, but they are essentially nocturnal and usually emerge from their roosts at dusk. Pel's Fishing Owl catches its prey by using a vantage point such as a stump or branch over the water, or sometimes a sandbank, and diving in feet first in the same way as the Asian fish owls. They certainly resemble the Asian species in their fish-catching adaptations, for they have unfeathered feet and tarsi, similarly sharp-edged spiny scales on their feet for gripping fish, poorly developed facial discs, and a relatively noisy flight. There is little definite information about the diet of African fishing owls. As well as fish, Pel's Fishing Owls are known to take frogs, crabs, mussels and even fruit, and Vermiculated Fishing Owls have been known to take crabs, prawns and small birds. It is probable that all three species feed primarily on fish and other aquatic animals, but that they take a wide range of other food items when opportunity offers. It is also probable that Pel's Fishing Owl is capable of taking larger prey than the other two species, for it is considerably bigger and more powerful, particularly in the structure of its feet.

Pel's Fishing Owl breeds in hollows and holes in large trees, or in large stick nests, probably abandoned by eagles, and has a clutch of 1 to 4 (usually 2) eggs. Most clutches have been recorded during the local dry season, so it is possible that breeding is timed to coincide with the period when rivers are low and clear, and fish easier to catch. Vermiculated Fishing Owls are known to use old stick nests, probably abandoned by other birds, and they also seem to breed in the local dry season. Nothing is known about the breeding biology of the Rufous Fishing Owl.

One of the best ways of locating Pel's Fishing Owl is to listen for it at night, for it is noisy and its calls carry for a considerable distance. Its most characteristic call is a deep, sonorous and musical double hoot which has been transcribed as 'hooomm-hut'. It is also said to have a hoot which rises to a screech and a terrifying wail. The voice of the Vermiculated Fishing Owl has seldom been heard, but a captive individual was recorded as uttering 'either a half-dozen short *hu's* in rapid succession, or a protracted quavering hoot'. The voice of the Rufous Fishing Owl seems to be undescribed.

Though the three African fishing owls are rather similar in general appearance and colour, they are not difficult to distinguish. Pel's Fishing Owl, which is the only one of the three species present over most of Africa, is easily recognized by its size, for it is up to 610 mm long and one of the largest owls in the world. The two smaller species are 460 to 510 mm long and best distinguished from each other by their colour. The Rufous Fishing Owl has bright rufous unbarred upperparts, whereas those of the Vermiculated Fishing Owl are sandy rufous and finely vermiculated with darker brown, the general effect being much more dull. The Vermiculated Fishing Owl has the ground colour of its underparts white, as opposed to sienna as in Pel's or rufous as in the Rufous Fishing Owl.

Pel's Fishing Owl
Scotopelia peli

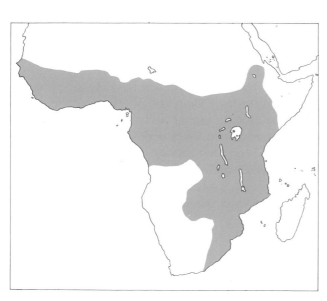

Scotopelia peli: forested banks of rivers, lakes and marshes.

Scotopelia bouvieri: riverine forest.

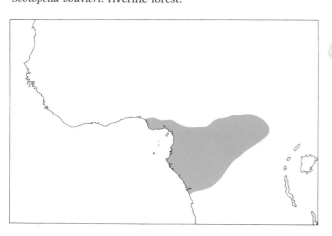

Pel's Fishing Owl *Scotopelia peli* (510 to 610 mm) is widely distributed in Africa, but the smaller Vermiculated Fishing Owl *S. bouvieri* (460 to 510 mm) is confined to forest rivers in West and Central Africa. Like all fishing owls, Asian as well as African, both species are largely nocturnal.

Vermiculated Fishing Owl
Scotopelia bouvieri

EAGLE OWLS

The eagle owls are among the largest and most magnificent of the owls, and are readily distinguished from all but the closely related Asian fish owls by a combination of their large size and possession of conspicuous ear tufts. They differ from the fish owls in having heavily feathered toes and tarsi, more pronounced facial discs, quieter flight and, of course, different feeding habits. As their name suggests, eagle owls are the nocturnal counterparts of such large birds of prey as the eagles and buzzards. With the exception of one apparently insectivorous species, they have a heavy, compressed, eagle-like bill and enormously powerful talons, and prey for the most part on mammals and birds up to the size of hares and game birds. Eagle owls are typical 'perch and pounce' hunters that sit and watch for their prey from a raised vantage point, and pounce on it from above. They are mainly nocturnal, depending on their acute hearing and excellent night vision to detect their prey, though they often venture forth before dusk and even hunt in broad daylight when food is scarce, or when they are forced to by the short summer nights.

The consensus of opinion recognizes twelve species of *Bubo*, although there are two species with particularly well-marked races that are recognized as good species by some authorities. The races in question are discussed below. Between them, the twelve recognized species have an almost cosmopolitan distribution, their role of large nocturnal predator being taken over by owls in other genera only in Arctic regions to the north of the tree-line, where they are replaced by the Snowy Owl, and in Australasia and the Pacific Islands, where they are replaced by the larger of the hawk owls. Within their enormous geographical range, the twelve eagle owls between them occupy just about all the available habitats from equatorial rainforest and mangrove forest to boreal forest, deserts and mountain-tops, the only essential prerequisite being the presence of at least a few trees or rocky outcrops to provide cover for roosting and nesting. For the most part, eagle owls segregate ecologically in a very clear-cut way, replacing each other either geographically or in different habitats, although the extent to which continents or lesser areas are subdivided into eagle owl niches varies greatly in different parts of the world. To take two extremes,

Populations of the Eurasian Eagle Owl *Bubo bubo* from southern or eastern arid regions tend to be paler, greyer and smaller than those from further north and west. This individual belongs to the race *B.b. nikolskii* (580 to 600 mm) from Transcaspia and Iran.

Above, right: The European race of the Eurasian Eagle Owl *B. b. bubo* (660 to 710 mm) is the largest and most powerful of all the owls. It is capable of killing young Roe Deer, foxes and such large game birds as Capercaillie, though its normal prey consists mainly of rats and other rodents. In recent years strict protection has restored Eagle Owl populations in Sweden and it is now becoming re-established in parts of Europe where it was previously rare or absent.

Map: *Bubo bubo*: in Europe, forested ravines, cliffs, rocky outcrops; elsewhere a variety of habitats from rainforest to desert.

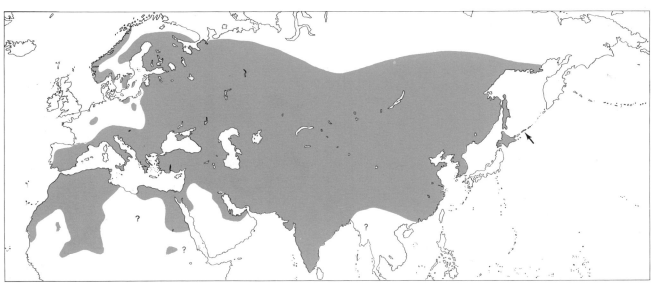

there is only one species of eagle owl in the whole of North and South America, compared with a total of seven in Africa, six of which are confined to the area south of the Sahara Desert.

The Eurasian Eagle Owl (*B. bubo*) is the best known species in the group, and also one of the most widely distributed. It ranges throughout most of Eurasia, from as far north as the Arctic Circle in Scandinavia, east across Russia to Sakhalin and the southern Kuriles, and south to the southern edge of the Sahara, to Arabia, Iran, India and southern China. As might be expected in view of its enormous range, the Eurasian Eagle Owl is very variable in both size and colour, the pattern of variation being similar to that of any other widely distributed Palaearctic species. Thus, it reaches its largest size, about 710 mm long, at

high latitudes and altitudes, and its smallest size, about 460 mm long, at the southern limits of its range, in North Africa, the Middle East and India. Similarly, it is relatively dark and brown in humid forested areas, and pale and sandy in arid desert and semi-desert regions. The variation is typically clinal, except in the case of two very distinct populations which have sometimes been regarded as distinct species. The more distinct of the two is known as the Pharaoh Eagle Owl (*B. b. ascalaphus*), and occupies suitable areas in the deserts of North Africa, Sinai, Arabia and the rest of the Middle East as far north and east as Lebanon, the Syrian Desert and the upper Euphrates. It is very different from the accepted populations of the Eurasian Eagle Owl, including those with which it comes into contact in the west and east of its range. It is

Eagle Owl *Bubo bubo*. An Eagle Owl's wings are large in relation to its body weight (wingspan: 1.5 m) and enable it to fly slowly and glide silently. Softened feathers on the edges of the wings also help to reduce the sound of its wingbeats, adding an element of surprise to its attack and enabling it to use its acute hearing to locate prey on the ground.

The Eurasian Eagle Owl typically nests on rocky hillsides or cliff-ledges but also makes use of the abandoned nests of buzzards and eagles. Most breeding territories hold several nest-sites which are used more or less regularly in rotation.

relatively small with weak talons, has pale plumage which is mottled rather than streaked, and is said to have a different voice. The two forms definitely interbreed to some extent in the Middle East, but the result is not primary intergradation, but rather a mixture of hybrids and typical individuals of both forms, which suggests that gene flow is very restricted. There is no recent information about the status of the two forms in northern Algeria, which is the only other area in which they are likely to come into contact, but both definitely occurred there in the last century, apparently without any sign of interbreeding. Obviously, the two forms are closely related and replace each other geographically, but it must remain largely a matter of taste whether they are regarded as separate species or not. Much the same is true of the Indian population of Eagle Owls that has been named *B. b. bengalensis*. It shows little sign of primary intergradation with neighbouring populations, and differs markedly from them in being smaller, darker and more richly coloured. In Europe the Eurasian Eagle Owl is typically associated with forested rocky outcrops, cliffs and ravines, but elsewhere it is found in all sorts of country, including dense coniferous or broadleaved forests, light woodland, mountains up to 4500 m, and deserts entirely devoid of trees. It tends to take larger prey than other owls but its diet is varied and includes mammals, birds, including other owls and even eagle owls, snakes, frogs, fish and insects; in fact, virtually anything that it comes across and can overcome. A study of the food of Eurasian Eagle Owls in Sweden showed 55 per cent of the prey animals to be mammals, 33 per cent birds, 11 per cent fish, and 1 per cent reptiles and amphibians, but no account was taken of insects or other invertebrates. The study showed that the most frequently recorded mammal and bird prey species were Brown Rats (18 per cent of the total of 484 items), assorted voles, mice and lemmings (18 per cent), Hooded Crows (9 per cent), assorted game birds up to the size of Capercaillies (9 per cent), hedgehogs (8 per cent), Red Squirrels (7 per cent), assorted ducks (5 per cent) and hares (4 per cent). Like other predators, individual Eurasian Eagle Owls sometimes learn to specialize on particular locally abundant prey species; some concentrate on Brown Rats, others on hedgehogs or squirrels; there is even a record of one individual in Switzerland that specialized on frogs, a total of

2397 bones of frogs being found in pellets from its territory. The proportion of different prey items in the diet can vary greatly according to the seasonal abundance of the prey. As an example 30 per cent of the diet of a bird in East Asia was made up of bats during the time when they migrated through its territory. On the other hand, Eurasian Eagle Owls are also opportunists and, being the largest and most powerful of all the owls, are capable of overcoming the most unlikely prey if they can take it by surprise. The Swedish study recorded such formidable prey items as 5 buzzards, 3 Goshawks, an Osprey and a wild cat, while foxes, porcupines and Peregrine Falcons have been recorded elsewhere. The heaviest recorded prey item is a Roe Deer weighing 13,000 g. To put this in perspective, a large Eurasian Eagle Owl weighs 3—4000 g.

Like many other owls, the Eurasian Eagle Owl is resident and strongly territorial throughout the year, although some mountain populations may be forced to descend to lower ground in winter. Most breeding territories hold several nesting sites which are used more or less in rotation. The sites are usually on cliff-ledges or the floor of rocky caves, in which case the nest itself is no more than a scrape in the ground, but sometimes the old abandoned nests of eagles or buzzards are taken over. Other nest-sites have included holes in trees, scrapes in the ground, usually near vegetation or boulders, and occasionally nests have been found in buildings. Up to 6 eggs are laid, 2 or 3 being the commonest number in Europe, and the clutch is usually completed early in the spring, often while there is still snow on the ground. Incubation begins with the laying of the first or second egg, and is carried out almost entirely by the female for 35 days. The young hatch asynchronously, the later ones generally dying unless food is exceptionally abundant. The male provides all the food for the young during the early stages of their development, both parents during the later stages. The young leave the nest when they are about five weeks old, although several more weeks elapse before they are capable of flying properly, and the parents continue to feed them to some extent for several months. This prolonged period of parental care is of great importance, for it provides the young with the time in which to learn the hunting skills upon which their subsequent survival depends. It is also important that the young should have the opportunity to learn to hunt while food is

abundant, and this is probably a major reason why Eagle Owls begin to breed so early in the spring. Early breeding ensures that the young are fledged by the end of June, leaving them several summer months in which to gain the necessary experience and skills.

In the New World the place of the Eurasian Eagle Owl is taken over by the Great Horned Owl (*B. virginianus*). The two species are very closely related. In fact, they differ only in relatively minor details of plumage colour and pattern, and must have become isolated from each other in comparatively recent times. The Great Horned Owl ranges more or less throughout North and South America, being absent only from the tundra regions of northernmost Canada and

Left: The sole representative of the genus in both North and South America, the Great Horned Owl *Bubo virginianus* (430 to 530 mm) occupies a remarkable range of habitats, from Alaska (where this individual was photographed) to the tip of South America. The largest birds are found in the northern parts of the range or at high altitudes in the Andes, where they have been recorded at 3000 metres or more.

Map: *Bubo virginianus*: wide range of habitats from boreal forests in north of its range to deciduous woodland and rainforest, desert and mountainous regions.

Over most of their range Great Horned Owls *Bubo virginianus* rear only one or two young per year, but in the far north they sometimes rear six or more in years when hares are very abundant.

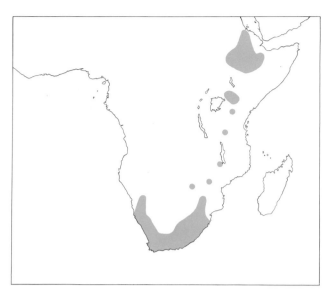

Bubo capensis: montane habitats, mainly above 1800 m.

Alaska. It is difficult to think of any bird, of any group, which occupies such a wide spectrum of habitats, for it occurs in the boreal forests of the far north, deciduous woodlands, the rainforests of the Amazon basin and Central America, coastal mangrove forests, the desert regions of both continents, and the mountains, reaching altitudes of more than 3000 m in the Andes of Ecuador. Like the Eurasian Eagle Owl, the Great Horned Owl varies clinally in both size and colour, the variation following the usual pattern. Thus, it is largest at high latitudes and altitudes, attaining a length of 510 mm in Alaska and 530 mm in the high Andes, and smallest in tropical lowland forest and desert areas, being only about 450 mm long in much of Central America and Mexico. Similarly, it is darker and more richly coloured in humid forests than it is in deserts or areas where there is snow for most of the year. To complicate matters, the Great Horned Owl has orange-breasted and white-breasted colour phases. However, the frequency of the two forms varies considerably from region to region, and conforms with the general pattern of colour variation. In central Canada and Alaska, for example, the white-breasted phase, which is ecologically the most appropriate, is almost totally dominant.

The feeding behaviour of the Great Horned Owl is similar to that of the Eurasian Eagle Owl though, being less powerful, the maximum size of prey that it can overcome is rather smaller. The populations that live in the boreal forests of northern Canada feed mainly on Varying Hares. Consequently, their numbers show a regular ten-year periodicity which corresponds with the regular and well-known ten-year cycle in the numbers of the Varying Hare. Similar cycles in the numbers of Eurasian Eagle Owls have been noted in Russia, though they are less well documented. The breeding biology of the Great Horned Owl is also similar to that of the Eurasian Eagle Owl, except that its clutch-size is more variable. Clutches of 6 eggs or more are not uncommon in the far north when hares are abundant, while clutches of 1 or 2 are the norm in tropical regions. The incubation and fledging periods are exactly the same.

Six species of eagle owls, half of the world's total, are confined to the area of Africa south of the Sahara Desert. Each of the six is much more restricted in its choice of habitat than the Great Horned Owl, or even the Eurasian Eagle Owl, for they segregate by sharing out the available habitats between them, rather than by replacing

Above and left: The race of the Cape Eagle Owl *Bubo capensis* (460 to 480 mm) that occupies the Kenya highlands and isolated mountains south to Zimbabwe is known as Mackinder's Eagle Owl *B. c. mackinderi*. In Kenya it is confined to areas above 1800 metres and often roosts in trees draped with picturesque Usnea lichens (above).

each other in different geographical regions. One of the six species, the Cape Eagle Owl (*B. capensis*), is closely allied to the Eurasian Eagle Owl and Great Horned Owl but, unlike them, it has a very restricted distribution, being confined to a series of isolated montane populations, some of which have been separated long enough to have evolved subspecific differences. One race is confined to the Ethiopian highlands; another, known as Mackinder's Eagle Owl (*B. c. mackinderi*) to the Kenya highlands, and outlying mountains as far south as Zimbabwe; and a third to the South African highlands. Apart from the fact that it occurs down to sea-level in southern Cape Province, the Cape Eagle Owl (which might more aptly be named the Mountain Eagle Owl) is confined to areas above about 1800 m, where it is associated with a mosaic habitat of montane grassland mixed with evergreen forest, and Afro-alpine moorland. It occurs to at least 4200 m on Mount Kenya.

The equivalent habitats at lower altitudes are occupied by the Spotted Eagle Owl (*B. africanus*) and Milky Eagle Owl (*B. lacteus*). In fact, the Cape Eagle Owl must occasionally come into contact with the latter species at altitudes of around 1800 to 2500 m, but its altitudinal range is basically complementary to theirs, and there can be little competition between them. The Cape Eagle Owl preys mainly on small mammals, such as rodents and hyraxes, but is known to take a wide variety of other food items including young antelopes, civets, hares, fruit bats, birds (including other owls and storks), snakes, crabs and insects. The nest is usually a shallow scrape on ledges or in caves in cliffs or on the ground among boulders or tree roots, but sometimes it is placed in the fork of a tree. The clutch is of 1 to 3 eggs, usually 2, and the incubation, which is usually done by the female, takes 34 to 38 days. The young fledge after 60 to 70 days in southern populations, and after 70 to 77 days in populations further north. However, they often remain dependent on the adults for another two months.

The Spotted Eagle Owl is very widely distributed in Africa south of the Sahara and has two well-defined races which replace each other approximately along the Equator. The northern form is much less spotted than the other, has greyer plumage, and brown rather than yellow

Right and far right: The southern race of the Spotted Eagle Owl *Bubo africanus* (300 to 400 mm) is very variable in colour but has two main phases, the commoner being grey (right, photographed in the Serengeti), the rarer, rufous or buff (far right, photographed in South Africa). Being one of the smaller eagle owls, it feeds to a greater extent than most on insects, but also preys on rodents, small birds and lizards. It occurs throughout the savannah regions of Africa and in suitable areas of eastern Arabia, being most numerous in lightly wooded rocky areas.

Bubo africanus: savannah and lightly wooded rocky areas.

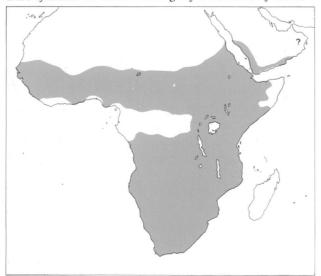

The race of the Spotted Eagle Owl that inhabits Africa north
of the Equator (*B. a. cinerascens*) differs from both the
southern African race (*B. a. africanus*) and the Arabian race
(*B. a. milesi*) in having dark brown rather than yellow or
orange eyes.

eyes. The Spotted Eagle Owl is not usually
regarded as being closely allied to the Eurasian
and Cape Eagle Owls, but the three species are
superficially similar, and replace each other rather
sharply in different areas and habitats. In fact,
they are sufficiently similar to have been
confused, even as museum specimens, in the
areas in which they occur in close proximity.
Spotted Eagle Owls have been misidentified as
Cape Eagle Owls, and examples of both species
from north-eastern Africa have been confused
with the Pharaoh Eagle Owl (the Saharan race of
the Eurasian Eagle Owl). The correct identification
of all three is hindered by their variability in
colour and markings, but the Pharaoh Eagle Owl
is generally more buff or cinnamon in colour than
the other two, while the Cape Eagle Owl is

distinguishable from the Spotted Eagle Owl by the
heavy blotching on its chest, and much coarser
barring on its abdomen. The Spotted Eagle Owl is
the smallest of the three, being 300 to 400 mm
long, compared with 460 to 480 mm in the other
two species. The Spotted Eagle Owl is probably the
most numerous of the African species, being
common throughout lightly wooded savannah
areas, particularly where there are small rocky
hills or kopjes. It is absent from rainforest, dense
woodland lacking in open spaces, and extensive
areas of treeless grassland. It feeds mainly on
small rodents, snakes, lizards and insects, but has
been known to kill prey as formidable as a Lanner
Falcon, and no doubt takes almost anything that
it can overpower. Spotted Eagle Owls generally
nest on the ground, often among rocks on a

Above and left: the Milky Eagle Owl *Bubo lacteus* (530 to 610 mm) is a large, powerful species capable of killing hares, hyraxes, hedgehogs, guineafowl and francolin. They sometimes nest in hollow trees but more commonly take over an abandoned stick nest of a large hawk or eagle. The significance of the characteristic pink eyelids of Milky Eagle Owls (obvious in the bird on the left) is unknown but they may have some signalling function.

Bubo lacteus: riverine forest of dense woodland with open glades.

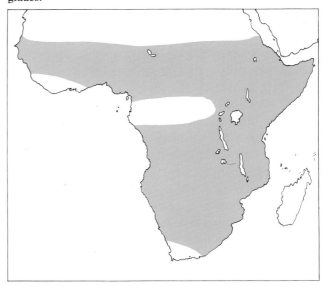

hillside, but use a wide variety of other nesting sites, including holes in trees and the abandoned nests of other birds. They will also nest in buildings and have even been known to use a suburban window-box. They lay between 1 and 6 eggs, the usual number being between 2 and 4, but as is usual among owls, the last-hatched owlet seldom survives. They breed in the dry season, from August to October in Kenya, for example, and from December to March in the northern Congo savannahs. As a result, the young fledge at about the beginning of the rainy season and have a long period with abundant food ahead of them, during which they can learn to hunt and to fend for themselves.

The Milky Eagle Owl (also known as Verreaux's Eagle Owl) is as widely distributed in Africa as the

Fraser's Eagle Owl *Bubo poensis* (390 to 450 mm) is one of three little known species that coexist in the equatorial rainforest of West and Central Africa. An isolated population in the Usambara Mountains of Tanzania is more commonly known as the Nduk Eagle Owl *B. p. vosseleri*.

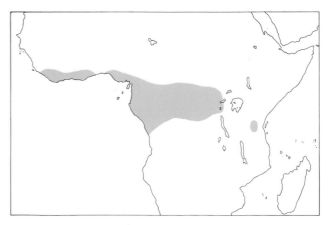

Bubo poensis: equatorial rainforest.

Right: The Akun Eagle Owl *Bubo leucostictus* (400 to 460 mm) and Shelley's Eagle Owl *Bubo shelleyi* (about 610 mm) are confined to the equatorial rainforest of West and Central Africa. Shelley's Eagle Owl is much more powerful than the other species and takes correspondingly larger prey, while the Akun Eagle Owl has a small bill and weak feet and is probably entirely insectivorous.

Bubo leucostictus: equatorial rainforest.

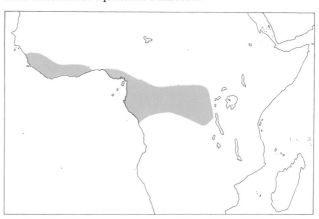

Map, below: *Bubo shelleyi*: equatorial rainforest.

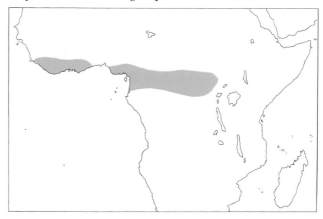

Spotted Eagle Owl, but not quite so numerous. It is most abundant in areas of savannah and semi-desert with stands of large trees. It is less common in dense woodland and absent from heavy forest, but it has a greater dependence on large trees than the Spotted Eagle Owl. However, the two species are only partially segregated by habitat, and they frequently live in close proximity in lightly wooded savannahs. Even then, there is probably little competition between them, for the Milky Eagle Owl is a large and powerful species, 530 to 610 mm long, that is capable of feeding on correspondingly large prey. In fact, it takes young monkeys, warthog piglets, hares, hedgehogs, herons, guineafowl and even adult hawks and other owls, including Spotted Eagle Owls, as well as such smaller fry as fruit bats, bush-babies, mice, snakes, frogs and insects. Milky Eagle Owls occasionally nest in hollow trees but

Shelley's Eagle Owl
Bubo shelleyi

Akun Eagle Owl
Bubo leucostictus

generally take over the nest of a bird of prey, sometimes forcibly. The enormous domed nests of Hammerkops are also very popular, particularly after they have been abandoned by their owner and the roof has fallen in. The Milky Eagle Owl usually lays 2 eggs, occasionally 1 or 3, and resembles the Spotted Eagle Owl in breeding during the dry season. It is said to lure predators away from its nest by means of a spectacular distraction display, in which it flops around feigning a broken wing, or even resorts to drunken flapping while hanging upside-down from a branch.

The remaining African species, Shelley's Eagle Owl (*B. shelleyi*), Fraser's Eagle Owl (*B. poensis*), and the Akun Eagle Owl (*B. leucostictus*), do not form a natural taxonomic group, but resemble each other in being rare, little known, and confined to dense equatorial rainforest. However, Fraser's Eagle Owl is also known from forest edge, clearings, secondary forest and plantations. All three are sparsely distributed through the forest regions of West Africa and the Congo basin, while Fraser's Eagle Owl has an additional isolated population in the Usambara Mountains of Tanzania. The latter population is known as the Usambara or Nduk Eagle Owl (*B. p. vosseleri*), and is now usually regarded as a separate species. Again, this is largely a matter of personal preference. If one is lucky enough to see them, there is little difficulty in distinguishing the three species. Shelley's Eagle Owl is 610 mm long and one of the largest and most powerful of all the eagle owls. It is heavily barred, both above and below, and its general colouring is very dark. Fraser's Eagle Owl is also strongly barred, but its general colour is more rufous, and it is small, only 390 to 450 mm long. The Akun Eagle Owl is about the same size as Fraser's Eagle Owl, but is less strongly barred and less rufous in colour. It is also distinguishable by the colour of its eyes, for they are bright yellow, while those of Shelley's and Fraser's Eagle Owls are brown. What little is known of the feeding ecology of the three species suggests that there is little competition between them. The Akun Eagle Owl may be entirely insectivorous, for it has been seen hawking for insects in forest clearings, and the stomachs of eight specimens that were examined contained only insects, particularly Orthoptera and Coleoptera. It also has strikingly small, weak feet, and a small bill; in fact, it seems to occupy a niche comparable to that of the African Cuckoo-

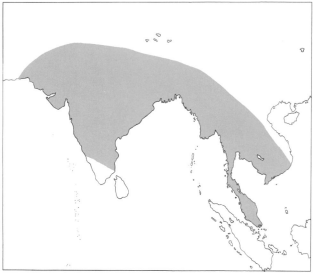

Bubo coromandus: riverine forest, patches of forest and groves of cultivated trees.

falcon among the diurnal birds of prey. Less is known about the prey taken by the other two species, but they probably take as wide a range of items as other eagle owls, with Shelley's Eagle Owl taking larger prey in view of its size. Fraser's Eagle Owl is known to take bush-babies, fruit bats, squirrels, mice, small birds, frogs, insects and occasionally even fruit. It is likely that Shelley's Eagle Owl takes similar items, together with bigger prey, such as small forest antelopes and forest guineafowl.

The eagle owl species in India and South-east Asia show some similarity to the African species in the way that they share out the resources of the region. Thus, the small, well-differentiated, Indian race of the Eurasian Eagle Owl occurs in lightly wooded rocky country, and is very similar in its general appearance and ecology to the African Spotted Eagle Owl; the Dusky Eagle Owl (*B. coromandus*) occurs in forest patches, riverine forest and groves of cultivated trees, and is more or less the equivalent of the African Milky Eagle Owl; and there are three species that are confined to heavy rainforest, just as there are in Africa. In fact, the parallel can be taken even further, for the high altitude Himalayan population of the

The Dusky Eagle Owl *Bubo coromandus* (430 to 480 mm)
of India, Indo-China and the Malay Peninsula
has a reputation for specializing in catching crows
and parakeets as they fly into roosts.

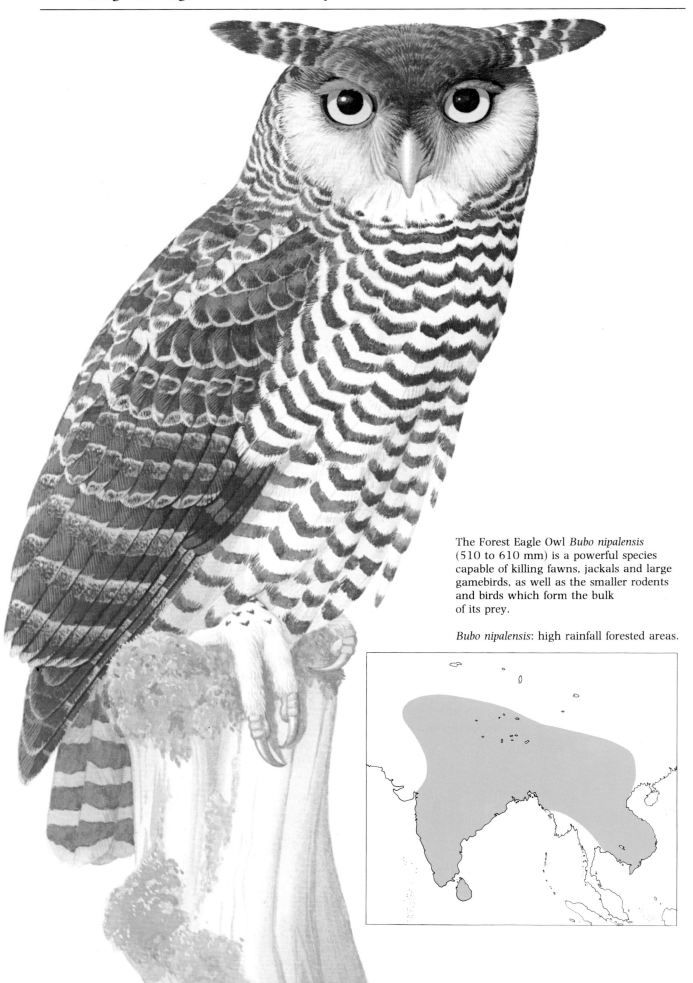

The Forest Eagle Owl *Bubo nipalensis* (510 to 610 mm) is a powerful species capable of killing fawns, jackals and large gamebirds, as well as the smaller rodents and birds which form the bulk of its prey.

Bubo nipalensis: high rainfall forested areas.

The Philippine Eagle Owl *Bubo philippensis* (about 400 mm) is unique among the eagle owls inhabiting tropical rainforest in having predominantly dark orange plumage.

Eurasian Eagle Owl can be considered as the ecological equivalent of the African Cape Eagle Owl. As in the case of the equivalent African species, the Indian race of the Eurasian Eagle Owl and Dusky Eagle Owl occur in close proximity over much of their range, though they generally remain segregated into their respective habitats. The two species are about the same size and catch very similar prey, notably rats, mice, lizards and insects. In addition, the Dusky Eagle Owl has a reputation for raiding birds' nests, and also for specializing in catching crows, parakeets and other birds at roost. The three Asian forest species, the Forest Eagle Owl (*B. nipalensis*), Malaysian Eagle Owl (*B. sumatrana*) and Philippine Eagle Owl (*B. philippensis*), are confined to the high rainfall forested region of the Himalayas, Indo-China, Malaysia, Indonesia and the Philippines. In contrast to the three African species, which coexist but take mainly different prey, these three species replace each other in different geographical parts of the region, as is clearly shown on the distribution maps. This is in spite of the fact that the two species that occur on the Asian mainland differ greatly in size, the Forest Eagle Owl being large and powerful, 510 to 610 mm long, and the Malaysian Eagle Owl relatively small and slight, 400 to 460 mm long. They might have been expected to coexist. Not much is known about the breeding biology of the Asian eagle owls, though the details that are available are in good agreement with those for other species, and need not be repeated. It should perhaps be mentioned, however, that the Indian eagle owls resemble the African species in breeding during the dry season, and presumably do so for the same reason.

So far no mention has been made of the calls of eagle owls, mainly because they are confusingly similar, and difficult to describe adequately. In fact, most species have a very varied repertoire of hoots, grunts, moans and clicks, while some are said to emit blood-curdling shrieks and screams. There is no doubt that eagle owls are noisiest prior to the breeding season, and that many of their calls are to do with maintenance of territory and courtship, but the precise significance of most is almost totally unknown.

Map: *Bubo philippensis*: tropical rainforest.

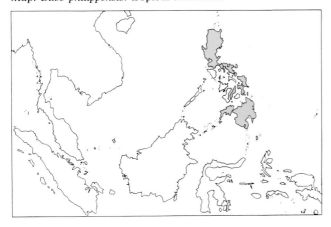

The Malaysian Eagle Owl *Bubo sumatrana* (400 to 460 mm) is a distinctive species with particularly long ear tufts. It is the only rainforest representative of its genus in its area and is relatively common throughout its range.

Bubo sumatrana: high rainfall forest areas.

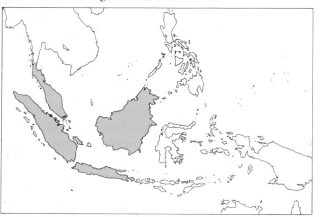

THE SNOWY OWL

Though the Snowy Owl (*Nyctea scandiaca*) is in a different genus from the eagle owls, and very different in appearance, it is quite closely related, and replaces them ecologically in the tundra regions to the north of the tree-line. It has a circumpolar distribution, breeding as far to the north as there is land that is not perpetually covered by ice and snow. It is, however, very dependent on lemmings during the breeding season, and does not often occur on many of the Arctic islands, such as Jan Mayen and Franz Josef Land, from which lemmings are absent; at best it is rare on such islands, as it is on Iceland and Spitzbergen. Snowy Owls are mainly sedentary, their wintering range in most years extending only a short distance to the south of their breeding range. However, once every four or five years they irrupt well to the south of their normal wintering range, occasionally reaching as far as southern Europe, the Balkans, northern India and China, the southern United States, and Bermuda.

The basis for the irruptions of the Snowy Owl is the regular periodicity in the abundance of their main prey species, particularly lemmings and Arctic Hares. Populations of lemmings, for example, rapidly increase when tundra conditions are good, only to crash when they eat out their food supply after four or five years. Arctic Hares fluctuate in abundance in a similar way, though they reproduce more slowly than lemmings, and have a longer cycle with a periodicity of about ten years. Populations of predators respond in turn, increasing and decreasing together with their prey. It is a decline in the availability of prey, at a time when their own numbers are at a peak, that is the cause of Snowy Owl irruptions. The

Right: The Snowy Owl *Nyctea scandiaca* (530 to 660 mm) replaces the eagle owls in Arctic tundra regions north of the tree-line. Its thick, pale plumage gives it protection from the cold and camouflage in the white winter landscape. Every four years or so, when populations of lemmings crash, Snowy Owls irrupt southwards well outside their normal range in search of prey. Map, page 82.

irruptions are particularly spectacular when populations of lemmings and hares crash together over extensive areas. However, the diet of Snowy Owls is by no means confined to lemmings and Arctic Hares. Like eagle owls, they are large, powerful opportunistic predators, and are capable of taking a wide variety of other prey, including ground squirrels, weasels, voles, birds ranging in size from finches to grouse, frogs, fish, insects and offal. They are crepuscular by choice, but are forced to hunt in daylight during the Arctic summer, when darkness is almost non-existent.

Snowy Owls breed more or less throughout the tundra region, though they particularly favour areas where there are numerous rocky ridges, outcrops or small hillocks, to provide suitable sites for nesting, and vantage points from which to hunt for prey. Their density varies considerably from year to year, but in suitable terrain, and in years when lemmings are abundant, there may be as many as one pair per 9 or 10 square kilometres. Snowy Owls lay their eggs in a scrape in the ground, usually at the base of a rock, but sometimes completely in the open. Like Eurasian Eagle Owls, and presumably for the same reason, they lay very early, often in mid-May while there

Nyctea scandiaca: Arctic tundra north of the tree-line, irrupting southwards when prey is scarce.

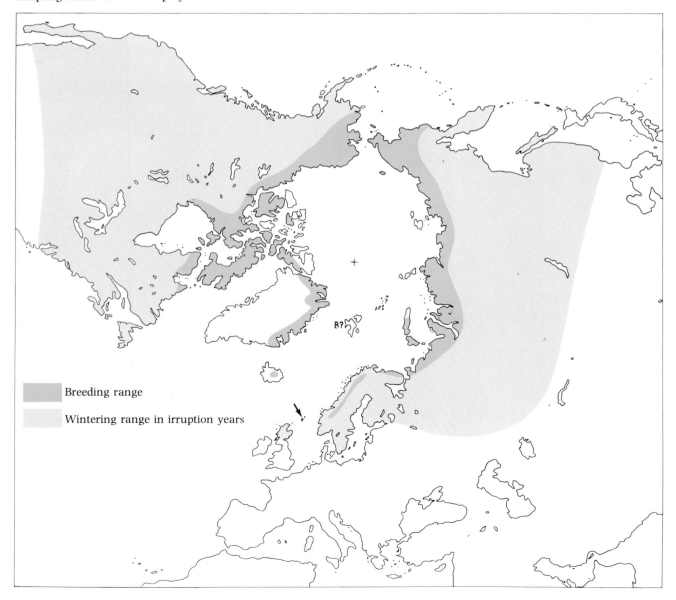

Breeding range

Wintering range in irruption years

is still snow on the ground. The clutch-size is very variable and depends on the abundance of lemmings and Arctic Hares; between 5 and 8 eggs is probably normal, but between 2 and 14 not unknown. Eggs tend to be laid every other day, but sometimes at longer and more irregular intervals, and large clutches often take three weeks or more to complete. Incubation, which is by the female, begins when the first egg is laid, so that a brood eventually consists of young of very different ages and sizes. However, the younger and smaller owlets soon die if there is insufficient food to go round, which ensures that the brood is quickly adjusted to the optimum size for the prevailing conditions. The actual incubation period per egg is 30 to 34 days, and the young fledge when they are about 43 to 57 days old, but the incubation and fledging period for the brood as a whole is, if course, much longer. Very few of the young survive, for predation by foxes and skuas is heavy, in spite of vigorous protection from the adults. There is also heavy mortality of the young when they attain independence, for the short Arctic summer gives them little time to learn the hunting skills that are so essential, particularly when food is scarce.

Male Snowy Owls *Nyctea scandiaca* attempt to divert the attention of intruders from their nest with spectacular distraction displays. They also help the breeding effort by feeding the incubating female, and later the young, but take no part in incubation.

CHAPTER SIX

Scops and Screech Owls

Otus, Ptilopsis, Lophostrix

The screech and scops owls of the genus *Otus* form a widespread group of about forty species, many of which, however, can be assembled into superspecies groups. They are nocturnal and eat mainly insects, the larger species also taking rodents and small birds, particularly in winter. Most live in the tropical regions of the world, except in Australasia where the genus is replaced by the hawk owls, *Ninox*, but there are a few in temperate regions, including the Common Screech Owls (*Otus asio* and *O. kennicotti*) of North America and the Common Scops Owls (*O. scops* and *O. sunia*) of Europe and Asia. These four species have all been well studied but there are many whose habits are almost unknown.

Two other genera are included in this chapter: the African White-faced Screech Owl (*Ptilopsis leucotis*) from African acacia savannahs has distinct features which justify placing it in a separate genus while the Maned Owl (*Lophostrix* or *Jubula lettii*) from West African rainforests and the Crested Owl (*L. cristata*) from Central and South American lowland forests, are considered here to be intermediates between screech owls (*Otus*) and eagle owls (*Bubo*).

In general, the *Otus* owls are small, ranging from starling to pigeon-size. They usually have long tufts with a light lining but sometimes these are almost indistinguishable, as in the Palau Spotted Scops Owl (*O. podarginus*) and the White-throated Screech Owl (*O. albogularis*). The facial disc is generally not as conspicuous as in most other owls, and they lack the distinctly bristled toes of *Ninox* and the silky chestnut and grey feather patterns of *Glaucidium*. *Otus* seems the

least specialized of all owl genera with the Vermiculated Screech Owl (*O. guatemalae*) from Central and South America the most unspecialized of all in appearance and voice. The more widely distributed species may be divided into a number of races of which the most isolated are often regarded as full species. Many species occur in two distinct colour morphs, grey and rufous, broadleaf forest species having the most prominent colour differences. The general effect of the plumage is cryptic, as in other owls, and each morph seems to select a roost to match its colouring. Rufous morph owls roost in foliage and grey morph owls roost against the bark of a tree trunk. In the northern U.S.A., grey Eastern Screech Owls (*O. asio*) are replacing rufous where conifer plantations are succeeding deciduous forests and rufous morph owls are almost absent from the mesquite woods of the central prairies, except where broadleaved trees have been planted around human settlements.

The name 'scops' is derived from the Greek *scopos*, 'look and watch'. This was a general name for owls, not necessarily given to the Eurasian Scops Owl. 'Screech owl' relates to the horse-like whinny of the Eastern Screech Owl, unfortunately an exceptional song-type in the genus.

Because there is little morphological variation among scops and screech owls, identification by plumage is not particularly easy and depends on finer points of patterning. Identification is often most readily confirmed by the voice, although the calls of a few species have still to be recorded and convergent song styles cause further difficulties. Within the basic scops and screech types of call there are many variations. In America the songs of screech owls increase in both length and strength from the Tropics to the Poles. The increase in length and strength of call with latitude is correlated with the larger territories that are needed as food supply decreases polewards: louder and longer songs carry further. Similarly in the Old World, the length of the accented songs of scops owls becomes progressively shorter across Asia to Africa and Europe.

Many restricted populations of screech and scops owls are now endangered species. Some could be easily eliminated by the felling of forests. Where typical forest species are on the retreat, however, those adapted to open woodlands and savannahs may gradually expand their ranges. Although the insectivorous habits of these owls are beneficial to man, many are still shot, or die from eating pesticide-contaminated insects.

SCREECH OWLS

NEW WORLD FOREST SCREECH OWLS

Dense forests, from lowland rainforests to mountain cloud forests, seem to offer more opportunities for owls to specialize than open woodlands and savannahs. At least, among the American screech owls the majority is adapted to forest habitats and among the widely distributed species are several groups so isolated that they are often considered to be separate species. Two clusters of species, called 'radiations', can be considered, one in Central America with extensions along the Andes into South America and the other in South America.

The Bare-legged or Cuban Screech Owl (*Otus lawrencii*) is often placed in a genus of its own (*Gymnoglaux*) because of its mottled appearance and lack of tufts. It breeds in cavities and trees in dense forests in limestone country, and is rather like the Burrowing Owl (*Speotyto cunicularia*) in appearance.

The least specialized of these forest species is the widely distributed Vermiculated Screech Owl (*O. guatemalae*) which forms a superspecies with the Puerto Rican Screech Owl (*O. nudipes*). It has an extensive range from Bolivia and Venezuela through Central America to Tamaulipas and Sinaloa in central Mexico, occurring in the upper tropical and subtropical forest zone in foothills and mountains. Continental birds have yellow eyes, those in Puerto Rico have hazel-brown eyes.

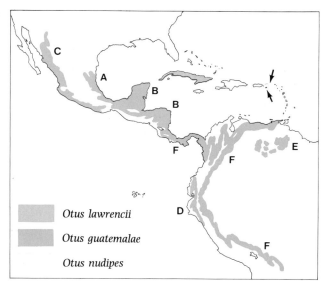

Otus lawrencii: sub-tropical forest, Cuba.
O. nudipes: upper tropical woods and forest on Virgin Islands and Puerto Rico.
O. guatemalae: upper tropical forest and woodland.
A *cassini* B *guatemalae* C *hastatus* D *pacificus* E *roraimae* F *vermiculatus*

The Cuban Screech Owl *Otus lawrencii* (200 to 230 mm) has some features, including its relatively long, bare legs, in common with the Burrowing Owl (*Speotyto cunicularia*). It is often put into a separate monotypic genus—*Gymnoglaux*.

Puerto Rican
Screech Owl
Otus nudipes

Santa Barbara
Screech Owl
Otus barbarus

The many New World *Otus* species are all about the same size, from 190 to 230 mm long. The two above are forest species. The Puerto Rican Screech Owl *Otus nudipes* is an island species and the Santa Barbara Screech Owl *O. barbarus* is found in a relatively small area of wet mountain forest. Maps, pages 85 and 87.

Right: The Cloudforest Spotted Screech Owl *Otus marshalli* (190 to 230 mm) lives in humid mountain forests of Peru and southern Ecuador.

Within this area the Vermiculated Screech Owl is divided into six distinct groups of several subspecies, some of which are so isolated and differing in plumage details that some authors treat them as full species, *cassini, hastatus, guatemalae, vermiculatus, roraimae* and the recently described *pacificus* group. Each subspecies group has both rufous and grey morphs.

On the edges of its range the Vermiculated Screech Owl seems to overlap with several other species but in fact the ranges do not simply overlap but interlock like parts of a jigsaw puzzle, each species preferring a particular elevation in the forested mountains or lowlands. This is a good example of the principle of competitive exclusion: two populations inhabiting the same area cannot display the same specialization. So wherever the

Vermiculated
Screech Owl
Otus guatemalae

Spotted
Screech Owl
Otus trichopsis

Otus trichopsis

Otus barbarus

Otus marshalli

Otus trichopsis: 'islands' of dry montane forest.
O. barbarus: wet mountain forest.
O. marshalli: cloud forests of eastern Peru.

The Spotted Screech Owl *Otus trichopsis* avoids competition
with its less specialized relative, *O. guatemalae*, by keeping to
dry mountain forest habitats. Both are around 190 to 230 mm.

As its popular name suggests, the Bare-shanked Screech Owl
Otus (ingens) clarkii (190 to 230 mm) is one of a number of
species that have more or less unfeathered tarsi. It also has
less well developed ear tufts than most *Otus* species.

different forest species meet, the Vermiculated
Screech Owl confines itself to more open places in
the forests but where no competition occurs it
penetrates denser vegetation.

Closely related to the Vermiculated Screech
Owls are two mountain forest species: the Spotted
Screech Owl (*O. trichopsis*) from 'islands' of dry
mountain forest from Arizona to Panama and the
Santa Barbara Spotted Screech Owl (*O. barbarus*)
in the wet mountain forest of northern Guatemala
and adjacent Chiapas. Where the two meet they
keep strictly to the dry and wet sides of the

mountains, respectively, leaving the lowland
forest to the Vermiculated Screech Owl.

In 1981 a new species was described from the
mountain cloud forest of Peru and named *Otus
marshalli*, the Cloudforest Spotted Screech Owl. It
most closely resembles the Santa Barbara Spotted
Screech Owl but is slightly taller. Its voice has not
yet been recorded. Its distribution approaches but
does not overlap with that of the Vermiculated
Screech Owl in the eastern Andes. The Cloudforest
Spotted Screech Owl is also similar to the larger
Bare-shanked Screech Owl (*O. (ingens) clarkii*)

from the mountains of Costa Rica to western Columbia. Like the Spotted and Santa Barbara Spotted Screech Owls, it probably evolved from the Vermiculated Screech Owl or its predecessor, possibly via the *roraimae* group.

It thus appears that there is a Central American 'radiation' originating in the Vermiculated Screech Owl and extending along the Andes into South America. Six new species seem to be emerging while one, the Puerto Rican Screech Owl (*O. nudipes*) is already completely isolated and three 'mountaineers', *O. trichopsis, O. barbarus* and *O. marshalli* are fully separated.

Six other species are found in South American forest habitats. They together constitute the South American radiation. The superspecies of Black-capped Screech Owls (*O. atricapillus*) inhabits tropical forests, being found also in lower subtropical deciduous forests. The superspecies is composed of three groups, now more or less isolated, but a few centuries ago probably still interbreeding. The Tawny-bellied *lophotes* group (also called *O. watsonii*) is found in Amazonian

Map: *Otus atricapillus* complex: The *lophotes* or *watsonii* group: lowland tropical Amazonian and Guyanan forest and central Brazil along rivers in remnant forests. The true *atricapillus* group: south-eastern Brazil to Uruguay, lower subtropical deciduous forest from lowlands up to 500 m. The *hoyi* group: north-western Argentina and adjacent Bolivia along the Andes slopes above 500 m. The *sanctaecatarinae* group: subtropical forest above 500 m, becoming isolated in outlined area.
O. ingens: the *ingens* group in the Andes at 1800-2500 m and the *clarkii* group in the mountains of Western Colombia-Panama-Costa Rica at 1000-1800 m.

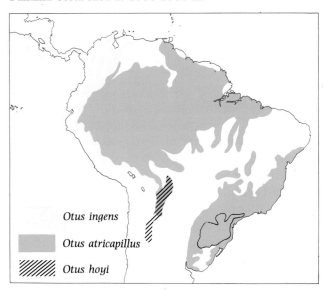

Black-capped
Screech Owl
Otus atricapillus

Rufescent
Screech Owl
Otus ingens

The Tawny-bellied Screech Owl *Otus watsonii* (190 to 230 mm) is one of several little known members of the genus that live in South American lowland rainforest (*O. atricapillus lophotes* group).

Left: The Black-capped Screech Owl *Otus atricapillus* (190 to 230 mm) belongs to a group of South American forest species which exploit different forest habitats and probably became isolated relatively recently. The Black-capped Screech Owl prefers lowland forest, while the Rufescent Screech Owl *Otus ingens* (190 to 230 mm) is found in the Andes at heights of up to 2500 metres.

Hoy's Screech Owl *Otus hoyi* (190 to 230mm) was observed in the montane forests of Salta province, Argentina in 1987 and described in 1989 as a new species, with a distinctive feather pattern, coloration and voice. This painting is based on a museum specimen.

and Guyanan forest areas and, in central Brazil, in remnant forests along rivers. The true Black-capped southern group (*O. atricapillus*) inhabits upper tropical dry and deciduous forest from Bahia to the Rio de la Plata, while the third, thought by some authors to be a separate species (*O. sanctaecatarinae*), is found in sub-tropical dry forests south of the Brazilian mountains. The *sanctaecatarinae* group has a less distinct 'cap' than the *atricapillus* group, and a more freckled plumage pattern. Nothing is known of its breeding biology.

In 1989 a new species was described from north-western Argentina, Hoy's Screech Owl, *O. hoyi*, which in voice is closely related to *atricapillus* from south-eastern Brazil but in coloration and appearance is a mixture of *atricapillus, ingens* and *marshalli*. It seems that different Andes altitudinal zones and separated mountain valleys will have more surprises in store as they are more intensely investigated.

The Rufescent Screech Owl (*O. ingens*) and the Bare-shanked Screech Owl (*O. clarkii*—which may be simply a side branch of *O. ingens*) closely resemble the *sanctaecatarinae* race. They are found in Andean forest habitats, the Rufescent Screech Owl between 1800 and 2500 m and the Bare-shanked Screech Owl between 1000 and 1800 m. Both species have yellow eyes and a variegated plumage pattern, but the Bare-shanked Screech Owl has developed farther away from the common features shared by the Black-capped and Rufescent Screech Owls. There is in fact a gradual reduction of facial tufts and discs, feathers on toes and nuchal collar in the sequence *lophotes, atricapillus, sanctaecatarinae, ingens, clarkii*.

The ultimate stage of this reduction, a complete lack of distinct tufts, is found in the White-throated Screech Owl (*O. albogularis*).

The White-throated Screech Owl *Otus albogularis* (190 to 230 mm) lives in humid forests in the Andes, above 2500 m. It has the darkest plumage of any *Otus* species.

Otus albogularis: temperate forest from Colombia to Bolivia.

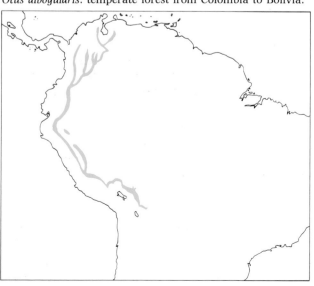

This mountain species, occurring in temperate forests in the Andes above 2500 m, is the darkest-looking *Otus*. It has often been regarded as a separate monotypic genus, *Macabra*, but it has sufficient similarities with the Black-capped, Rufescent and Bare-shanked Screech Owl complex, and with the Vermiculated Screech Owl for it to be regarded as an *Otus*. In colour and general appearance it resembles the Solomon Islands Hawk Owl (*Ninox jacquinoti*), a case perhaps of convergent or parallel evolution between species from different areas belonging to different genera.

As in Central America, it is possible to trace a radiation of forest species, starting with the *O. atricapillus* complex (*lophotes-atricapillus*), expanding via *sanctaecatarinae* into the sub-tropical zone in the Andes (*ingens, clarkii*) and by some process which is not yet clear, giving rise to a temperate forest species (*O. albogularis*) with a voice resembling that of lowland *O. atricapillus*.

SCREECH OWLS OF OPEN WOODLAND

There is a group of New World screech owls that lives in open woodland, savannah and even cactus desert regions and, due to deforestation, these species continuously expand their ranges. They have a generally paler and greyer plumage than the forest-dwellers, in accordance with their drier habitat. The pale facial disc surrounded by a dark rim contrasts particularly with the dark faces of the forest species. There is a collar around the nape, the tarsi are well feathered and the tail is short. Tail feathers tend to be longer in the forest species, to give them greater manoeuvrability among dense vegetation. Together the open country screech owls form a superspecies ranging from Alaska to Argentina and include the Eastern and Western Common Screech owls (*O. asio* and *O. kennicotti*, sometimes considered together as the Common Screech Owl of North America), the Choliba Screech Owl (*O. choliba*) of South America and some less well known Central American species: *O. cooperi, O. lambi* and *O. seductus*.

The Choliba Screech Owl occurs in all open woods and even in open places in the forests from Buenos Aires to Costa Rica, at elevations up to the temperate zone in the Andes. In the winter they descend to the valleys. One group (*roboratus*) has also adapted to the scrub steppes of the Upper Marañon valley and is sometimes regarded as a separate species, the Roborate Screech Owl (*O. roboratus*). It resembles Cooper's Screech Owl

The Choliba or Tropical Screech Owl *Otus choliba* (190 to 230 mm) has the shorter tail characteristic of open-country owls. It has both red and grey morphs, the red being adapted to hunting in dense foliage and the grey to more open terrain in the dry woodlands and savannahs of South America.

Cooper's Screech Owl *Otus cooperi* (190 to 230 mm) is a little known Central American species, living among giant cactus and palms as well as in open woodland and the mangrove swamps of the Pacific coast.

Map: *Otus seductus*: dry inland woodland.
O. cooperi: low scrub and mangrove, Central America, Pacific.
O. choliba roboratus: scrub steppes of upper Marañon valley.
O. choliba: dry woodland and savannah.

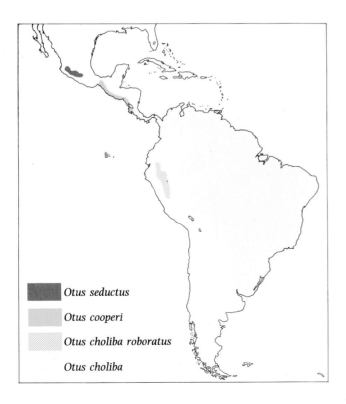

Otus seductus

Otus cooperi

Otus choliba roboratus

Otus choliba

(*O. cooperi*) which lives in low scrub and mangrove on the Pacific coast of Central America. Cooper's Screech Owl is slightly larger than the Choliba Screech Owl, has some bristles on its toes and has a gruffer, louder voice.

Even larger and with more bristled toes and a louder voice is the Balsas Screech Owl, (*O. seductus*) from the interior of the Rio Balsas valley and Colima in Mexico. It prefers drier inland woods rather than coastal mangroves. Between these two is a smaller species with no bristles on the toes and a mellower voice: Lamb's Common Screech Owl (*O. lambi*) from the southern valleys of Oaxaca, Mexico, down to the mangrove coast of the Gulf of Tehuantepec. Lamb's Screech Owl is like an Eastern Screech Owl, settled away from the main distribution in the United States and with reduced wings. Its voice, too, is closer to the Eastern Screech Owl's, while the voices of Cooper's and the Balsas Screech Owl are more similar to that of the Choliba species.

The Eastern and Western Common Screech Owls (*O. asio* and *O. kennicotti*) have been well studied. They survive well in captivity and will sometimes nest or roost in boxes. The Eastern Common Screech Owl lives to the east of the Rocky Mountains in mixed woodland and is replaced to the west of the Rockies and in Mexico by the Western species, which lives in cactus desert, riverside woodland and mesquite scrub. The two meet and perhaps partially overlap in the Big Bend of the Rio Grande (U.S.A.—Mexico border) where some mixed pairs have produced hybrid offspring. The two can be most easily distinguished by their different voices. Around the Gulf of Baja California, is a vinaceous group with a wine-coloured wash over their plumage.

Insects form the main diet of these owls. They are taken in the air with a loud snap of the bill or seized on the ground or on a branch with the feet. Insect-eaters are often migratory when they live outside the tropics but the Common Screech Owls are essentially non-migratory although there is a downward movement from the mountains to the plains in winter. In this, they differ from the partially migratory European Common Scops Owl. In Canada, Screech Owls become inactive in bad weather and survive on an accumulation of fat laid down in the autumn. Surplus food is cached in winter roosting cavities. Winter is also the period when most non-insect food is taken. Small mammals, including flying squirrels and bats, birds, frogs, reptiles and invertebrates have been found in Screech Owl stomachs and ducks and poultry are sometimes attacked.

Male Screech Owls maintain their territories for about ten months of the year. The size of the territory varies and there is usually neutral ground between them. The males are probably solitary from September through the winter. They start calling in February, the courtship notes being heard most frequently within 20 to 30 minutes after sunset. The male flies about his territory, settling on branches to call and peer about but, if no female appears, he starts to hunt. Late in February, or in early March, the females appear in the territories. The male attempts to approach the female, courting her by running up

The Eastern Common Screech Owl *Otus asio* (190 to 230 mm) is widely distributed in North American woodland east of the Rocky Mountains. Its relatively short wings give it considerable manoeuvrability in dense woodland.

Map: *Otus asio*: mixed woodland, east of Rocky Mountains, northern limit not sharply defined.
O. kennicotti: cactus desert, riverside woodland and mesquite scrub, west of Rocky Mountains. The two species overlap and interbreed in the Big Bend of the Rio Grande. A vinaceous group is found in the area shown by dotted line.
O. lambi: Southern Oaxaca to coastal mangroves.

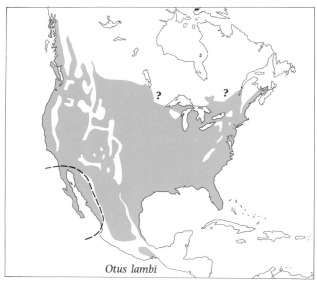

Otus lambi

The Western Common Screech Owl *Otus kennicotti* (190 to 230 mm) is closely related to the Eastern Common Screech Owl and has similar habits. Where their ranges overlap, mixed pairs have produced hybrid offspring. Only the extreme northern races, along the British Columbian-Alaskan coast, have red morphs, but some Californian races show a wine red gloss over the grey coloration. Southern races are mainly insectivorous but the larger-sized northern races also take small mammals, bats, and birds as large as ducks and poultry.

and down a branch, crouching and uttering rasping calls. When the pair has formed, these calls and the initial courtship cease. A couple of weeks later the female selects one of the winter roosting cavities as a nest-site. The pair may leave the territory for a while, presumably to concentrate on feeding and the male also feeds the female, to help provide material for the developing eggs. While hunting they keep in touch with a duet, the male uttering a tremolo and the female replying at a higher pitch. Eventually she gives up hunting and the male feeds her throughout the 26 days that she is incubating the 3 to 7 white eggs.

When brooding is finished, the female helps the male to feed the owlets. Small items of food are placed directly in the owlets' bills but large prey is thrown into the nest for the young to tear to pieces. The owlets leave the nest when four weeks old but for another five or six weeks they continue to receive food from their parents. From this stage the young utter guttural calls, while until the silent months of January the adults' 'whinny' or scream, a tremulous whistle, can be heard. The Western Screech Owl produces no whinny, but a double trill instead.

Screech Owls defend their nests vigorously. They will attack and kill animals larger than themselves, earning the description of 'feathered wild cats'. Human intruders are sometimes attacked near the nest. The owls swoop down, striking the head, while uttering hollow sounds and snapping the bill. Roosting owls 'play possum' when disturbed, becoming motionless, as if mesmerized. One wild owl was weighed while in this state, lifted off its perch with a spring balance hooked under its bill. When alarmed, Screech Owls assume a concealment posture in which the ear tufts are raised and the facial disc and eye slits are arranged so as to distort the usual outline and pattern of the owl. This posture is adopted when a flock of sparrows approaches, presumably to avoid being mobbed.

Giant Scops Owl
Otus gurneyi

White-fronted Scops Owl
Otus sagittatus

POSSIBLE OLD WORLD SCREECH OWLS

In some forests of Oriental Asia, which presumably have not changed much throughout different climatic events, there are at least three species of uncertain affinity between scops and screech owls; unfortunately little is known of their voices and breeding habits. The Lesser Sunda Scops Owl (*O. silvicolus*) from the lowlands of Flores and Sumbawa is very dull in general appearance, much as the Vermiculated Screech Owl *O. guatemalae*. The White-fronted Scops Owl (*O. sagittatus*) of the Malay Peninsula and northern Sumatra has a marked white throat, as in the South American White-throated Screech Owl (*O. albogularis*). The Giant Scops Owl (*O. gurneyi*) from the southern Philippines, with its striped body plumage, is very much apart. It is often considered a different monotypic genus *Mimizuku* but has enough in common with *O. sagittatus* to keep it within *Otus*. These three species reflect, no doubt, different early stages in the complex evolution of the scops and screech owls.

The largest members of the genus *Otus* are two Oriental species—the Giant Scops Owl *O. gurneyi* (about 300 mm) and the White-fronted Scops Owl *O. sagittatus* (250 to 280 mm). The Giant Scops Owl is sufficiently distinct from other scops or screech owls to be placed in a monotypic genus—*Mimizuku*—by some authors. The White-fronted Scops Owl, noteworthy for its unusually long tail and rufous plumage, inhabits primary forests of the Malay peninsula and possibly also northern Sumatra.

Otus gurneyi: highland forest, Marinduque and Mindanao Is.
O. sagittatus: highland primary forest.

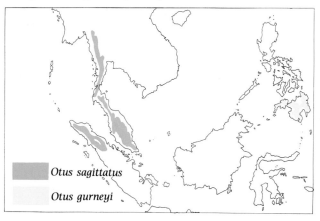

Otus sagittatus

Otus gurneyi

SCOPS OWLS

In the Old World the scops owls have evolved along similar lines to the American screech owls, to fill similar ecological niches in both forest and open country. Geographical and climatic changes have left isolated species with restricted distributions over Africa, the Orient and oceanic islands. They are the remnants of once more widely spread populations and their affinities are obscure. For a few, neither breeding season, food nor even voice are known.

The greatest ecological differentiation is seen in

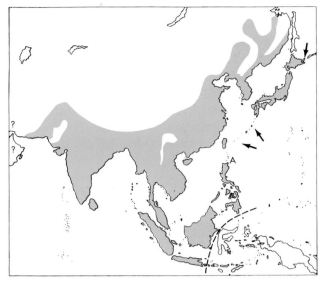

The Collared Scops Owl *Otus bakkamoena* (190 to 230 mm) is a widely distributed Asiatic species of light woodlands, savannah-like habitats and even suburban gardens. As a result of forest clearing, its range is expanding rapidly in South-east Asia, but only at the expense of forest representatives of the genus.

Otus bakkamoena: light woodland and savannah, parks and gardens. A = *O. (bakkamoena) megalotis*, mountains of northern Luzon.

South-east Asia where the ranges of the Collared (*O. bakkamoena*), Rufescent (*O. rufescens*) and Spotted (*O. spilocephalus*) Scops Owls overlap. The Rufescent Scops Owl inhabits the lowland primary rainforests and is thus the ecological counterpart of the Tawny-bellied Screech Owl of the Amazonian forests in Brazil. Similarly the ecological counterpart of the Choliba Screech Owl of South American savannahs and dry woods is the Collared Scops Owl.

Unlike their New World counterparts the Common Screech Owls, which are split up from north to south into six species (see above), the Collared Scops Owls form one huge interbreeding species from the tropical woodlands of Java to the temperate valleys of eastern Siberia. On northern Luzon, a rather larger race is often regarded as a separate species (*O. megalotis* or *whiteheadi*). The morphal differences are shades of brown rather than grey and rufous phases. The natural habitat in South-east Asia is the open savannah-like grassland and mangrove swamps of the coasts but through the felling and opening of the primary forest, the Collared Scops Owl is spreading inland as the forest species decline. It lays 4 or 5 eggs in the north of its range where it nests in spring but lays only 3 or 4 eggs in the south where it breeds during the period of maximum rainfall. In the northern parts of its range, it has denser plumage on its tarsi and, in Japan and China, even the toes are well feathered.

Closely related is Rajah's Scops Owl (*O. brookii*) of the sub-tropical mountains of Sumatra, Kalimantan and Java. It resembles the large Collared Scops Owls from the Chinese mainland, from where it may have colonized the Indonesian mountains, developing its brighter colours in the different climatic conditions. Similarly, *O. megalotis* can be considered a colonist from northern China into the mountains of northern Luzon.

The Rufescent Scops Owl *Otus rufescens* (150 to 180 mm) of the Malay Peninsula and the Greater Sunda Islands is strictly confined to lowland primary rainforest, being replaced by the Collared Scops Owl *O. bakkamoena* in secondary forest, scrub and gardens and by the Spotted Scops Owl *O. spilocephalus* at altitudes above 1000 metres.

Otus rufescens: lowland primary forest.

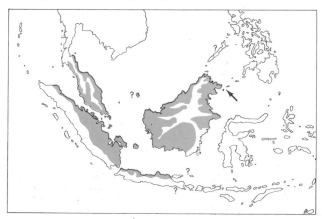

Rajah's Scops Owl
Otus brookii

Lesser Sunda
Scops Owl
Otus silvicolus

Rajah's Collared Scops Owl *O. brookii* (about 230 mm) from the mountains of Sumatra, Java and Kalimantan and the Lesser Sunda Scops Owl *Otus silvicolus* (about 230 mm) from Flores and Sumbawa. *O. silvicolus* is like a larger version of the South American Vermiculated Screech Owl (*O. guatemalae*), and, like it, is a forest species. *O. brookii* is a mountain bird, like a larger, more warmly red-brown Collared Scops Owl (*O. bakkamoena*).

Map: *Otus brookii*: subtropical mountain zones of Java, Sumatra and Borneo.
O. silvicolus: lowland forests of Sumbawa and Flores.

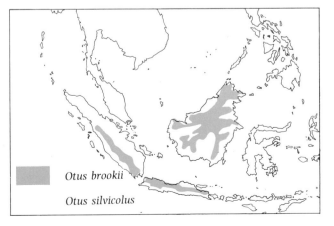

Otus brookii
Otus silvicolus

MOUNTAIN SCOPS OWLS AND RELATED SPECIES

In the oriental region are several isolated mountain populations of scops owls. The best known of all is the Spotted Scops Owl (*O. spilocephalus*). It is found throughout the oriental mountains, from the Himalayas to southern China and Taiwan, through Indo-China, Thailand and the Malay Peninsula into northern Sumatra and the mountains of Kalimantan. The races on the Andaman Islands (*balli*) and Taiwan (*hambroecki*) are often regarded as distinct species, but are still so close to *O. spilocephalus* as to be considered conspecific. The Greater Sunda Spotted Scops Owl (*O. angelinae*) from the mountains of central and southern Sumatra and Java, the Philippine Spotted Scops Owl (*O. longicornis*) from the mountains of Luzon and Negros, the Flores Spotted Scops Owl (*O. alfredi*) from the mountains of Flores (above 1000 m) and the Palau Spotted Scops Owl (*O. podarginus*) from lowland mangrove swamps of Palau Island are sufficiently distinct to be regarded as different species. It is a pity that much of the habitats of these birds is endangered before they have been thoroughly investigated.

The Spotted Scops Owl nests in dense jungles

The Spotted Scops Owl *Otus spilocephalus* (about 180 mm) occurs in montane forest throughout the Oriental region, from the Himalayas to Malaysia. In the Himalayas its metallic call notes have caused it to be called the Himalayan bell-bird. The Andaman Spotted Scops Owl *O. balli* (about 180 mm) is an island form of the Spotted Scops Owl which has become isolated and has evolved differences which some consider give it specific status. The classification of island forms is often disputed since it is difficult to prove whether they can interbreed successfully and are therefore all one species.

A *Otus spilocephalus*: Himalayas to Malay Peninsula and China; also on Borneo and northern Sumatra; not Java.
B *O. (spilocephalus) balli*: Andaman Islands
C *O. (spilocephalus) hambroecki*: Taiwan.
D *O. longicornis*: northern Luzon.
E *O. (longicornis) nigrorum*: Negros.
F *O. angelinae vandewateri*: mountains of Sumatra.
G *O. angelinae angelinae*: mountains of Java.
H *O. alfredi*: mountain forests of Flores above 1000 m.
I *O. podarginus*: mangroves of Palau Islands.

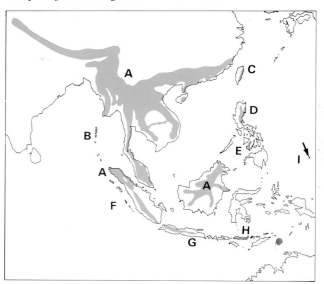

Andaman Spotted Scops Owl
Otus balli

Spotted Scops Owl
Otus spilocephalus

and shaded gullies from 1000 m to 3000 m and descends after breeding to the warmer lowland valleys. Its metallic notes, recalling a hammer on an anvil or mule bells, have caused it to be called the 'Himalayan bell bird'. Voices of most of the island races have not yet been recorded but the voice of *hambroecki* on Taiwan resembles that of the continental *O. spilocephalus*.

Whereas the various Spotted Scops Owls *O. spilocephalus*, *O. angelinae*, *O. longicornis* and *O. alfredi* can be considered to form one superspecies arisen from the Rufescent Scops Owl (*O. rufescens*), the Palau Spotted Scops Owl (*O. podarginus*) may have originated from the *O. manadensis* complex, to be discussed next.

THE OCEANIC SCOPS OWLS

This is a group of owls on islands off the continental shelf (beyond the 200 m depth line). The best known of these is the Magic Scops Owl (*O. manadensis*) of Sulawesi, Lesser Sunda islands, Moluccas and Philippines, with a gentle, single call note.

On the Moluccan and several Philippine islands is the larger sized *magicus* group, with a harsher, coarser voice. More to the east is the rare *beccari* from Biak, north of New Guinea and to the north of Luzon and in the Riu Kiu Islands is the form *elegans*, with a mellower voice, comparable to that of the *mentawi* group on the Mentawi Islands, off west Sumatra. Together they are called the *Otus manadensis* complex. They occupy the same ecological niche as the Collared Scops Owl but exclusively on extra-continental islands where the Collared Scops is not found. Because of its coloration and isolated distribution, the *mentawi* group is often considered a separate species.

On the other side of the Indian Ocean there is a similar group of scops owls centred around Madagascar. The typical form of the so-called Ruddy Scops Owl (*O. rutilus*) is found on Madagascar, with subspecies on Pemba (*pembaensis*, sometimes regarded as a separate species), the Seychelles (*insularis*, also often treated as a separate species) and the Comoris (*capnodes*). The Pemba population is known to nest near the ground on heaps of dead material. It seems that the Ruddy and Magic Scops Owls are related even though they are now well separated by the expanse of the Indian Ocean. They probably had a common ancestor on the Asian mainland, that is to say they simply evolved out of the Collared Scops Owl.

Flores Spotted Scops Owl
Otus alfredi

Mentawi Scops Owl
Otus mentawi

Palau Spotted Scops Owl
Otus podarginus

Magic Scops Owl
Otus manadensis

Ruddy Scops Owl
Otus rutilus

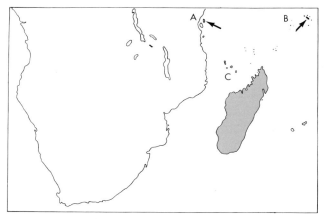

Otus rutilus complex: *O. rutilus rutilus*: Madagascar.
A *O. rutilus pembaensis*: Pemba Island.
B *O. rutilus insularis*: Seychelles.
C *O. rutilus capnodes* Comores.

Left: The Flores Spotted Scops Owl *Otus alfredi* (about 190 mm)
and the Palau Spotted Scops Owl *O. podarginus* (about 220
mm) represent the Spotted Scops Owls on the islands of their
names. The Magic Scops Owl *O. manadensis* (190 to 230 mm)
is the best known of the scops owls on the oceanic islands of
South-east Asia. The Mentawi Scops Owl *O. mentawi* (about
180 mm) is part of the same complex but because of its
isolated distribution and darker coloration is often considered
a separate species. The Ruddy Scops Owl *O. rutilus* (190 to
230 mm) is now widely separated from the Magic Scops Owl
but may have evolved from a common ancestor.

Map: *Otus manadensis*: widely distributed in oceanic islands of
South-east Asia.
A *manadensis* group: Sulawesi and Lesser Sunda Islands.
B *magicus* group: northern and southern Moluccas.
C *beccarii*: Biak Island.
D *elegans* group: many small Philippine and Riu Kiu Islands.
E *mentawi* group: Mentawi Islands, off W. Sumatra.

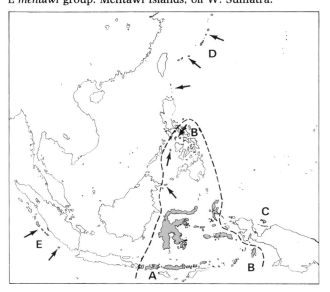

THE COMMON SCOPS OWLS

The Oriental Common Scops Owl (*O. sunia*) which
is often wrongly considered to belong to the same
species as the European Common Scops Owl (*O.
scops*), occurs in Asia. It lives in riverside
woodland from Palestine to the Aral Sea, Iran,
and Turkestan and is found again in India,
southern China, eastern Siberia to Japan and the
Philippine islands of Mindanao and Mindoro,
where the habitat is savannahs, parks and dry
woods. The western and eastern populations are
roughly separated by the Sind desert in India. The
western group is more commonly known as the
Striated Scops Owl (*O. brucei*), but it probably
interbreeds with the eastern population of the
Oriental Scops Owl in the upper Indus region.
Populations living north of the January 0°C
isotherm are migratory. The western (*brucei*)
population migrates to the Indus valley and the
Bombay region while the north-eastern part of the
sunia population flies to southern China and Indo-
China. From Asia Minor to Baluchistan, the Aral
Sea and Lake Balkhash, the European and
Oriental Scops Owls overlap. Oriental Scops Owls
arrive at the breeding grounds towards the end of
March, one month earlier than the European
birds. They take up residence in riverside
woodland whereas the European species prefers
mountain woods and apple orchards. The two can
be distinguished by their calls. There are also
small differences in plumage.

The southern, non-migratory races of the
Oriental Scops Owl (Philippines to Arabia and
Socotra) start to breed at the end of February.
Migratory populations breed a month later. The
eggs are thus hatched before the monsoons start
and the owlets are flying before the rains cease;
their development coincides with the maximum
supply of insect food.

Some very rare specimens taken in the
Philippines (*mirus*) are much smaller and more
brightly coloured than specimens from the
continent. They are very like the North American
Flammulated Scops Owl (*O. flammeolus*) and this
makes it easier to believe that this species
originated in Oriental Asia and only relatively
recently colonized North America. Another
aberrant group occurs in the Andaman, Nicobar
and northern West Sumatran islands (*nicobaricus,
umbra*). Yet another small form inhabits Socotra
(*socotranus*). This is often regarded as belonging to
the African Common Scops (*O. scops senegalensis*)
but it looks quite different and is more like the

Flammulated Scops Owl
Otus flammeolus

Oriental Scops Owl
Otus sunia

Otus sunia: western populations (*O. s. brucei*), riverside woodland; eastern populations, savannahs, parks and dry woods. Dotted line shows probable limit of distribution. Populations breeding north of the 0°C January isotherm migrate in winter to China and India.

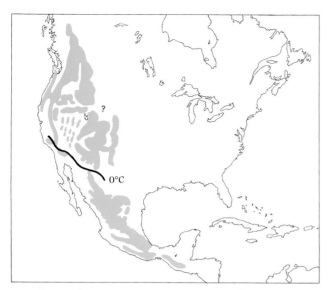

Otus flammeolus: temperate zone, mountain forest, Populations north of the 0°C January isotherm migrate in winter to Central America.

Left: The Oriental Common Scops Owl *Otus sunia* (160 to 180 mm) and the Flammulated Scops Owl *O. flammeolus* (160 to 170 mm) occupy similar ecological niches in Asia and North America respectively. In the Middle East the Oriental Scops Owl overlaps in range with its European equivalent *O. scops* but the birds avoid competition by occupying different habitats. The European species prefers mountain woodland, the Oriental species riverine woodland.

The European Common Scops Owl *Otus scops* (160 to 190 mm) ranges over most of Africa and into Asia, though African populations are sometimes separated as a distinct species— *Otus senegalensis*. Throughout its range it inhabits relatively open woodland and similar habitats.

south Arabian race *pamelae* (Oman to Yemen). Although there are at present no signs of breeding populations in the middle of the Arabian peninsula to connect Yemen birds with those from the Middle East, it is quite likely that they did exist in earlier times.

The North American Flammulated Scops Owl (*O. flammeolus*) is the smallest *Otus* in North America. The northern populations are summer visitors only, leaving after a short season of about four months to return to the central American mountain forests. Three or 4 eggs are laid in a hollow tree or in the old nests of squirrels or flickers. Several territories may occur in a tight group, sometimes with overlapping boundaries. These groups of territories may belong to families of owls for there is usually a space between one group of territories and the next.

In Africa the Common Scops Owl inhabits

Otus scops: woodland, parks, gardens; in north also birch and conifer forest. In Africa, savannah and dry woodland. Birds north of the palm limit migrate southwards in winter.

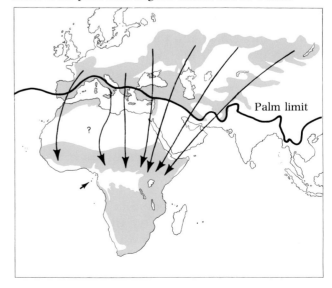

savannahs and dry woodlands. It is now thought by some authorities to be a separate species, (*O. senegalensis*); its links with the European bird probably date from the time, a few thousand years ago, before the Sahara desert was formed, when the Central African massifs were still covered with woodland. Breeding dates vary north and south of the Equator. In the north breeding begins in April, in the south in September. In both areas this is in advance of the wet season, so that the young are becoming independent as the rains bring out the insects.

The European Common Scops Owl (*O. scops*) lives from North Africa and Iberia across Europe and Asia Minor to the Urals, Baluchistan, and through Siberia to Lake Baikal. In the northern part of its range, north of the palm limit, the European Scops Owl is migratory, moving to spend the winter in the African savannahs between the Sahara and the rainforests. Owls from Siberia travel to Ethiopia, a distance of 7000 to 8000 km that may take two months to cover.

Unfortunately, their migration routes take them over countries where considerable numbers are shot. The long journey also depletes the fat reserve and pesticides that have accumulated in it from contaminated insect food pass into the nervous system and kill the bird. Non-breeding summer visitors are found in southern Scandinavia and around Moscow.

The habitat of the European Scops Owl is the more open country of woodland, parks, orchards and towns. Its food is mainly insects but it also takes lizards, small mammals and birds. The nest is built in holes in trees, in ruins, in old crow nests or occasionally on the ground. The 4 or 5, rarely 6, eggs are laid mostly in early May in southern Europe. They are incubated for 24 to 25 days by the female and the owlets leave the nest when 3 weeks old. The family may stay together on migration. There is a variety of calls but a characteristic evening sound of southern Europe is the short whistle, 'giu' or 'pliu', repeated at regular intervals of two seconds and easily distinguishable from the tremolo 'prru' heard in Africa. Each whistle is apparently single but is rarely made up of a tremolo. Male and female may sing in a duet, the female higher pitched and less regular. Winter visitors from Europe to Africa can best be distinguished from the African Scops Owls by their longer slender wings. Only the southernmost African race is difficult to distinguish from the European Scops.

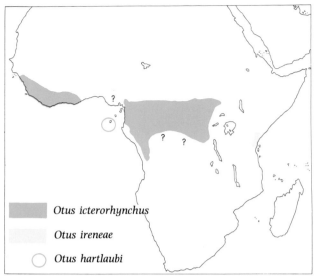

Otus icterorhynchus: tropical forest.
O. ireneae: coastal forest.
O. hartlaubi: highlands of São Tomé island

AFRICAN FOREST SCOPS OWLS

The Oriental, African and European Scops Owls all inhabit open woodland and gardens but in Africa they have close relatives which are well adapted to both lowland rainforest and mountain forest. These now form isolated populations, left behind in restricted habitats as climatic change has affected the vegetation.

The Sandy Scops Owl (*O. icterorhynchus*) is found in the forests of Ghana and Cameroon, perhaps extending to Liberia. On the other side of the continent is the rare Sokoke Scops Owl (*O. ireneae*) of coastal Kenya. Its existence is threatened by forest clearance and bird collecting. The São Tomé Scops Owl (*O. hartlaubi*) is known only from the highlands of São Tomé island in the Gulf of Guinea. It may have originated from migrating European Scops which settled and adapted to the mountains of the island. The fact that no similar bird has developed on the mountains of Cameroon and Guinea can be regarded as an indication that the European and African Scops, when meeting, are mutually exclusive, and thus still closely related.

Sokoke Scops Owl
Otus ireneae

Sandy Scops Owl
Otus icterorhynchus

São Tomé Scops owl
Otus hartlaubi

The São Tomé Scops Owl *Otus hartlaubi* (160 to 190 mm) is related to the European Scops Owl and confined to the island of São Tomé in the Gulf of Guinea. The Sandy Scops Owl *Otus icterorhynchus* (180 to 200 mm) and the Sokoke Scops Owl *O. ireneae* (160 to 180 mm) are two small, closely related species with forest ranges on opposite sides of Africa. The Sokoke Scops Owl must be considered endangered as it is restricted to the remnant Sokoke forest on the Kenyan coast.

Map: *Ptilopsis leucotis*: thorn scrub and savannah.

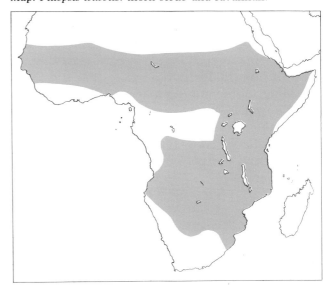

PTILOPSIS

The African White-faced Screech Owl, recognized as a genus of its own named *Ptilopsis leucotis*, has two song races, one of which strikingly resembles the South American Choliba Screech Owl. It often breeds on the ground in open savannah. The unusually distinct facial disc, heavily banded plumage, aberrant wing formula, orange-red eyes and slightly diurnal habits differ from any *Otus* and its ear openings are twice as large as those of any *Otus* of the same body size. Apart from locusts and other insects, they frequently prey on rodents in acacia thorn bush and the way they

Possibly the most attractive of all owls, the White-faced Screech Owl *Ptilopsis leucotis* (190 to 240 mm) is a species of the African acacia savannah. It usually breeds in abandoned stick nests of small hawks or plantain-eaters, but sometimes uses holes in trees or even the thorny, domed nests of Buffalo Weavers. Map, page 105.

tear large prey such as birds and rats and swallow the pieces, makes some authors believe the species is more closely related to *Asio* than to *Otus*. During the Pleistocene glaciation and the spreading of the mountain and lowland forest the only two areas suitable for *Ptilopsis leucotis* were the Kalahari desert and the Horn of Somalia. This may explain the song differences between the southern and northern populations.

CRESTED AND MANED OWLS

The genus *Lophostrix* is considered by some to be related to *Otus* owls on one side and to the *Bubo* eagle owls on the other. Recent studies have also suggested that it may have links with *Pulsatrix*,

the spectacled owls of South America. It contains two species, the Maned Owl (*L. lettii*) and the Crested Owl (*L. cristata*), neither of which are well known. They are intermediate in size between *Otus* and *Bubo*, the Maned Owl particularly resembling a large-sized version of the White-fronted Scops Owl. The Maned Owl lives in tropical forests from Liberia to Cameroon and Northern Zaire. The Crested Owl is tropical American, dwelling in forests from southern Mexico to central Brazil. The two species are probably relics of a group that spread around the Tropics and have only survived in the old forests that were not changed during the period of climatic cooling. About all that is known of these owls is that they eat mainly insects, but one Maned Owl had plant material in its stomach.

The Maned Owl is often given a genus of its own, *Jubula*, but considering the variation within other owl genera (e.g. *Otus*) and the Maned Owl's similarities to the Crested Owl, there is no reason to separate the two species into different genera. Similarly, Crested Owls from Central and South America are often seen as two species (*stricklandi* and *cristata*) but are sufficiently alike to be regarded as one.

Maned Owl
*Lophostrix
lettii*

Crested Owl
Lophostrix cristata

The affinities of the two rainforest
species in the genus *Lophostrix*—the
African Maned Owl *L. lettii* (about 439 mm)
(left) and the Central American Crested Owl *L. cristata*
(about 280 mm)—are not at all clear. Some authorities
consider that they are related to the tropical wood owls *Pulsatrix*,
others that they form a link between *Otus* and the eagle owls *Bubo*.

Map: *Lophostrix lettii*: old tropical forest. The western and
eastern populations still look very alike.

Map: *Lophostrix cristata cristata*: tropical forest of Amazonia.
L. cr. stricklandi: tropical forest of Central America.

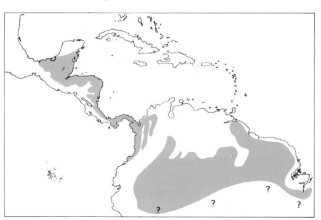

CHAPTER SEVEN

Wood Owls

Pulsatrix, Ciccaba, Strix, Asio

Pulsatrix, Ciccaba and *Strix* owls are grouped under the name 'wood owls', because they look so much alike, and are generally forest-dwellers. This chapter also includes six species of the genus *Asio*, most of which are also owls of woodland. The Striped Owl (*Asio clamator*) and the Long-eared owls (*Asio otus, A. stygius* and *A. madagascariensis*) can be regarded as wood owls, but the two Short-eared species (*A. flammeus* and *A. capensis*) are entirely owls of open country.

The twelve species of *Strix* are of almost world-wide distribution, absent only from the Australian region. The genus *Ciccaba* with four species, and the genus *Pulsatrix* with three species, are found only in Central and South America. Because of their tropical occurrence these seven species can conveniently be distinguished from *Strix* as 'tropical wood owls'. *Asio* species are found in every continent except Australasia, but do not occur in India or South-east Asia.

Although all three *Pulsatrix* species are larger and heavier than *Ciccaba* owls, and have stouter beaks and feet and more colourful plumage, there is obviously quite a close relationship between these seven species from tropical America. The African Wood Owl (*Strix woodfordii*) was formerly seen as the only member of the genus *Ciccaba* in the Old World, but now it appears that African and South American wood owls are not closely related. Instead, *Strix woodfordii* probably has relatives in tropical Asia, with which it may have had geographical contact in a not too distant geological past.

Wood owls in general, and those occurring at high latitudes in particular, are very stocky, or chunky, and have very loose, fluffy, and thick plumage. In this respect they differ from those *Asio* owls which hunt largely on the wing in open country. (Open-country owls which fly frequently, such as the Short-eared Owls, have a slimmer appearance than forest owls and have relatively smaller heads.) The most significant difference between *Asio* species and the other wood owls is, however, the presence of ear tufts. The Striped Owl has ear tufts which are well developed and project at the sides of the head; the three species of Long-eared Owls have conspicuous tufts placed vertically on the top of the head, while the two Short-eared species have only rudimentary ear tufts.

All *Pulsatrix, Ciccaba* and *Strix* owls are medium to large owls, with a large round head, no ear tufts, and, usually, dark eyes; exceptions are the Great Grey Owl (*Strix nebulosa*), Hume's Owl (*S. butleri*) and the Spectacled Owl (*P. perspicillata*), all of which have bright yellow eyes.

Most wood owls range in length from 300 to 500 mm: exceptions are the Great Grey Owl and the Ural Owl (*Strix uralensis*) which, like many other birds of prey living in cold countries, are larger than related species from warm countries and have many more downy feathers. Northern wood owls are also greyer and paler than their tropical rainforest relatives, which tend generally to be darker and brownish. Generally wood owls seem to show a clear trend in coloration and size in accord with Gloger's and Bergmann's rules, respectively. Gloger's rule (that coloration of a species becomes progressively darker from north to south of its range) seems to be broadly

Pulsatrix perspicillata: tropical rainforest; also in dry open woodland.

The appropriately named Spectacled Owl *Pulsatrix perspicillata* (430 to 460 mm) inhabits dense equatorial and tropical forests in the New World and is as opportunistic in its hunting as most other owls, preying on creatures as diverse as rodents, bats, small birds, crabs and insects. Juveniles (left) are often known as 'white owls' as if they were a different species. The reddish eye colour is caused by reflection of the photographer's flash from the retina.

applicable also to inter-specific comparisons of plumage colours among northern forest owls; the most northern Great Grey and the Ural Owls are light and grey, with very little brown colour while more southerly owls, such as *Strix aluco* and *Asio otus* are darker and have much more brown in their plumage. Bergmann's rule, that size decreases progressively from north to south, is also nicely demonstrated in Eurasian *Strix* owls. The largest one, *S. nebulosa*, lives furthest to the north, followed in latitudinal range by the medium-sized Ural Owl, *S. uralensis*, and then by the smaller Tawny Owl, *S. aluco*, which lives further to the south. The same trend continues southwards with the smallest of all, Hume's Owl (*S. butleri*), from the deserts of the southern palaearctic region. This is a fairly orderly pattern even though there is considerable overlap between the ranges of the Great Grey and the Ural Owls, and rather less overlap between the Ural and Tawny Owls, and between the Tawny and Hume's Owls.

All three *Pulsatrix* species have dark faces, outlined by light 'spectacles'. Although all species are believed to be fairly common in their ranges, very little is known about their life except that

they are mainly nocturnal and prefer to live in humid forests. They usually nest in tree-holes and lay only 2 eggs; incubation and fledging periods are still unknown. The juveniles leave the nest well before they are able to fly and due to their conspicuous white plumage have been called 'white owls' as if they were a different species. Reports indicate that the juveniles pass through several plumage stages before losing their whiteness, but moulting is not, however, well enough known to be described reliably. *Pulsatrix* owls feed on mammals (including bats), birds, lizards, insects and even crabs, if they are living near water as they often do.

The Spectacled Owl (*P. perspicillata*), a very large hornless owl, is dark brown above and light yellow-ochre below, with narrow white 'spectacles', a white patch on the front of the neck, and a dark brown belt across the breast. The large eyes are bright yellow and the tail is short. It occurs from southern Mexico to Argentina and six subspecies are recognized. One of these extends from Mexico to Panama, and the others are found in Venezuela, the Guianas, Trinidad, Brazil and Peru. In areas where the humidity and rainfall are high—for example in the tropical zone west of the Andes of Colombia and Ecuador—plumage colours are more intense. Spectacled Owls are about 430 to 460 mm long and, as is usual among owls, the females are somewhat larger than the males: males weigh from 590 to 760 g, females from 765 to 980 g. The smallest birds are those found in equatorial regions, while the largest occur in regions with lower mean annual temperatures.

Although fairly common over much of their range, spectacled owls live mainly in dense rainforest and are rarely seen, so we still know remarkably little of their daily routine, breeding, biology and diet. However, they do not always avoid cultivated areas, and can sometimes be found in trees shading coffee plantations. Their most frequently heard call is a series of six short, dry, rattling hoots, lacking in resonance and similar to the tapping of a woodpecker—in Brazil they are known locally as 'knocking owls'. They respond readily to imitations of their calls and so are probably territorial. Members of a pair sometimes indulge in bouts of antiphonal calling, each bird's call having a slightly different tone. Birds rest by day in thick foliage but this is not an exclusively nocturnal species and they are sometimes active on cloudy mornings and

Juvenile Spectacled Owls *Pulsatrix perspicillata* take up to five years to attain fully adult plumage, moulting through a complicated series of intermediate plumages in the meantime.

evenings. Like many other owls they nest in a hole in a tree and, according to the few available records, lay only 2 eggs. In Surinam a nest with eggs was recorded in August, but nestlings have been seen emerging from other nests between mid-April and mid-June. In Trinidad the breeding time is January to April. Chicks leave the nest before they can fly well, and are fed for some time by their parents before they become independent. During this time they call for food with a persistent, hoarse 'kweer'. Juveniles are white with brown wings, and have brown spectacles which contrast sharply with their white head. An owlet in captivity took five years to attain adult plumage, but a shorter time may be normal in the wild: all *Strix* and *Asio* wood owls attain adult plumage during their first year.

Spectacled owls feed on small mammals and insects, including grasshoppers and large caterpillars. They also take quite large mammals, including two species of spiny mice, completely covered in spines like a hedgehog. In the mangroves they are said to feed on crabs. Elsewhere birds and even bats are included in their food.

The two other *Pulsatrix* species, the Rusty-barred Owl (*P. melanota*) and the White-chinned Owl (*P. koeniswaldiana*) are both relatively rare

The White-chinned Owl *Pulsatrix koeniswaldiana* (about 430 mm) and the Rusty-barred Owl *P. melanota* (about 480 mm) are poorly known species, but they are likely to resemble the Spectacled Owl in most aspects of their ecology.

Rusty-barred Owl
Pulsatrix melanota

White-chinned Owl
Pulsatrix koeniswaldiana

Map: *Pulsatrix melanota* and *P. koeniswaldiana*: tropical rainforest and more open woodland.

Pulsatrix melanota

Pulsatrix koeniswaldiana

species about which little is known. The Rusty-barred Owl occurs in Ecuador and Peru. It is similar to the Spectacled Owl, but has white eyebrows and white tail bars, and white underparts barred with chocolate brown. It is about 480 mm long. The White-chinned Owl also has a white-barred tail, but has yellow-orange on the eyebrows and underparts. It is about 430 mm long, and occurs in southern Brazil. The two species are probably similar in ecology to the Spectacled Owl, but their nesting and feeding habits are not sufficiently well known to be described.

Owls of the genus *Ciccaba* largely replace those of the temperate zone genus *Strix* in the tropical forests of America. Where the ranges of the two genera overlap, as they do in Mexico and southern South America, tropical *Ciccaba* owls occupy lower altitudes. Other *Ciccaba* owls are found in tropical South America, where they probably compete with the three *Pulsatrix* species, which prefer to be near water in their jungle environment. Recent DNA-DNA hybridization data indicate that *Ciccaba* is not recognizable as a genus and some authors put all *Ciccaba* into *Strix*. As the relation between *Pulsatrix* and *Ciccaba* owls in Central and South America is not fully investigated, four *Ciccaba* species still form a genus in this book.

Ciccaba owls have a round, hornless face, with an almost fully developed facial disc and conspicuous eyebrows; wings and tails are long. Almost nothing is known of their ecology, except that they are largely nocturnal, preying on insects, rodents and small birds. Like many other owls they nest in holes in trees or in abandoned nests of raptors, and they lay one or two white, rounded eggs. Like *Pulsatrix* species they have a series of juvenile plumages.

The Mottled Owl (*C. virgata*) is dark brown with light spots above, and white or tawny, heavily streaked with deep brown below. Widely distributed through the neotropics from Mexico to north-eastern Argentina, it has many local variations of size and colour. Birds in the southern part of Tamaulipas, as well as southern Mexico, Central America and northern South America, are smaller with fine, distinct barring above; those restricted to Venezuela, northern Colombia and the extreme eastern end of the isthmus of Panama are brown, with fine light tawny barring, and those in the Amazon Valley, also finely barred, are larger and more reddish-brown with chrome-

Ciccaba virgata: tropical forest, woods, plantations and fields.

Living in tropical habitats from southern Mexico to northern Argentina, the Mottled Owl *Ciccaba virgata* (305 to 355 mm) is the most widely distributed of this New World genus.

The Black and White Owl *Ciccaba nigrolineata* (330 to 380 mm) is more a species of forest borders and clearings than its close relatives.

orange markings. The pale parts of the juveniles are yellow-orange, and the face is white. In captivity one chick took 8 months to attain adult plumage. Adults are about 305 to 355 mm long, and weigh 176 to 248 g.

This is a fairly common but solitary and nocturnal species occurring in a variety of habitats including lowland forest, second-growth deciduous woodland and thickets, plantations and open fields up to 1900 m. Breeding starts in April or May, when two dull, white eggs are usually laid, in tree-holes or in raptors' old nests. Incubation and fledging periods are still obscure. In Mexico the call has been described as a somewhat guttural hoot but in Trinidad it is said to be a long, drawn-out single note with a rising inflection, resembling a whistled screech. Food is reported to be mainly small mammals, but small birds, insects and reptiles are also taken.

Little is known about the three other *Ciccaba* species beyond their general appearance and distribution. The Black and White Owl (*C. nigrolineata*) is white barred with dark brown below and on the upper back, and dark brown elsewhere above. It is rare and local from southern Mexico to western Ecuador, and is found in rainforest and clearings from sea-level to 900 m. It also occurs in second-growth woodland, ravines near rivers and flooded swampy woodland, and is probably mainly nocturnal. The bulk of its food probably consists of large insects, including beetles, tettigoniids, and cicadids but it also takes rodents and bats. Its calls consist of a nasal, long drawn 'who-ah' with an upward inflection and also a repeated, deep explosive resonant 'whoof'.

Ciccaba nigrolineata: forest borders.

Though basically an Amazon forest species,
the Black-banded Owl *Ciccaba huhula* (305 to
355 mm) is nowadays often found in banana
and coffee plantations. The closely related
Rufous-banded Owl *C. albitarsus* (about 305 mm)
represents the genus in the high altitude
forests of the Andes.

Black-banded Owl
Ciccaba huhula

Rufous-banded Owl
Ciccaba albitarsus

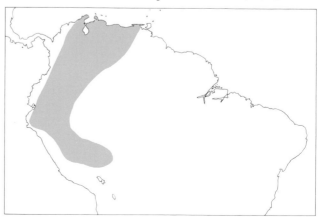

Left, map: *Ciccaba huhula*: rainforest; also coffee and banana
plantations.

Ciccaba albitarsus: humid temperate forest to 3700 m.

The Black-banded Owl (*C. huhula*) is an Amazon forest species seldom found above 200 m. Its habits are probably similar to *C. nigrolineata* and it has been reported as common in banana and coffee plantations. Like *C. nigrolineata* it is also mainly dark brown and white but is barred with white above as well as below; birds living in south-eastern Brazil have darker bars. It is slightly smaller than *C. nigrolineata* (305—355 mm). The Rufous-banded Owl (*C. albitarsus*) lives mainly in the cloud forests of 2000 m up to 3700 m. Again, it is nocturnal, solitary and little known. It is about 305 mm long, with brown upperparts and breast, barred with chrome-orange, and a belly spotted boldly with white.

The twelve species of owls of the genus *Strix* are represented in every continent of the world except Australia. They are easily recognizable by their disproportionately large, round head, with its particularly well-defined facial disc; they have no ear tufts. The wings are wide and rounded, and the longish tail is also rounded. With one exception they are nocturnal birds of forest and woodland. The exception is the Great Grey Owl (*S. nebulosa*) which is also the only member of the genus to be found in both Old and New Worlds. Prey consists mainly of small mammals, which are captured on the ground, and, according to the locality, small birds, bats, fish, amphibians, molluscs, worms, insects and other invertebrates supplement this staple diet. The generic name *Strix* is derived from the Greek *Strizo* to screech, and most of the owls in this genus are very vocal.

Eggs are commonly laid in tree hollows and in the old nests of large hawks. No nest material is added. Nearly all the species nest at times in tree stumps or on the ground, though Tawny and Ural Owls (*S. aluco* and *S. uralensis*) occasionally forsake woodlands for buildings. A clutch of 2 or 3 eggs is common for the Barred Owl (*S. varia*) and the Spotted Owl (*S. occidentalis*) in North America as well as for the Tawny Owl in India. In Europe Tawny and Ural Owls lay 2 or 4, other *Strix* species 1 or 2 eggs, while the circumpolar Great Grey Owl lays 4. (Tropical owls normally lay smaller clutches than more northerly species; the average clutch size in equatorial Africa is 2.5, as opposed to 4.6 in mid-Europe). Incubation, by the female alone, lasts 26 to 30 days. The interval between eggs is normally from 2 to 7 days, but there is a record of a Great Grey Owl laying at twelve-day intervals. Incubation usually starts with the first egg, and the young are brooded for about 3 weeks, while the male provides food for both female and chicks. The owlets leave the nest when they are 4 to 6 weeks old, remaining with their parents and usually being fed by them for the rest of the summer.

Species with a generalized diet—such as the Tawny Owl and the Ural Owl—show site tenacity. Still others may show a mixed strategy, females tending to be more nomadic than males. This is the case, for instance, in Great Grey Owls. Great Grey Owls, Barred Owls, and Ural Owls often attack animals or people who approach their fledglings or nest. They strike and lacerate the scalp and face with their sharp talons: at least five people are known to have lost an eye in this way. Tawny Owls, too, have been known to attack intruders.

In the Old World, Tawny and Ural Owls are the ecological equivalents of the North American Barred and Spotted Owls. Moreover, these four *Strix* species seem to be very close relatives which some taxonomists do not accept as well defined and separated species.

From breeding experiments in captivity it has been noted that there is no genetic barrier against hybridization between the Ural and the Tawny Owl as sibling species. And it has also been postulated that in the wild, lack of a partner of its own species could stimulate the Ural Owl to choose the wrong mate. No field records of hybrids are known, but a female Tawny Owl crossed with a male Ural Owl in captivity, produced fertile eggs and two viable young, a female and male. The female later showed full breeding behaviour but never laid an egg while the male was back-crossed successfully both with Tawnies and Ural Owls. Characteristics of so called F1 hybrids' plumage followed intermedial heredity, but their voices were dominated by the Tawny Owl. Thus, the most important barrier for species isolation is thought to be the specific voice.

The genetic barrier between the Barred and Spotted Owls in North America may be even weaker than that between the Eurasian species. There are already at least two known cases where a Spotted Owl has bred with the more common Barred Owl. Unofficially, the offspring are called Sparred Owls and are believed to be quirks of nature. The hybrid has similar markings on the back of its nape and head to those of the Barred Owl. Its breast looks more like a Spotted Owl but it has a larger white area and a bigger buff patch below the neck. Where the Spotted Owl has round spots on top of its head, the hybrid has rectangular bars. Its facial colouring is between that of the two parent species. The bars on its tail resemble a Spotted Owl but are farther apart.

As the Barred Owl expands its range from the east coast to the west in North America, Spotted Owls may be threatened not just by the destruction of their habitat but by hybridization which drains their gene pool.

The Barred Owl is a largish brown and white, nocturnal, round-headed Owl, without ear tufts, but with black eyes, a barred breast, and a striped abdomen. It resembles both the Great Grey and the Spotted Owl. Its barred breast, black eyes, and smaller size distinguish it from the former, its striped abdomen and paler coloration from the latter. Body length is 405 to 610 mm; males weigh from 468 to 774 g, females, usually larger, from 610 to 1051 g. Its range extends from Canada to Guatemala. Throughout the mountains of central Mexico these owls are larger and darker, barred in dark brown and pale off-white. Guatemalan birds are smaller (about 350 mm long) also darker, and heavily tinted with medium yellow-orange. Juveniles are sienna-brown to cinnamon-brown, barred above and below with pale yellow-orange and white.

The Barred Owl is clearly closely related to the Eurasian Ural Owl and is its ecological equivalent in the temperate zone forests of the New World. In Canada and the north-eastern United States it is a bird of coniferous or mixed woods, rather than of deciduous forests, but in the southern part of its range it seems to prefer denser, darker forests, with mature trees, especially those near swamps and streams. However, it is often seen hunting away from these forests in open country and around farms. Barred Owls sometimes hunt and even hoot during the day-time, especially in cloudy weather. Best known of its hoots is the sound described as 'who cooks for you, who cooks for you all', but it can also sound like the barking of a dog—and spit like a bobcat. It nests in early spring, starting to lay in January in Florida and April in eastern Canada. It prefers to nest in the hollow of a tree, but suitable hollows are scarce and the owls are more often forced to appropriate an old nest of some other species. Sometimes it has been found nesting on the ground, in a hollow it has dug itself. The owls do not bring any new material to the nest. Favoured holes may be used for many breeding seasons—even for 20 to 25 years, if the tree remains standing long

enough. The usual clutch is of 2 or 3 eggs, though up to 5 have been recorded, and incubation, by the female alone, lasts about 28 days. The young are brooded for about 3 weeks, while the male provides food, and the owlets take about 6 weeks to fledge. It is some time, however, before they reach full independence.

Barred Owls feed mainly upon mammals such as mice, squirrels, hares and shrews, with smaller numbers of fish, amphibians, reptiles, and birds. Insects are only rarely eaten. In the southern United States, where the favoured habitat is swampy woodland, crayfish, frogs, and various kinds of fish (apparently caught by wading) are the most important food items. Laboratory experiments have demonstrated that Barred Owls can capture live deer-mice in complete darkness on a bare floor, locating quarry by sound alone.

Barred Owls remain within the breeding range in winter, though the more northerly breeders tend to move south. In seasons of deep snow, when mice are difficult to uncover, great flights of Barred Owls move from the north to New England and further south to areas where prey is more easily available.

The Spotted Owl (*S. occidentalis*) a largish, hornless, round-headed owl with black eyes, is the other species of *Strix* which occurs only in North America. It resembles the Barred Owl but is on average slightly smaller; it is a much darker and richer brown, the top of its head and hind-neck are spotted with white, and its abdomen is barred instead of striped. About 405 to 480 mm long, males weigh 518 to 694 g and females 548 to 760 g. This rather rare bird is permanently resident from south-western British Columbia to central Mexico. Geographical isolation of three different subpopulations has caused some morphological differences, giving a reason to separate the Northern Spotted Owls (*S. occidentalis caurina*), the Californian Spotted Owls (*S. o. occidentalis*) and the Mexican Spotted Owls (*S. o. lucida*). A recent study has found no genetic variation between a California owl and the northern Spotted Owl, but significant differences were found in the blood proteins of the Mexican Spotted Owl if compared with the previous two. Scientists now believe that the Mexican Spotted Owl should be reclassified as a full species in its own right.

The favourite habitats of Spotted Owls are dense, mainly coniferous forests and wooded ravines. They nest in tree cavities or snags, the

The Barred Owl *Strix varia* (405 to 610 mm) seems to adapt easily to logged areas and has recently expanded its range from the east coast to the west in the USA. Like a number of other thoroughly nocturnal owls, it is capable of catching its prey in total darkness, locating it by sound alone. However, in most normal conditions it also makes use of its keen night vision.

Map: *Strix varia*: coniferous or mixed woods in north; denser forests near swamps and streams in south.

old nests of other birds of prey, or in crevices in cliffs. Spotted Owls lay two or three eggs, usually only two, and very rarely four. Little seems to be known about the development and behaviour of the young. This owl takes a wide variety of prey including flying squirrels, deer-mice, wood rats, bats, shrews and moles, small and medium sized birds, amphibians, and such insects as crickets, cockroaches and beetles. Its main vocalization is an explosive high-pitched hooting, likened to a baying hound, and usually comprising a series of three to five hoots. A dove-like 'who-whoo-whoo-whoo' has also been noted. The Spotted Owl is a decidedly nocturnal species, seldom moving about in the daytime unless it is disturbed at its roost. Adults are very tame.

Lately the Spotted Owl has received more publicity than any other owl in the world, and has acquired an imposing political stature. This inoffensive brown owl has become a symbol and the star of a drama set in North America's ancient coniferous forests. The US government has declared the owl a 'threatened' species that can survive only in the old growth forests of northern California, Oregon, Washington and southern British Colombia. One pair of owls needs as much as 900 hectares of ancient forest to thrive and raise their young and in the Pacific north-west only 3000 to 5000 pairs are still living in the monarch forest. Citing its own research, the timber industry has asserted that the owl is not threatened; rather it is the loggers, truckers and mill hands who are the endangered species. And as they are much more numerous, this is bad for the owl. The forestry association

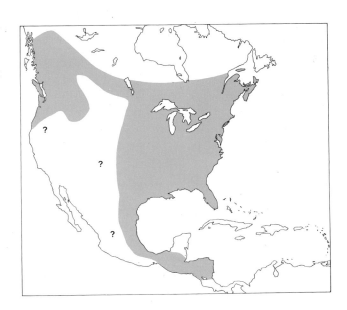

predicts 100,000 jobs will be lost over the next ten years if the industry is banned from logging the owl's habitat. However, in June 1990, the US Department of the Interior listed the Spotted Owl as threatened and established a recovery team, with responsibility to develop a Recovery Plan for the species, the completion of which is expected by Fall of 1991.

The population in Mexico is also very rare and local according to ICBP. In addition to displacement by Barred Owls, they are also preyed on by Great Horned Owls. Although it is hoped that the owl will be able to adapt to a habitat other than dense coniferous forests, as its nearest relatives the Tawny and Ural Owl have done, it is an indicator species and reflects the health of the forest. At stake as well as the owl are the last stands of ancient forest in North America. Clearly, the Spotted Owl has ruffled its feathers to save the old growth—if it is not too late; nine-tenths of the virgin woodland of the Pacific north-west has been hauled to the mill already.

Two species of the genus *Strix* occur exclusively in South America: the Brazilian Owl (*S. hylophila*) and the Rufous-legged Owl (*S. rufipes*). Neither species appears to be rare in woodland regions,

Rather similar to the Barred Owl in appearance, the North American Spotted Owl *Strix occidentalis* (405 to 480 mm) favours dense mature coniferous forests and wooded ravines in rocky mountainous country. Northern, Californian and Mexican populations have become isolated; the Mexican Spotted Owl *S.o. lucida* is probably a separate species.

Strix occidentalis: dense coniferous forest and wooded ravines.

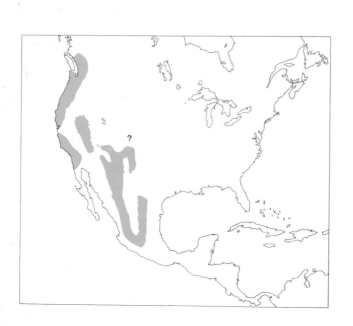

but very little is known about their living and breeding habits. The Brazilian Owl occurs, as its vernacular name suggests, in south-east Brazil as far as Paraguay and northern Argentina. The plumage of the Brazilian Owl is dark brown with yellow-orange stripes above, and white with dark brown and yellow-orange diagonal stripes below; the breast is heavily tinged in medium yellow-orange. The species is a little smaller than the Tawny Owl: two males weighed between 315 and 340 g and two females 345 and 365 g respectively. The total length is about 355 mm.

In captivity in Germany Brazilian Owls laid eggs between December and mid-March. Eggs were laid either into a flat depression on the cage floor, or into a nest-box which stood on the ground. The incubation period is 28—29 days and only the female incubates while the male looks for food. The development of the young as well as the pattern of parental care bears marked similarities to that of the Tawny Owl, proving this species to be correctly placed in the genus *Strix*. In captivity, the first young left the nest-box at 35 days, the second two days later. At this time the female became very aggressive and attacked the keeper viciously. By 4 months the young owls were fully feathered and closely resembled the adults. The young ones began breeding at the age of 12 months, again in parallel with the development of the Tawny Owl.

The Rufous-legged Owl occurs from the Paraguayan chaco, Salta in Argentina and Chile, south to Tierra del Fuego, and is also a rare breeder in the Falkland Islands. It is sepia above, with fine white barring and patches of yellow-orange all over, and evenly barred underparts. In northern Chile the facial discs appear to be strongly barred in dark brown and white, while in southern Chile they are dark orange. The nesting and breeding habits have not so far been studied in detail. The Rufous-legged Owl's length is 330 to 380 mm, which is more or less the same as the Brazilian Owl. It is not known if these two closely related species ever live near to each other, or if they are ecologically separated in the areas where their ranges slightly overlap.

The Brazilian Owl *Strix hylophila* (about 355 mm) and the Rufous-legged Owl *S. rufipes* (330 to 380 mm) are the only two exclusively South American *Strix* species. They are not rare but little is known about their habits. Map, page 120.

Brazilian Owl
Strix hylophila

Rufous-legged Owl
Strix rufipes

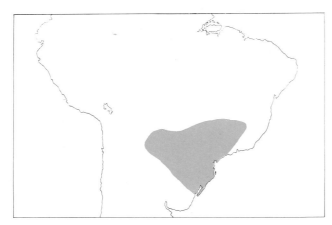

Strix hylophila: found only in Brazil.

Strix rufipes: mature forest, steppe, Argentina to Tierra del Fuego, also occasionally on Falkland Islands and South Georgia.

Found mainly in the north of both Europe and North America, the Great Grey Owl (*S. nebulosa*) is one of the most elusive birds of the taiga, able to vanish easily in the damp, mossy pine forests. It has the largest and most perfectly circular facial disc of all the owls, possibly indicating an advanced sense of hearing, which it shares with other *Strix* owls. Its massive head may be as much as 510 mm in circumference. The fierce-looking yellow eyes are noticeably small (12.5 mm in diameter compared with those of, for example, a Tawny Owl which are 16 to 17 mm). Plumage is dusky grey, irregularly marked with dark and white on the upperparts and broadly streaked below. In flight it shows distinctive orange-buff patches on the wings, and the long feathers of the head and neck give it a rather cylindrical appearance. Great Grey Owls of northern Europe and Asia tend to be lighter and more finely barred on the belly than North American ones, and also seem to be more completely streaked below. Juveniles are olive-brown, darkly barred as well as spotted with white above, and completely barred below; broad black face-markings extend from the eyes to the ear coverts. The owlets attain their adult plumage in less than 5 months.

The Great Grey Owl is one of the largest of all owls, varying from 610 to 840 mm (Europe 610 to 710 mm, N. America 635 to 840 mm). However, the volume of its feathers, which provide insulation from the cold conditions in which it lives, make it appear much larger than it really is and, whereas female Eagle Owls weigh up to 4000 g, male Great Grey Owls weigh only 535 to 1100 g and females no more than 1900 g.

Great Grey Owls are found mainly in the northern coniferous forests on both sides of the Atlantic, but in many areas, e.g. central Europe, they are scarce and unevenly distributed. The southernmost nest ever found in Europe was in the forest of Bielowieza in Poland, where this owl was last reported in 1955. It is said to be the rarest owl in Europe, but so many have been recorded in northern Europe during the last forty years, that this is hard to believe. In Finland its range has extended southwards since about 1930.

In northern Europe Great Grey Owls occur mainly in dense spruce and pine forests. Nests are usually near forest edges, and they have also been recorded in pinewood in the middle of marshes and occasionally in birchwoods. It seems likely that the availability of a suitable nesting site is more important than the exact habitat. Although it is usually thought of as an inhabitant of remote places it has been found breeding close to farmhouses. Great Grey Owl territories are probably very small, since nests have often been found close together—in Finland two as little as 49 m apart, and in another case within 400 m of one another. Within their small territories Great Grey Owls tolerate the presence of other birds of prey; Ural Owls, Hawk Owls and Tengmalm's Owls (*Aegolius funereus*) have nested undisturbed near Great Grey Owls, though all compete with the Great Grey for voles.

The Great Grey Owl *Strix nebulosa* (610 to 840 mm) generally breeds in the abandoned nests of diurnal birds of prey. Though it is such a large species, it is relatively conservative in its hunting behaviour, preying almost entirely on voles and shrews. Being so dependent on voles, it is forced to irrupt well outside its usual range whenever vole populations crash and northern populations move south even in normal years.

Map: *Strix nebulosa*: northern coniferous forests.

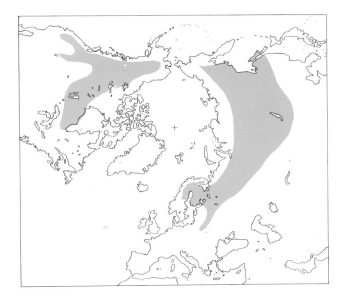

In northern Europe Great Grey Owls regularly make their homes in the old nests of goshawks, buzzards, or even Golden Eagles. About 13 per cent of nests are on the top of stumps, and six times a nest has been found in a hollow dug by the bird on level ground. Many investigators have claimed that the Great Grey Owl builds its own nest, but recent research in both Europe and North America has not revealed any kind of nest-building activity. Like the Ural Owl the Great Grey Owl does not bring any new material to the nest, but merely deepens it. In hawks' nests the twigs which it moves from the middle of the nest accumulate at the brim and these may be misinterpreted as an addition of the owl's. Sometimes the owl may excavate a thin hawk's nest too deeply, and the bottom may drop out. The Great Grey Owl has never been known to nest in a hole, although holes or crevices are typical nest-sites for other *Strix* owls.

In Finland Great Grey Owls have been heard calling as early as mid-February. The call is a deep-toned, booming sequence of notes, 'hoo-hoo-hoo', often rising, and repeated at regular intervals. The voice is, however, very weak, and its carrying power is only about 500 m. They often snap their mandibles together to produce a loud noise—probably a stylized biting movement given as a warning, as it seems to occur in situations where a bird is on the defensive. Great Grey Owls are often absurdly tame. In North America in winter, birds can be enticed to fly down to dead mice cast in their direction on the end of a fishing line. They may then be caught for ringing with a hand net.

Dates of egg-laying vary from mid-April to mid-May. Of 122 clutches recorded in northern Europe, clutch-size varied from 1 to 9, with an average of 4.2. Clutch-size fluctuates in accordance with vole populations (see below). It is interesting that the Great Grey Owl, nesting in open sites, has more oval-shaped eggs than its hole-nesting cousins the Ural and Tawny Owls. The female incubates for about 30 days, during which time the male brings her food. The female will attack intruders near the nest, particularly after the chicks have hatched. Chicks hatch at intervals of 2 or 3 days and leave the nest at the age of 3 weeks. They are reluctant fliers and spend a long time simply moving about in the branches of the nest tree. Even after 6 to 8 weeks they are usually found near the nest, and they keep together and may stay within the territory for several months, while the female keeps constant watch.

The male alone hunts during breeding and, as long as the nestlings are small, the female tears the prey he brings to pieces before feeding them. Hunting may occur at any time of the day, but seems to be less successful in strong sunshine and during the middle of the night; at least the feeding frequency is then at its lowest. Prey is captured by pouncing on it from a suitable perch, usually a small tree. In winter mice are located by sound and then caught by the owl plunging through the snow. Great Grey Owls favour open country such as marsh and cleared forest for hunting. They feed on small voles and shrews, occasionally taking frogs and birds ranging in size from finches to jays. Many hunters have claimed that in winter they feed on larger animals, such as hares and big game birds, but in fact small mammals are always the most common food. Great Greys seem reluctant to change from small voles and shrews to other foods, and for this reason they do not normally stay in their territory all winter, unless voles are very numerous. Usually they lead a nomadic life, irrupting through the coniferous zone eastwards and westwards as well as to the north and south in response to food availability. The greatest invasions of these owls into northern Europe always occur when vole populations are at their lowest in northern Russia. They may migrate as far as southern Sweden and Germany and, if there are plenty of voles available for food, then the owls remain to breed in southern Finland and Sweden. When voles become scarce, the owls move back to the east and north again.

The Ural Owl (*S. uralensis*) is rather like a large, pale, long-tailed Tawny Owl, with greyish-white to brownish-white plumage, boldly streaked with dark brown. The streaks are particularly long and well-defined on the underparts. The long tail is noticeably barred, and is tipped with white. As the bird flies along it gives an impression of ghostly near-whiteness. The facial disc, which

Above right: The Ural Owl *Strix uralensis* (about 585 mm) is less nocturnal than some other *Strix* species and has smaller eyes. Its hunting peaks are late evening and early morning.

Map: *Strix uralensis*: old coniferous or mixed forest; now often found in heath forest, spruce bogs.

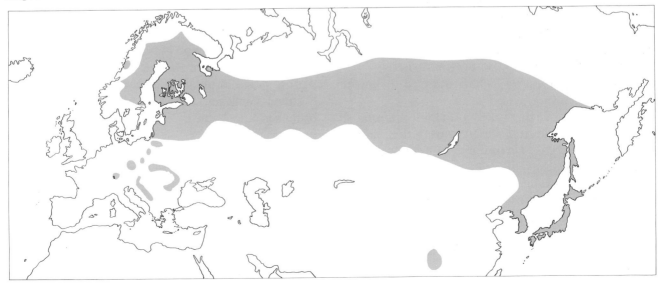

forms an almost perfect circle on the round head, is off-white and unmarked, making it easy to distinguish the Ural Owl from the Great Grey Owl with its lined face. The blackish-brown eyes are not as big as those of some of the other *Strix* species, for the Ural Owl is less completely nocturnal. It is about 585 mm long, the female weighing 520 to 1020 g and the male 451 to 825 g.

Ural Owls are distributed over a large area of Europe and Asia. Some populations are geographically isolated, and between nine and eleven subspecies are recognized. The very isolated Chinese subspecies is the darkest of all, with blackish-brown markings. In general, the populations in Europe and Asia are darker than those in the middle of the range. The Ural Owl population has recently increased in northern Europe, and the increase has produced change and variety in the owl's choice of nest-sites and habitats. The most common nesting habitat used to be old coniferous or mixed forests, far from human habitation. In the last fifty years, however, the nesting habitat has become more varied. Damp heath forests are now the most common habitat, though the species also nests regularly in dry heath forests and in spruce bogs. In Finland the first nests near civilization were found in the 1950s and about fifty nests in buildings or holes near houses are known to the author. Until the end of the 1950s stumps and holes in trees seem to have been the preferred nesting sites and, until the beginning of the 1960s, old twig nests of other large birds were becoming more and more common. In 1960 the widespread use of boxes began, and since the mid-1960s nest-boxes have been used more often than any other type of nest-site, although occasionally buildings, flat ground and rock faces are chosen. Like the Great Grey Owl, the Ural Owl does not bring any new twigs to the nest, but merely rearranges the material it finds there to make the nest deeper.

The Ural Owl feeds mainly on small mammals, such as bank, field and water voles, but it also takes squirrels, weasels and even hares, frogs and beetles and a variety of birds. Finches, thrushes and even such game birds as Hazel Hens and Black Grouse have been recorded. Its ability to change over to food other than small mammals is greater than, for instance, that of the Great Grey Owl, and it is therefore able to remain in its territory throughout the year.

The Ural Owl *Strix uralensis* takes a greater range of prey items, including more large species, such as hares and game birds, than its close relative the Great Grey Owl *S. nebulosa*. As a result, it is able to remain on its territory throughout the year.

Right: The Tawny Owl *Strix aluco* (355 to 460 mm) is the commonest and most familiar owl throughout most of Europe. Though woodland is its preferred habitat, it is very adaptable and has even colonized the centre of cities where there are large wooded parks and gardens.

The breeding season is variable, and is mainly controlled by the severity of winter. In northern Europe spring hooting and duetting may begin from early March. The two-part call of the Ural Owl has a barking quality. The female has a variety of calls at the nest, including a barking note of warning to the young, and various gobbling, chuckling and hissing calls. They signal aggression by snapping their bills loudly. The number of eggs varies from 2 to 6. The average clutch-size in Finland is 3, and seems to be clearly influenced by the number of voles that are available. Eggs appear between late March and mid-May. Incubation lasts 27 to 28 days and the young fledge in about 5 or 6 weeks. The Ural Owl is called *slaguggla*, 'attacking owl', in Swedish, because of its habit of attacking intruders at the nest.

The Tawny Owl, *S. aluco* is a moderately large, mottled brown bird with a large head. It is usually rufous brown above, mottled and streaked with dark brown, with conspicuous whitish patches on shoulders and wings. The underparts are buff, broadly streaked and faintly barred with dark brown, while wings and tail are barred. In Europe there is also a grey adult phase of

Map: *Strix aluco*: in Europe broadleaved forest and parkland; in eastern mountains, tall coniferous forest up to 300 m.

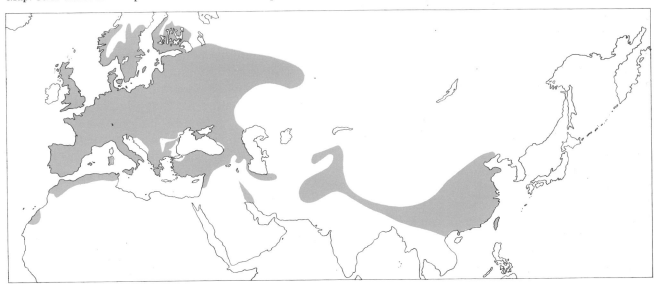

plumage, although this is rare in Britain. The Tawny Owl is 355 to 460 mm long. As with most owls, the female is larger than the male, although they look similar. Females weigh 410 to 800 g and males 410 to 550 g.

The Tawny Owl is probably the commonest and most familiar owl over much of Eurasia and north-west Africa. It is usually associated with deciduous forests where it may attain densities of six to seven pairs per square kilometre but in western Europe it is also found in tree-dotted farmland, parkland and conifer plantations; in the Himalayas and in the Burmese and Chinese mountains it is characteristic of tall coniferous forests up to about 3000 m. Tawny Owls have such a wide choice of food, and are so tolerant of man, that they have been able to maintain and even increase their numbers in a changing environment. Some have even colonized the centres of large cities such as London. In Finland, Tawny Owl nests are typically found near civilization.

The typical hooting of the Tawny Owl has been described as the most musical of all the European owls. It can be heard all through the year, but especially in autumn when territories are being established. It is hard to see how this beautiful quavering song has been converted into the popular 'tu-whit tu-whoo' so often quoted as the typical owl call. It is perhaps interesting to note here that owls which inhabit thick woodland areas rely on voice to proclaim their territories and so are more vocal than open-country owls.

In Europe, breeding usually begins in mid-March. The owl chooses a hole or nest-box in a tree, but occasionally uses the old nest of a crow, magpie, sparrowhawk or heron. There are even records of Tawny Owls rearing chicks on the ground, in rabbit burrows or buildings—curious choices for such a traditionally tree-based species.

In the north of their range, Tawny Owls vary their clutch-size according to vole abundance, just as Great Grey Owls do. In Finland the clutch-size in 188 nests averaged 3.3. The number of eggs varied from 1 to 6 and two nests with 8 eggs have been recorded. However, in Britain clutches of 2 or 3 eggs are most common (range 2 to 7 eggs) and clutches of 5 or 6 eggs are very rare (12 out of a total of 580 records). Here fluctuations in the abundance of small rodents have very little influence on clutch-size but a marked effect on the proportion of birds which attempt to breed each year. When mice and voles are very scarce no owls may even lay eggs. Incubation, by the female alone, starts with the second egg; food is brought to the nest by the male. There may be an interval of 48 hours to a week between the laying of each egg, depending on the weather. The eggs are incubated for about 30 days and the young brooded for about 3 weeks, the male again providing food.

The Tawny Owl is usually considered to be a thoroughly nocturnal species but this is not strictly correct. When feeding young, 20 per cent of all visits to the nest are made between sunrise and sunset and even during incubation the male not infrequently brings prey to the female in broad daylight. Tawny Owls possess colour vision and their visual acuity in daylight is only slightly less than that of man.

The Tawny Owl usually hunts by waiting quietly on a perch, watching and listening before pouncing on its prey. Earthworms are caught by a different technique. The owl stays on the ground until it sees or hears one emerging from its burrow. It then hops across and seizes the worm in its bill. The Tawny Owl can catch mice in very dark conditions, probably locating the prey entirely by sound, as its visual sensitivity in darkness has been shown to be only two and a half times better than man's (though about a hundred times better than that of a wholly diurnal bird like the pigeon). Its large ear openings and the difference in the shape and size of the two ears probably help it to find its prey, which is usually small mammals, birds, frogs, earthworms and insects. Occasionally it will snatch fish from streams, ponds—even from ornamental goldfish ponds. Tawny Owls are very adaptable feeders and during bad vole years they change their diets to include many more birds. They are thus able to spread into densely built-up areas, where mammals are scarce, and can live in close proximity to man.

Closely related species usually manage to avoid competition, either by living in different areas, or by occupying different parts of the environment, or adopting different ways of life, in the same area. Thus two closely related species in the same area may have different hunting techniques and so avoid competition. The ecology of the three *Strix* species, the Tawny, Ural and Great Grey Owls, has now been studied over several years in Finland, where their area of sympatry covers—especially in good vole years—almost the entire southern and central country. It was formerly

Tawny Owls *Strix aluco* are among the most nocturnal of owls and feed mainly on Wood Mice and voles, which they detect while perched quietly on a branch, watching and listening. This bird is carrying a Wood Mouse to its young.

was estimated. In 6 months a Tawny Owl requires about 18 kg, a Ural Owl about 23 kg and a Great Grey Owl about 27 kg of food. Thus the amount eaten is directly proportional to the weight of the bird. While it might seem efficient for the largest bird to take the largest prey, almost the reverse is true. The Great Grey Owl, which is the largest, takes only small mammals (for example in the study period more than 650 field and bank voles but only 11 of the much larger water voles), while Ural and Tawny Owls take fewer of the smaller species and more of the larger. In addition, the smaller Ural Owl took more larger mammals (including a hare) and more game birds, and both Ural and Tawny Owls took mice, rats, frogs and fish. Great Grey Owls took fewer birds—many fewer than Tawny Owls, which were particularly severe predators of thrushes and small birds.

Quantity of prey taken by one Tawny, Ural, and Great Grey owl during six months.

Food taken in a period of six months	Tawny 18 kg	Ural 23 kg	Great Grey 27 kg
Moles, shrews and bats	34	22	25
Field and bank voles	174	201	654
Water voles	16	43	11
Squirrels and weasels	1	7	1
Mice and rats	23	18	12
Hares	—	1	—
Game birds	1	3	1
Jays	1	2	1
Thrushes	57	24	2
Small birds	54	5	5
Frogs and fishes	28	13	3
Total number of prey	389	339	715

Although they take the same foods, these three closely related species apparently show quite distinct food preferences. The Great Grey Owl stands out as a predator of small mammals. Its lightly built skeleton and long, rather slender claws, which spread widely on the ground, seem well adapted for capturing voles and other small, fast-moving creatures on the ground. The short, strongly curved claws of the Tawny on the other hand seem well fitted for grasping birds in the air, and the strong thick claws of the Ural Owl are appropriate for its role as a predator of larger

believed that these three species occupied different geographical ranges without any major overlap and so did not enter into any competition with each other. In Finland, however, this is not the case and the three species may nest within a few hundred metres of each other. The Tawny, Ural and Great Grey Owls also breed sympatrically in large areas of the U.S.S.R., in south-eastern Poland, and in part of Sweden. It is therefore of interest to see how the similar species in such close proximity try to avoid direct competition. This comparison concentrates on four ecological parameters: hunting activity, food, breeding habitat and nest-site and includes comments at the end on mate and nest-site fidelity.

From studying the feeding biology of these owls, the half-yearly food consumption of each species mammals. It was concluded from the food studies that both Ural and Tawny Owls are catholic predators and food generalists, while the larger Great Grey Owl is a small rodent specialist. Thus, the food niches of Ural and Tawny Owl are about 2.5 times broader than the Great Grey Owl's.

The three species also to some degree avoid competition by hunting at different times. Activity studies during the breeding season showed that the Tawny Owl is the most nocturnal of the three, hunting almost exclusively at night until the young are big and hungry, when they also bring food home in the daytime. The Great Grey Owl is the most diurnal. The peaks of its activity are the early morning and late evening hours, but it only ceases feeding the young at noon. The Ural Owl fits between the other two, showing a so-called biphasic activity, with the highest peak in hunting during the late evening and a lower peak in the early morning. To a small extent, it also remains active during the day. The Great Grey Owl's breeding habitat was found to be the most catholic among the three; it breeds in forests of all kinds. Habitat selection of the Tawny Owl is the most restricted, but overlaps extensively with that of the Ural Owl. The Tawny Owl is almost exclusively a hole-nester (92 per cent of nest-sites studied), while nest selection by the Ural Owl is quite catholic, including nest-boxes and holes (53 per cent), stumps (23 per cent), and twig nests (20 per cent). The Great Grey Owl uses mainly twig nests (79 per cent) and stumps (13 per cent), and may even lay on the ground (3 per cent). Great Grey and Tawny Owls are therefore not likely to compete for the same nest-sites, while competition for nest-sites may be keen between Ural and Tawny Owls. Occasional competition between Great Grey and Ural Owls may also occur. When measured by the four parameters (activity, food, breeding habitat, and nest-site), the Ural Owl has the widest niche. The niche of the Tawny Owl is only 73 per cent and the Great Grey Owl's only 48 per cent of that of the Ural Owl. These results suggest, however, that competition among the three species is common, and should be taken into account when providing artificial nest-sites (boxes or platforms).

It has been more or less a dogma that the Ural Owl and the Tawny Owl are very faithful to their breeding sites and that their pair-bond is life long. Finnish ring recoveries (19,383 Tawnies and 12,067 Ural Owls ringed between 1913 and 1986) suggest that 98—100 per cent of Ural Owl males, 90—95 per cent of the females and 80—90 per cent of both sexes of Tawnies are faithful to their previous nest-site. Fidelity to the mate seems to be almost absolute (95—97 per cent) in the Ural Owl, but much less so (only 80—85 per cent) in the Tawny Owl. The Great Grey Owl is a nomadic species, although some pairs have been recorded on their territories over many years.

Some 796 Great Grey Owls have been ringed in Finland between 1913 and 1986, but the ringing has not yet yielded enough recoveries to say anything conclusive on nest-site tenacity or mate fidelity. However, in Sweden two interesting long-distance recoveries support the nomadism of this species. Two adult females marked in their nests in Norrbotten in 1974 and 1977 were both recovered in Finland. The first female was controlled breeding in the Finnish Lapland in 1983, 300 km north-east of the ringing site, and in May 1979 the second female was found dead in eastern Finland, 430 km south-east of the ringing site. During the last invasion (1983—84) it was noted that more than sixty per cent of the Great Greys were birds of more than one year old, and judging from their weight, the majority were females. Therefore, it seems likely that adult males are more sedentary than adult females, which is in accordance with the much larger samples of *Aegolius funereus* ringed in Finland.

Hume's Owl (*S. butleri*) is mentioned in the Old Testament (*Isaiah 34:14*), but was more officially described in 1878 by Mr Hume in the Mekran coast of southern Baluchistan where, however, nothing is known of its present occurrence. Today, this 300 to 330 mm long *Strix* Owl is known to live in wide areas in the Arabian Peninsula, and is not rare in the lower Jordan valley and around the Dead Sea. It has also been recorded recently in Oman and in the arid Egyptian Red Sea mountains near the Roman ruins of Medinet Nugrus in Wadi Nugrus, where the species was discovered on 16 February 1982.

The colour of the upperparts varies from dark browny-buff to paler brown-buff with sparse, dark brown streaks. The facial disc is a buffish-grey with delicate brown barring round the disc below the eye, the iris of which is yellow or orange-yellow. The underparts are whitish, well marked with orange-buff, particularly on the upper breast. In the field, Hume's Owl looks like a small sandy-brown Tawny Owl, but is somewhat smaller. Two females weighed only 214 and 220 g. In flight it appears to have a proportionally longer wing than

Hume's Owl *Strix butleri* (about 330 mm) is a desert owl which is much lighter in colour and somewhat smaller than the Tawny Owl. Recently it has been found in many new places in the lower Jordan valley and around the Dead Sea where its range comes within 20 km of the Tawny Owl's.

Strix butleri: palm groves and rocky outcrops in desert.

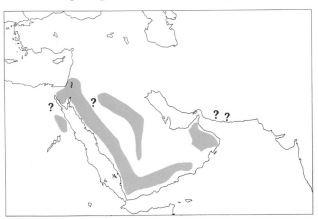

the Tawny Owl, and it perches at an angle, rather than upright like the Tawny.

Most of the records of this owl are from cliffs and steep-sided wadis with only minimal vegetation (acacia). It is therefore thought that rocks are an essential medium for its life-style, and presumably rock holes are used for nesting. The main breeding season in Israel is believed to be February to April. So far only one nest has been positively identified: in 1974, in a well at Nahal Sekher in the western Negev. In this case, a clutch of eggs was laid in early May, hatching between 10 and 21 June. The chicks remained in the nest for about 28 days, until 17 July.

Its call is a longish hoot followed quickly by two short double notes—'hoooo-huhu-huhu', and is soft compared with that of the Tawny Owl. The usual call lasts about two seconds and can be repeated at 15 second intervals. Calling generally starts about 20 minutes after sunset and may continue all night, and sometimes after dawn.

Hume's Owl feeds on small mammals such as rock gerbils, small birds, grasshoppers, scorpions, reptiles and insects. It often hunts animals crossing roads in the dark and unfortunately many owls are killed by cars while doing so. In five years Aronson collected 15 Hume's Owls killed by cars in Israel, demonstrating that this owl is far from rare at least in that country. However, due to their wholly nocturnal life-style they are likely to be found only after a careful search in suitable habitats.

The African Wood Owl (*S. woodfordii*) is the only member of the genus *Strix* living in the sub-Saharan part of the African continent. It is 305 to 335 mm long and has warm red-brown upperparts with white spotting on the wing coverts and scapulars. On the underparts it is barred russet and white. Its facial disc is dark, but there are prominent white eyebrows and lores. The large eyes are dark brown. The tail is barred and protrudes beyond the wing tips. Juveniles are similar but paler and the head is creamy. At the age of 5 months they are indistinguishable from adults. The sexes are alike.

This is the commonest owl in forests and woodlands in Africa south of the Sahara. It is by no means restricted to forest habitat but also occurs in coastal bush, pine plantations and near villages. More recently the birds have even become established among the suburbs of some large towns. Personally I reared one African Wood Owl which was found with a broken wing in a garden in the middle of Abidjan, Ivory Coast.

The African Wood Owl is strictly nocturnal in its habits, and roosts in dense foliage or in thick creeper. It is not particularly afraid of humans and will easily nest near houses. It catches prey by dropping on to it from a perch, but the main food, insects, is caught in flight. Insect prey includes beetles, weevils, grasshoppers, crickets, moths, caterpillars, mantises, cicadas and termites. It also eats small rodents, frogs and birds such as bulbuls, shrikes and doves. There is one record of a snake as prey.

Several calls have been described, but only two basic calls are used to maintain contact and during courtship. The call of the female owl is a high-pitched 'eee-yow', to which the male answers with a low, gruff 'hoo' or with the full 'hoo-hoo, hu, hu, hu, hu, hu', which is also the major call of both sexes. It is a rapid call, in which the last five syllables are emitted unevenly with a syncopated rhythm. Soft 'oop, oop, oop' and single 'hoo' calls combined with bill-clacking are delivered in the presence of a nest intruder.

The usual nest-site is a natural tree-hole; such sites are normally well protected above, but open hollows have been used as well. Occasionally it breeds in an old raptor nest or on the flat ground, under a log or at the base of a tree. One to three eggs are laid between July and October. The incubation period is some 31 days and the nestling period between 30 and 37 days. Unlike the northern hemisphere *Strix* species, the African Wood Owl is not known to attack observers at the nest, even after dark.

Three Wood Owls are found only in India and South-east Asia: the Brown Wood Owl (*Strix leptogrammica*), the Mottled Wood Owl (*S. ocellata*), and the Spotted Wood Owl (*S. seloputo*).

Patches of dark orange and white spotting on the head and mantle, as well as on the upper breast, are peculiar to the Mottled Wood Owl. Its back, wings, and tail are mottled brown and white, the facial discs are dusky white with black lines forming distinctive concentric circles, the throat white and the underparts barred. There are three races, which occur in India and Arakan. Varying in length from 380 to 460 mm it lives in open, semi-cultivated areas, and in tamarind groves from the plains up to an altitude of 830 m. Its voice is a loud single hoot.

The Spotted Wood Owl of Malaysia is 380 to 475 mm long, and may be distinguished from the Brown Wood Owl by its dark grey-brown

Map: *Strix woodfordii*: forest and woodland

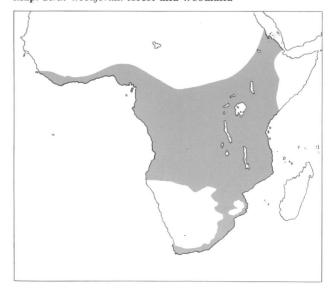

Left: The African Wood Owl *Strix woodfordii* (305 to 355 mm) is the only *Strix* species in sub-Saharan Africa. Like most species in the genus, it is largely nocturnal and preys on rodents, small birds and insects.

The Mottled Wood Owl *Strix ocellata* (380 to 460 mm) and the Spotted Wood Owl *S. seloputo* (380 to 475 mm) are lowland species that inhabit relatively open and semi-cultivated areas, the Mottled Wood Owl in India, and the Spotted Wood Owl in Burma, the Malay Peninsula, Java and Palawan.

Mottled
Wood Owl
Strix ocellata

Spotted Wood Owl
Strix seloputo

Left, map: *Strix seloputo*: lowland, open semi-cultivated areas.

Strix ocellata: open semi-cultivated areas and tamarind groves up to 830 m.

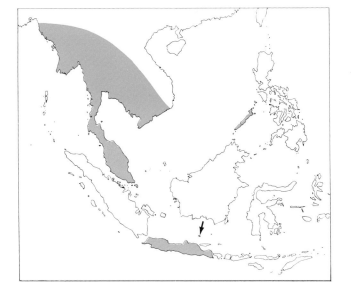

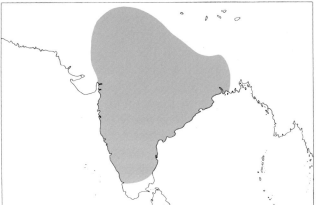

colouring, the white spots on the forehead, crown, and mantle and the very sparse, broken white barring on the back. Distinct white patches on the wing coverts are barred in grey-brown. The face is tawny and there is a white patch at the throat; the underparts vary from white to tawny, with widely spaced brown barring. Although largely nocturnal, it often emerges to hunt before sunset and it feeds mainly on large beetles. Spotted Wood Owls are not rare, but are of more frequent occurrence in the north than in the south of Malaysia. It is a bird of lowland forest and scrub, sometimes even occurring in town parks and around villages, and is frequently encountered in pairs. Nests have been recorded but little is known of this owl's breeding biology. Among its variety of calls is a distinctive series of musical but low-pitched notes, ending with a prolonged, deep 'hoooo'.

The Brown Wood Owl is the largest of the three, measuring from 460 to 530 mm long, except in Indonesia, where the birds are smaller. It is rich dark brown above, darker on the head, with dark brown wings, faintly barred with paler brown and with a whitish patch. The facial discs are pale to rufous-brown and the eyes are surrounded by a black ring. The eyebrows are whitish, as is the throat. The breast is washed with dark brown. The rest of the underparts are light buff, heavily barred with thin dark brown lines. Juveniles have almost completely white heads. It is an uncommon resident in India but occurs east through the Indo-Chinese and Malaysian subregions to southern China, Taiwan and Hainan Island. It usually nests in pine, deciduous, moist temperate, and evergreen forest from the plains to 2800 m but it has been recorded up to 4300 m. In Borneo it inhabits lowland primary forest. Brown Wood Owls prey not only on the smaller mammals and birds, but also on pheasants, jungle fowl, larger squirrels, and monitor lizards. In Ceylon, where it is semi-diurnal, it also eats fish. In Borneo, and possibly elsewhere, birds nest in December—January, laying 2 eggs in a tree-hole. It has a wide variety of calls including a rapid series of four hollow-sounding hoots with the emphasis on the first, the sequence being repeated every ten seconds.

The six owls of the genus *Asio* fall into two widespread, but usually ecologically distinct, groups: Long-eared owls, distributed throughout the temperate zones of the northern hemisphere, in tropical America, and locally in Africa and

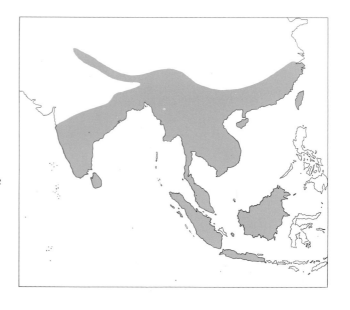

Madagascar, are dark, nocturnal owls of woodland; Short-eared owls, which are found at one season or another nearly everywhere in cold and temperate regions, are pale of plumage, predominantly diurnal, and inhabit open country.

Long-eared and Short-eared owls are among our most effective mousers; meadow mice, voles and other small mammals top the list of prey species taken, supplemented by birds, insects and occasionally frogs and fish. Long-eared owls usually nest in an abandoned nest of another large bird, such as a heron, crow or hawk. Mountain birds frequently nest on the ground. They lay 4 to 5 eggs, in peak vole years 8 to 10. Short-eared owls nest in a slight hollow on the ground near a clump of vegetation in marsh or meadow, laying 2 or 4 eggs in Africa, 4 to 7 in other parts of the world: during years of vole abundance the number increases, with 9, 13 and even 14 eggs recorded in a single clutch. Both Long- and Short-eared owls normally raise one brood, but produce a second in response to a plentiful supply of food, for example when rodents are abundant. Females alone incubate, starting when the first egg is laid. Incubation takes about 26 days; Long-eared owl chicks leave the nest at 23 or 24 days, Short-eared at 12 to 17 days. Both are migratory, especially the most northerly breeding birds. They have relatively longer wings than sedentary species, which no doubt help them in their long annual journeys to the breeding grounds.

The Striped Owl (*A. clamator*) ranges from Mexico to Bolivia and Brazil. Its upperparts are tawny-ochre, boldly striped with sooty brown,

Ranging from Mexico to Bolivia and Brazil, the Striped Owl *Asio clamator* (305 to 380 mm) is a little known species which looks and sounds very much like the Long-eared Owl *A. otus*. Because of these similarities it has recently been included with *Asio* although it was earlier considered to be a separate genus, *Rhinoptynx*. Map, page 134.

Above left: The Brown Wood Owl *Strix leptogrammica* (460 to 530 mm) is the South-east Asian representative of the genus. Like other large wood owls, it feeds on a great variety of prey items up to the size of large rodents and small game birds.

Left, map: *Strix leptogrammica*: deciduous moist temperate and evergreen forest to 2800 m; in Borneo, lowland primary forest.

while below it is white or buff, with narrow brown streaks. It has short wings and a long tail, the flight feathers and tail being barred with sooty brown. It is usually between 305 to 355 mm long and one weighed 385 g. Larger birds, 330 to 380 mm long, occur on the island of Tobago. Its striped underparts and white face and throat, as well as its larger, stouter grey beak and feet, distinguish it from other Long-eared owls found in tropical America.

Striped Owls occur in a wide variety of habitats from rainforests and deciduous seasonal forest to savannahs, marshes and even suburban areas. They can be encountered singly or in pairs but have also been recorded roosting in scattered groups of up to a dozen birds. Nests are on the ground among grass. One nest beneath a citrus orchard in Panama contained two young but a captive pair which produced ten clutches of 3 or 4 eggs (average 3.3) only ever raised one chick

Asio clamator: deciduous and lowland seasonal forest.

fawn. Island forms from the Canaries and Madeira are darker than Eurasian birds.

Long-eared Owls are found in light broad-leaved coniferous forests, riverine forests with willows and poplars, copses and clumps of trees in natural and cultivated steppes, and also in parks and large gardens—though it rarely breeds in large towns. Like many other species, it nests in twig nests made and abandoned by other birds of prey. Nesting begins in March or early April, and 4 to 6 eggs are generally laid. (In Finland the average clutch-size is 5.4.) Incubation begins with the first egg and usually lasts about 26 to 28 days. The young leave the nest when they are 23 or 24 days old but cannot fly until they are 34 days old. Breeding success is dependent on the availability of voles, which affects the number of pairs which breed, the number of clutches produced, the number of eggs laid and the survival of the owlets. Peak vole years seem to occur every four years.

The Long-eared Owl is one of the most nocturnal owls in the world but when feeding fledged young in summer it often hunts before sunset. During the day it sleeps in dark places close to tree trunks, preferably in conifers. Its food, predominantly voles, mice and rats, is caught in open, grassy places and along forest edges; it also takes small birds, numerous other species of small mammals, and large insects. The Abyssinian Long-eared Owl (*A. otus abyssinicus*) tends to feed on somewhat larger prey than the Long-eared Owl, mainly small mammals including rats up to 90 g in weight. It also appears to be strictly nocturnal. As is well known, these owls have remarkably good eyesight at night. Even more remarkable is their precise three-dimensional hearing, based on a facial disc shaped to trap sound, and asymmetrical ears located in different positions on either side of the head, enabling the birds to catch rodents in darkness. Their completely noiseless flight makes it possible for them to take the unsuspecting animal by surprise. Long-eared Owls are mainly sedentary, but in general the northern populations move south or west in winter.

per nesting attempt. Incubation, which began with the first egg, was by the female alone and lasted 33 days. The main prey appears to be small mammals. The usual calls are a melancholy, long shrill 'wheeyoo' and a series of staccato hoots.

The Long-eared Owl (*Asio otus*) is distributed in a belt right round the northern hemisphere, including many of the larger islands, between latitudes 30 and 65° N, at heights up to and sometimes exceeding 2300 m. It is also found in Africa, where it is sometimes separated into a distinct species (*A. abyssinicus*). Very like the Short-eared Owl (*A. flammeus*) although less stocky and with much longer ear tufts, its upperparts are freckled and mottled with buff and grey-brown, and its buff underparts boldly marked with dark streaks and fine cross-barring. It is 280 to 405 mm long, and the body weights of male and female vary from 245 to 400 g. The Long-eared Owl shows tremendous colour variation, not only over its considerable world range, but also in local populations, and varies from a deep chestnut brown nearing black to a fairly pale

Above right: The Long-eared Owl *Asio otus* (280 to 405 mm) hunts at night over open country, but retires by day to roost in dense cover. It is a mainly sedentary species, though the most northerly populations move further south in winter.

Map: *Asio otus*: light broadleaved and coniferous forest, riverine forest, trees in cultivated land.

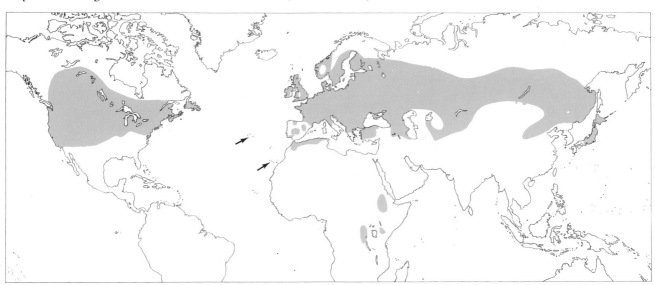

The Madagascar Long-eared Owl
Asio madagascariensis (about 320 mm) may be no more than an island race of the Long-eared Owl *Asio otus*, but it is usually given specific status on morphological grounds.

Map: *Asio madagascariensis*: humid forest.

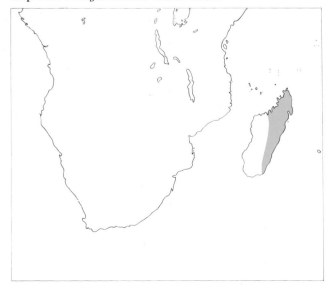

The Stygian Owl *Asio stygius* (380 to 460 mm) shows remarkable variability in its breeding behaviour, nesting in old nests in trees in Central America and on the ground in Cuba.

Map: *Asio stygius*: forests, often mountains.

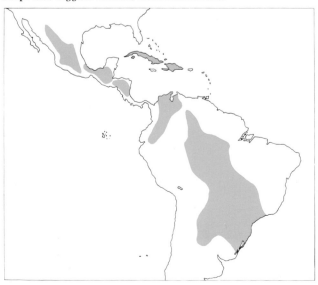

The Madagascar Long-eared Owl (*Asio madagascariensis*) is very similar to other Long-eared owls but has always been treated as a separate species on morphological grounds. It is slightly smaller (330 mm) and darker than the Long-eared Owl and has more orange-yellow in its plumage. Its distribution is apparently confined to the humid forests of eastern Madagascar and to an area around Sambrino.

The Stygian Owl (*A. stygius*) is a large, dark owl with prominent ear tufts, found in forests and often in mountains from Mexico to northern Argentina. Like the Madagascar Long-eared Owl, it is very closely related to the Long-eared Owl. Its upperparts are sooty black, more or less mottled with white or buff; underparts are buff to yellow-buff, heavily spotted and streaked with sooty black. It varies in size from 380 to 460 mm and often feeds on bats. In Mexico it nests in trees, like the Long-eared Owl, but in Cuba it is said to lay its two white eggs on the bare ground like the Short-eared Owl. Such adaptability has, of course, tremendous survival value for this owl, because it may well be able to live and breed successfully in open areas if its wooded habitat is threatened.

The Short-eared Owl (*A. flammeus*) is a very widely distributed species, breeding throughout the Old and New Worlds between latitudes 40°N and 70°N, as well as in the southern half of South America, in Hawaii, the Galapagos, the West Indies, the northern end of the Andes, and the mouth of the Orinoco in Venezuela. Over the main European, Asian and North American parts of the range there is only one subspecies, but seven different subspecies are described from other areas.

Short-eared Owls are birds of grassland, tundra, marshes and dunes over which they move in search of prey with a buoyant, moth-like flight. For this reason they have longer, narrower wings than other medium-sized owls. They have a distinctive dark carpal on both the upper and the

The Short-eared Owl *Asio flammeus* (330 to 430) coexists with the closely related Long-eared Owl over much of Eurasia. Both species hunt over open country, preying largely on voles, but the Short-eared Owl differs from the Long-eared Owl in being mainly diurnal and in roosting and nesting on the ground. Map, page 138.

lower surface of the wings. The body is pale below, boldy streaked with dark brown—except for the lava-coloured Galapagos race, which is streaked and barred below like a Long-eared Owl. The back is boldly mottled in pale buff and dark brown. The brilliant, lemon-yellow eyes are surrounded by dark-tipped feathers, in pale facial discs. Size varies from 330 to 430 mm, the body weight of females from 280 to 390 g, and that of males from 200 to 360 g. All short-eared owls display much smaller ear tufts than their close relatives the long-eared owls. They are always birds of open country and it is possible that they do not need special 'outline' recognition signals as much as their woodland-living relatives. They have a spectacular display flight and a rasping high-pitched 'wak, wak, wak' heard only on their breeding ground. Other calls are described as a repeated 'toot-toot-toot', a jackdaw-like 'tyak, tyarrp' and a harsh flight note. Generally, however, these are rather silent birds.

The nest is invariably built of grasses on the ground near marshy areas. Their territories can be as little as 15 to 20 hectares in size, which means that there may be up to seven pairs per square kilometre. Incubation begins with the first egg, which is normally laid in late April or early May. The eggs are laid at intervals of 24 hours and, on average, incubation lasts for about 26 days. The young wander from the nest when they are about 12 to 17 days old but do not fly until they are 31 to 36 days old.

The Short-eared Owl is to some extent able to match its reproductive effort to the prospective food supply; in good rodent years clutches of up to 14 eggs may be laid. In a study of this species

Asio flammeus: open country.

In the northern parts of its range, the clutch-size and breeding success of the Short-eared Owl *Asio flammeus* is correlated with the four year cycle of abundance of voles. This clutch is about average. Note the egg-tooth on the bill tip of this newly hatched chick; it is shed soon after it has been used to break out of the egg-shell.

The Short-eared Owl has an immense range and has even colonized remote oceanic islands. This bird, photographed in the Galapagos Islands, belongs to the race *A. f. galapagensis* which is as tame as most of the other birds of the Archipelago.

in Finland, an area of 20 square kilometres supported 40 pairs, which on average laid 7.3 eggs (range from 4 to 9); 4—7 owlets per nest reached adult age. From these territories about 300 pellets were collected and over 600 prey animals identified. On the basis of this material it was possible to calculate how much the population of 40 owl families ate during the breeding season. The owls stayed in the area between 15 April and 31 July: from 5 June onward 40 pairs fed 4.7 young per nest. One Short-eared Owl ate, on average, 80 g in a day, and produced a pellet for every 30 to 90 g of food taken. The population as a whole consumed about 1500 kg during the April to July period, divided between different groups of prey as follows:

field and bank voles	41988 individuals
shrews	4241 individuals
mice and rats	2706 individuals
water voles and squirrels	261 individuals
small birds	690 individuals
owlets	85 individuals

The owls thus ate over 41,000 voles and altogether around 50,000 small mammals. Feeding mainly on harmful rodents, they are indeed a good friend to the farmer. However, although the Short-eared Owl is obviously an efficient mouse-trap, what influence this predation has on the dynamics of rodent population is not understood.

Although the year of this study was a remarkable year for voles, the owls ate in addition almost 700 small birds: similarly the number of owl chicks eaten, 85, seems high. These were the one to three chicks which disappeared from each nest: the strongest young eat the weakest, ensuring that at least some of the brood survive. It is not surprising that such an opportunist species has spread widely over the temperate land masses, and even succeeded in colonizing remote oceanic islands.

In Finland both Short-eared and Long-eared Owls coexist in the same area, sometimes nesting as little as 30 m apart without interfering with each other. They even catch the same kind of prey without apparently adversely affecting each other's hunting success. However, as Short-eared Owls are diurnal and Long-eared Owls mainly nocturnal, together they can exploit the habitat throughout the twenty-four hours without directly competing with each other.

The African Marsh Owl *Asio capensis* (305 to 380 mm) is an ecological equivalent of the Short-eared Owl, living in similar open grassy or marshy habitats and differing only in being rather more nocturnal.

Asio capensis: open grassy or marshy habitats.

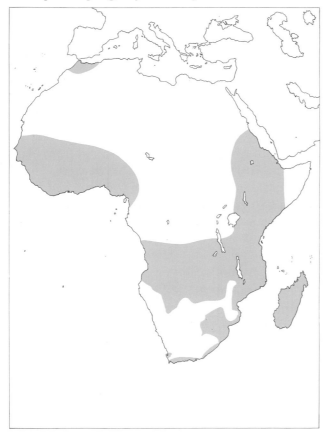

The African Marsh Owl (*A. capensis*) is a uniform earthy colour without markings on the upperparts except for barring on the tail. The underparts are pale and faintly barred. The pale patch near the wing tips is a conspicuous feature in flight. It is difficult to separate this species from the Short-eared Owl, although it differs in having uniform coloration and a darker face with a characteristic ring of dark feathers around the eyes. The ear tufts are short but more visible than in the Short-eared Owl. Body length is 305 to 380 mm.

The African Marsh Owl nests on the ground, usually in a well sheltered hollow under a grass tuft. In April (Morocco) or during the last 3 months of the year (Nigeria), it lays a clutch of 2 to 4 white eggs, sometimes up to 6. The eggs hatch at two-day intervals. The young spend 2 or 3 weeks in the nest and are then probably fed nearby for another 2 or 3 weeks. It is similar in habits to the Short-eared Owl, but lives mainly on large aquatic insects and also frogs, lizards, mice and small birds. It is a common species, made conspicuous by its habit of flying around a few hours before sunset. Perhaps because it inhabits a relatively restricted habitat, it is frequently gregarious and can sometimes be flushed in flocks of as many as 30 to 40 birds. Its call is a frog-like croak, uttered singly or in rapid succession and used during courtship or in alarm near the nest when disturbed.

CHAPTER EIGHT

Hawk Owls

Ninox, Sceloglaux, Uroglaux, Nesasio, Surnia

The name 'hawk owl' has been given both to a group of southern hemisphere owls of the genera *Ninox, Uroglaux* and *Sceloglaux*, and to a single, probably unrelated northern genus, *Surnia*. *Nesasio*, a little known genus from the Solomon Islands, is also included in this chapter.

As the name implies, species of these genera are more hawk-like than other owls: some have longer or narrower wings and longer tails but the main difference appears to be some reduction in the size of the stiff discs of feathers around the eyes, which otherwise are the main distinguishing features of the owls. In the southern group of species it is conceivable that the distinctive facial feathering was never developed, suggesting that these genera have not evolved so far as other owls from the ancestral condition. Almost lacking facial discs, the head is proportionally smaller and more rounded in smaller species, strong-browed and more aquiline in a very large one, with the eyes and bill appearing more prominent. In the small species of the genus *Ninox* these modifications are to some extent reduced by the presence of short, stiff feathers which form a pair of prominent 'eyebrow' ridges over the eyes.

Apparently associated with the simple, reduced facial discs are small, symmetrical ear-openings. The very nocturnal owls with elaborate facial discs usually also possess specialized, asymmetrical ear-openings which enable them to pinpoint the position of their prey by hearing in conditions where sight cannot be used. As the hawk owls lack this special adaptation they must presumably rely almost entirely on sight for their successful hunting.

The single species of Northern Hawk Owl (*Surnia ulula*) ranges right around the northern hemisphere through the great coniferous forest belt of the boreal and sub-Arctic zones. Only remotely related to its southern counterparts, the modifications which it shows are almost certainly adaptations evolved to fit a particular niche in the ecology of these regions, rather than ancestral characters retained from the south. Characters shown by the hawk owls in general are not peculiar to them alone, for they are shared in varying degrees by other species too. The name 'hawk owl' is due to an accident of resemblance which occurred to the person who first gave them the name, but does not necessarily indicate a real and consistent difference setting them apart from other owls.

The southern hawk owl complex consists of around eighteen species. Its distribution suggests that the group may once have been dispersed more widely over the earth's surface, but has now been displaced elsewhere and is successful only where competitors are few. These species provide most of the medium-sized owls of the Indonesian and Australasian regions, existing side by side with the larger owls of the genus *Strix*, barn owls (*Tyto*) and small owls of the genus *Otus*. In Australasia, where *Bubo, Strix* and *Otus* are absent, hawk owls produce a wider range of species to take advantage of the wider range of vacant ecological niches.

Over much of their range the species of hawk owl replace each other geographically with little overlap. In the main, species occupy large single islands or groups of smaller islands. The Oriental

Hawk Owl, *N. scutulata*, is an exception, with an extensive distribution on the Asiatic mainland from Sakhalin to India and Malaysia. Migratory, it has spread also to the Andaman and Nicobar Islands where its resident range overlaps that of several other small species of *Ninox*. Sulawesi (formerly Celebes) has two similar sized species of hawk owl with similar ranges which differ in ecological preferences.

The most complex situation occurs in Australasia. Here the hawk owls are unchallenged by other genera, except barn owls (*Tyto*), and in some regions three different species coexist. They provide a good example of the more general rule that where several closely related species share the same geographical range they tend to evolve size differences which enable them to concentrate in the main on a different range of prey, or to exploit different parts of the environment, so that they do not normally compete with each other.

Through most of Australia and New Zealand the small Boobook or Morepork Owl (*Ninox novaeseelandiae*) is present. It occurs also in one corner of southern New Guinea, although in lowland areas there it is largely replaced by the similar-sized Sooty-backed Hawk Owl (*N. theomacha*). A rare forest species, the small Papuan Hawk Owl (*Uroglaux dimorpha*) is also present to some extent. In north and east Australia, eastern New Guinea and the Moluccas, the larger Barking Owl (*N. connivens*) occurs in the same range as these smaller birds. In south-eastern Australia a third, larger species, the Powerful Owl (*N. strenua*) occurs with the other two types, replaced in northern Australia and in New Guinea by the almost equally large Rufous Owl (*N. rufa*). In New Zealand the Laughing Owl (*Sceloglaux albifacies*) was a similar large bird which coexisted with the Boobook Owl but is now thought to be extinct.

Within the main genus, *Ninox*, the best-known species are the three southern Australian owls. The study of these species by David Fleay (1968) has provided a good background to the life and habits of the whole group. One interesting fact that one might have suspected from their lack of specialization of hearing (see above) is that, although these birds usually roost by day among branches or in cavities, they are capable of hunting by day and use sight in catching their prey. Smallest of the three is the Boobook Owl, *N. novaeseelandiae*, which is about 360 mm long. It is the most widely distributed, occurring in a wide range of habitats from thick forest to arid, open areas of sparse trees, or in open places where there are caves or rock crevices to roost in. It has also moved into urban areas where there are trees. Its wings and tail are not markedly long, the head is relatively large and rounded, the facial disc is fairly well-developed, and it has prominent brows of whitish feathers. Its eyes are large, with pale greenish-yellow irides.

The Boobook Owl's plumage is patterned with whitish spots along the edges of the mantle and on the wing coverts; wings and tail are barred, and there are dark irregular streaks on the breast. Its plumage varies in intensity of colour and markings from pale sandy-brown to deep rufous, with yellowish-buff on paler parts. Its facial disc is dark, its legs long, slender and downy. The Boobook Owl is best known for its clear disyllabic call of 'morepork', a call that in the earlier days of settlement was attributed to a member of the nightjar order, the Tawny Frogmouth. In addition, the owl may use a staccato, rapid low note in 'conversation' between individuals, and it also has a cat-like single yowling call. Young birds have a shrill, trilling whistle.

These owls feed very extensively on insects, but they also take mice, small birds and similar small creatures. They nest and roost in tree cavities. They will also roost in the foliage of trees, but are vulnerable to mobbing, particularly by the various honeyeaters. Sometimes it is only a noisy little band of honeyeaters, taking it in turns to peer into a hollow branch, that betrays the presence of an owl. The clutch is usually of 2 or 3 or, rarely, up to 5. The male prepares the nest-hollow, but the eggs are incubated by the female for about 33 days, the male bringing her food while she is on the nest and remaining nearby at other times. The young are downy and white. The first plumage is white around the face and on the underside, with dark facial discs. They leave the nest after about 5 or 6 weeks and moult into adult plumage at about 3 months.

The Barking Owl, sometimes called the Winking Owl and therefore having the Latin name *Ninox connivens*, is at 380 to 430 mm long, the next in size of the group. Wing, tail and legs are all fairly long, but its most striking feature is the reduced facial disc which is less conspicuously developed than on some of the harriers. Its head is rounded and its large eyes with their yellow irides appear rather close together on either side of a prominent bill. The plumage pattern is similar to that of the

Above and right: The Boobook Owl *Ninox novaeseelandiae* (about 350 mm) occupies a wide range of habitats in Australia and New Zealand. Both Boobook and an alternative name—Morepork—are phonetic renderings of its clear disyllabic repeated call. It nests in tree cavities and feeds its young mainly on insects, but to a lesser extent on small rodents, birds and lizards. Like other hawk owls, it is largely nocturnal, in spite of having a reduced facial disc and hunting probably mainly by sight.

Map: *Ninox novaeseelandiae*: thick forests, also open areas with sparse trees or rocks.

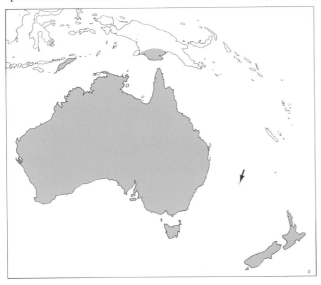

Boobook Owl but without the facial and mantle markings, with few wing spots, and with heavily striated underparts. As with the Boobook Owl, the intensity of plumage colour varies considerably throughout the range.

Barking Owls are sparsely distributed and, being birds of forest, particularly savannah forest, they have a more limited range than the Boobook. They frequently roost on branches of trees, probably having less to fear from mobbing than the smaller Boobook, and they occasionally hunt by day. In most owls the female is bigger than the male, but in these larger hawk owls, the male is bigger than the female, indicating that the ecology and behaviour of these owls are different from those of other owls.

The species gets its popular name from its disyllabic call, an abrupt dog-like double bark, higher-pitched in the female. It also produces the long-drawn strangled scream, like a frightened woman, which has sometimes been attributed to various other species.

As with the Boobook Owl the male prepares the nest-hollow. The nest itself may be in a tree cavity at any height from the ground upwards, and the male bird prepares it by scraping and

Left: With its very reduced facial disc and long tail, the Barking Owl *Ninox connivens* (380 to 430 mm) is particularly hawk-like in appearance. Large enough not to be seriously threatened by mobbing birds, it often roosts quite conspicuously and sometimes hunts by day.

Ninox connivens: forest, particularly savannah forest.

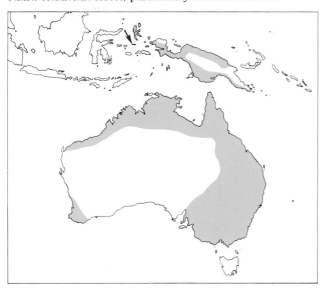

rotating on it. The female then lays her clutch, usually of 2 or 3 eggs, at three-day intervals. The female incubates, fed and guarded by the male, who may attack intruders. Incubation begins with the first egg and takes about 37 days, the young leaving the nest at about 5 weeks. In first feather they are greyish, patterned like the adults on back and head, but with a pale forehead, a white collar, white underside with dark grey streaking and a reduced facial disc forming a narrow dark mask across their yellow-irised eyes. Barking Owls feed mainly on mammals—rabbits, rats, mice, the smaller marsupials, such as possums and gliders—but will also take birds of various species up to crow size, and at times large insects, these appearing to be a more important prey in the northern part of the range.

The largest of the hawk owls, the Powerful Owl (*N. strenua*) is 630 to 650 mm long and occurs only in south-east Australia. Probably the most hawk-like, least owl-like, of the group, its wings and tail are fairly long, and its legs long and strong, with big, powerful feet. The bill is large and prominent, made more obvious by bold brows which slant back from it over the eyes, giving a low forehead and a rather flattened crown. The plumage is dark brown above, thickly barred and spotted with white. The underside is marked with dark narrow chevrons. The face is dark, and the irides yellow. As in the Barking Owl, the male is the larger bird. In this species the disyllabic call is a deep 'who-whoo', higher-pitched and shorter in the female. Other calls are deep, gruff contact calls used between members of a pair; and the young have a shrill whistling call.

The Powerful Owl occurs in the forested gullies of the south-eastern region of Australia. It roosts in trees, in a sheltered spot with a good view around. Paired birds roost together just prior to nesting, when the female occupies the nest-hole and the male roosts nearby. In spite of his size the male tends to be less aggressive than the smaller Barking Owl, although the female may attack if she considers that the young are threatened. The nest cavity, which is situated high in a large tree, is prepared by the male. The female lays 2 eggs only, at a four-day interval. Incubation, by the female alone takes about 38 days. During incubation, and the early period when the young are small, all food is brought by the male. Young Powerful Owls are white on breast and head with a few scattered dark streaks, and heavily barred in brown and white on back, wings and tail.

Male Powerful Owl *Ninox strenua* (630 to 650 mm) at daytime roost. Powerful Owls choose roosting places high in a tree, where they have a clear view for some distance around.

Map: *Ninox strenua*: forested gullies.

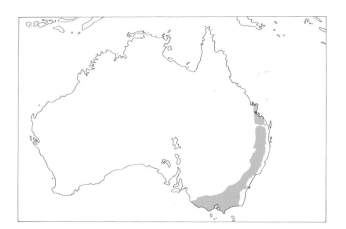

There is a little streaking on the forehead, and the small patches of feathers that replace the facial disc form a narrow, dark mask around their yellow-irised eyes. They leave the nest at about 7 weeks and mature in 7 to 9 months. The principal food is climbing and gliding marsupials, rabbits and rodents, but many birds, and occasionally large insects, are also taken.

To the north of its range, the Powerful Owl is replaced by the Rufous Owl (*N. rufa*) a smaller species some 450 to 550 mm long. Although smaller, it appears to be a more aggressive species and, from experiments with recorded voices of both birds, it would appear that they are mutually intolerant. The plumage of the Rufous Owl is finely barred all over. It is dark brown with fine buffish barring above, and on the underparts it is pale buff with fine brown bars. Its forehead and throat are pale and its yellow-irised eyes are set in a dark face. With the same strong-browed appearance as the Powerful Owl, and a similar though softer voice, it is a bird of rainforest and the thicker savannah woodland, and within these areas is usually found close to watercourses.

The nest is a cavity high in a large tree, and the clutch is of 2 white eggs similar to those of the Powerful Owl. Like the Powerful Owl it feeds on arboreal marsupial possums and gliders, but it takes birds up to the size of sparrows, flying foxes and many large insects. Rufous Owls occur in the wooded areas of north and north-east Australia, and through the lowland forests of New Guinea, but neither this, nor any comparable large *Ninox* owl exist in the Indonesian and Philippine regions. Their niche is apparently filled in most of these areas by the wood owls *Strix leptogrammica* and *S. seloputo*, while the Solomon Islands have the Fearful Owl (*Nesasio solomonensis*), small in body but with proportionately very large bill and feet.

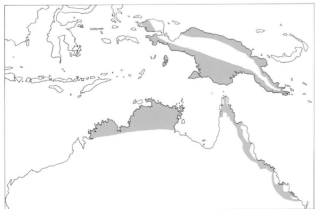

Above left: Female Rufous Owl *Ninox rufa* (400 to 500 mm) at a nest hollow in a forest tree. Two eggs are usual: here one owlet can be seen at the entrance to the nest.

Map: *Ninox rufa*: rainforest, thick savannah woodland, particularly near watercourses.

Within the Australasian region the genus *Ninox* provides a range of species which utilize a wide food spectrum from insects to medium-sized arboreal mammals. As one begins to move northwards from this region, however, the genus provides only a series of rather similar, medium-sized owls of the Boobook type. In New Guinea the Boobook Owl occurs in some southern savannah regions, but the typical owl of the lowland forests is the Sooty-backed Hawk Owl (*N. theomacha*). This is 200 to 250 mm long, plain brown above and below, with blackish-brown face and yellow irides: there may be a few white spots on the scapulars. The Sooty-backed Hawk Owl has a disyllabic call, basically similar to that of the Boobook, but specifically distinct. Like the Boobook, it feeds mainly on insects. Its range extends to some of the islands, where it shows considerable variation. On the D'Entrecasteaux and Louisade Archipelagos, for example, the birds are a little larger and have some white markings on the underside.

These forms on the Archipelagos indicate how bird populations change when isolated on islands. Gradual differentiation from the parental form occurs and, where differences become constant in the population, taxonomists recognize them as geographical forms or subspecies. If isolation continues, the populations may diverge to a point where interbreeding ceases, and the island forms become a separate species. Where bird populations occur on different islands from each other it is usually difficult to say exactly when this point has been reached. But one may sometimes have the situation where an island population becomes

The Sooty-backed Hawk Owl *Ninox theomacha* (200 to 250 mm) replaces the closely related Boobook Owl in the lowland forests of New Guinea.

Right: The New Ireland Hawk Owl *Ninox solomonis* (230 to 310 mm), Admiralty Islands Hawk Owl *N. meeki* (200 to 250 mm), Solomon Islands Hawk Owl *N. jacquinoti* (230 to 310 mm) and New Britain Hawk Owl *N. odiosa* (200 to 230 mm) are four members of a large group of closely related hawk owls which have speciated on various of the numerous Australasian islands and archipelagos. Maps, page 150.

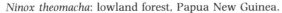

Ninox theomacha: lowland forest, Papua New Guinea.

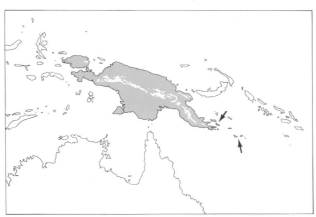

New Ireland Hawk Owl
Ninox solomonis

Admiralty Islands
Hawk Owl
Ninox meeki

Solomon Islands Hawk Owl
Ninox jacquinoti

New Britain Hawk Owl
Ninox odiosa

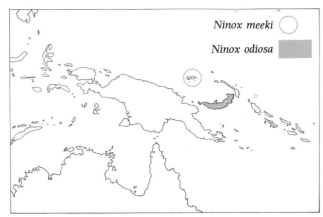

Ninox meeki: confined to Manus Island, Admiralty Islands.
N. odiosa: forest, lowland hills to 600 m, New Britain.

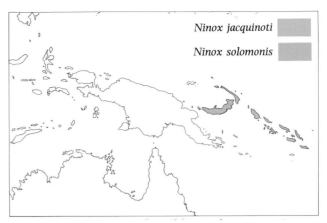

N. jacquinoti: forest to 1500 m, Solomon Islands.
Ninox solomonis: forest, hills and lower mountains on New Britain, New Ireland and New Hanover (not Solomon Islands).

differentiated from a parental, mainland stock and later a second invasion of the island by the parental stock occurs. By this time the two forms may have diverged to a point where they behave towards each other as separate species. The Solomon Islands Hawk Owl (*N. jacquinoti*) is regarded as a separate species from the New Guinea bird. Within the Solomons it has begun to produce slightly different forms on each of the larger islands. It differs from the smaller Sooty-backed Hawk Owl in being marked with transverse barring on the underside, the colour of the underside varying from one island to another.

On the island chain of the Bismarck Archipelago, adjoining both New Guinea and the Solomon Islands, several separate species have evolved. The Admiralty Islands Hawk Owl (*N. meeki*) is limited to Manus Island in the Admiralty Islands. It has streaking on the breast and its buffish-brown upper parts have irregular whitish barring. New Britain, New Ireland and New Hanover Island share the New Ireland Hawk Owl, unfortunately misnamed *N. solomonis*. This species is about 230 to 310 mm long and is also barred on the breast. New Britain has in addition its own endemic species of hawk owl, *N. odiosa*. This is a smaller species than the last, 200 to 230 mm long and more like the Boobook Owl in plumage, with white eyebrows and white spotting on its rufous-brown back. Its head is also spotted and the white underside is streaked and barred in brown. At the western end of New Guinea yet another form occupies the Moluccas. The Moluccan Hawk Owl (*N. squamipila*) has a larger size range—250 to 360 mm—approaching that of the still larger Barking Owl, which is also present in the northern Moluccas. The former shows

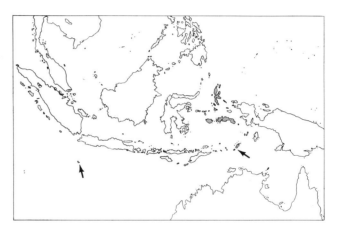

Ninox squamipila: Moluccas and scattered islands.

Ninox perversa: deep, virgin forest, Sulawesi.
N. punctulata: open forest; cultivated areas with trees, Sulawesi.

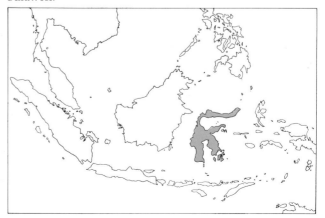

The Moluccan Hawk Owl *Ninox squamipila* (250 to 360 mm), shows typical island variation in its colour markings.

The Ochre-bellied Hawk Owl *Ninox perversa* (200 to 260 mm) and Speckled Hawk Owl *N. punctulata* (200 to 260 mm) represent the genus in Sulawesi, replacing each other in rainforest and more open habitats respectively.

Ochre-bellied Hawk Owl
Ninox perversa

Speckled Hawk Owl
Ninox punctulata

typical island variation in colour and markings, ranging from deep brown to yellowish-brown on different islands, with the variably barred underside white or yellowish-brown.

Further west again, Sulawesi (Celebes) has two similar small species, 200 to 260 mm long, the Speckled Hawk Owl (*N. punctulata*) and the Ochre-bellied Hawk Owl (*N. perversa*). The Speckled Hawk Owl is finely spotted above, and barred on the flanks; the Ochre-bellied one has only a few spots on the wing coverts and is streaked below, with a dark breast and yellow-orange belly. The Speckled Hawk Owl is a commoner, more widely spread bird, occurring in more open forest and in cultivated areas with some trees. It has a trisyllabic call note of two short, low-pitched notes followed by a longer high-pitched one. The Ochre-bellied species is a bird of the deep virgin forests, a habitat which the Speckled Hawk Owl seems only occasionally to penetrate. It is a scarce and little-known species.

To the north the Philippine Islands have a single *Ninox* species, the Philippine Hawk Owl (*N. philippensis*) though in winter the Oriental Hawk Owl is a visitor to this region. The Philippine bird is small, only 150 to 200 mm long, and varies considerably from island to island, being plain or buff-spotted above, and white, with streaking, or brown, with barring, on the underside.

The Oriental Hawk Owl (*N. scutulata*) is a bird of the Asian mainland, and overlaps with some of the other species on its winter migrations. Between 200 to 250 mm long, it is distinguished by a uniformly dark brown back and white underparts, with heavy streaking or spotting. In the Andaman and Nicobar Islands the local subspecies is dark above and below: it overlaps in distribution with the endemic Andaman Hawk Owl (*N. affinis*) which is similarly marked. The Andaman Hawk Owl probably evolved from stocks of Oriental Hawk Owls which invaded earlier and became genetically distinct: the local race of Oriental Hawk Owls which at present share their habitat represents a later invasion, on which the same selection for darker plumage seems to be operating.

Oriental Hawk Owls are slightly better known than other hawk owls. They occur in all types of forest and also in partly cultivated or scrub areas where trees are present. In very thick forest they are usually found close to watercourses and they also inhabit the mangroves of coastal zones, where they feed on small crabs in the mud as well as on a wide range of insects, amphibians, reptiles, small birds and mammals. They nest, usually, in a hole in a tree, laying a clutch of 3 to 4 eggs. Oriental Hawk Owls have a typical disyllabic call, rendered by a Japanese writer as 'poppow' and in India as 'oo-uk'; but some authors state that the Malayan race has a monosyllabic note. If so, it resembles the Andaman Hawk Owl, which is also said to have a monosyllabic call.

Ninox affinis: confined to Andaman Islands.

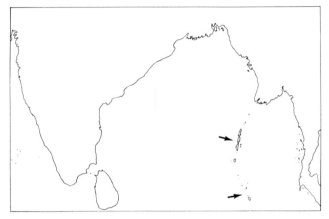

Ninox superciliaris: forest, Madagascar.

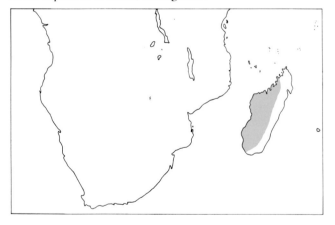

Ninox philippensis: confined to Philippine Islands.

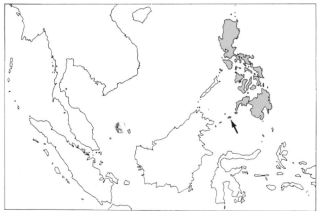

The Madagascan Hawk Owl (*N. superciliaris*), restricted to western Madagascar, is closely akin to the Oriental Hawk Owl. A small species, 230 to 280 mm long, it remains well isolated from the others of its genus, and resembles owls of the northern hemisphere in having grey and brown plumage phases. It is a forest bird, roosting in trees or in small caves of rocky ravines, and sometimes flies by day. Its diet ranges from insects and reptiles to small birds and mammals.

The Andaman Hawk Owl *N. affinis*
(200 to 250 mm),
Philippine Hawk Owl *N. philippensis*
(150 to 200 mm) and
Madagascar Hawk Owl *N. superciliaris*
(230 to 280 mm) are all island representatives
of the genus *Ninox*.
The Madagascar Hawk Owl is the only
one outside the Oriental and Australasian regions.

Andaman
Hawk Owl
Ninox affinis

Madagascar Hawk Owl
Ninox superciliaris

Philippine Hawk Owl
Ninox philippensis

The Oriental Hawk Owl *Ninox scutulata* (200 to 250 mm) is an Asiatic species with an extensive range from Sakhalin to India and Malaysia. Northern populations are migratory, moving south and augmenting the numbers of resident tropical populations.

The Laughing Owl (*Sceloglaux albifacies*) and the Papuan Hawk Owl (*Uroglaux dimorpha*) are both specialized and possibly relict forms. They are sufficiently differentiated from the other species to have been separated in special genera—of which they are the only representatives. The Laughing Owl is, or was, a large owl of open country and may in the past have been present over most of New Zealand. Like other species endemic to New Zealand it suffered from successive invasions of man and of new predators—possibly also diseases—which he brought with him. On the Chatham Islands, which have for long been densely occupied by man, they are known only as sub-fossil bones. On the main islands of New Zealand the species gradually decreased and was last seen in the 1930s: it may now be extinct.

The Laughing Owl had an overall length of 390 to 450 mm. The rounded head, with prominent eyes and bill, were typical of this group of birds, but the pale facial disc of stiff feathers seems to have been a little more strongly developed than in most of the hawk owl species. In general, plumage was yellowish-brown with darker brown streaking: wings and tail were brown with brownish-white barring, and its long legs were yellowish-buff. Its conspicuous features were whitish streaking and feather edges on wings, mantle and nape, and the whitish facial disc which accentuated the dark brown irides of the

Ninox scutulata: all types of forest and cultivated scrub where there are trees; in thick forest near watercourses; also in mangroves near coast.

Right: The Papuan Hawk Owl *Uroglaux dimorpha* (300 to 330 mm) is a rare forest species about which extremely little is known. Half of its length is accounted for by its long tail and it is actually a smaller bird than the Sooty-backed Hawk Owl (*Ninox theomacha*) with which it coexists.

Map: *Uroglaux dimorpha*: lowland forest, Papua New Guinea.

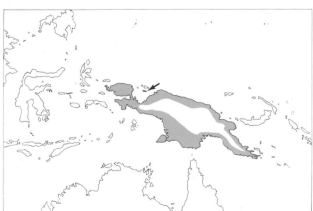

eyes. The Laughing Owl occurred on rocky outcrops in open places or along forest edges; the rocks provided roosts and nesting sites, and may have limited the distribution of the species. As with many other owls, their food consisted of a wide range of small creatures, including the indigenous rats and introduced mice, small birds, reptiles, insects and earthworms. The voice was varied. Harsh cacklings, strident shrieks, yelping, mewings, chucklings, and a 'cooeying' call were all noted at various times. The nest, in a dry cavity under a boulder or in a rock crevice, was lined with a little dry grass and accommodated 2 rather rounded white eggs, with slightly roughened surfaces; there is a record of a clutch of 3 eggs from a captive bird. Nesting and egg-laying occurred from August to October. Incubation took about 25 days and young were reared in October to November. The female took care of most, perhaps all, of the incubation, and responsibility for the downy, yellowish-white young. The male brought food to her at the nest.

The other species of southern hawk owl, the Papuan Hawk Owl (*Uroglaux dimorpha*), is still extant, but comparatively less is known about it. It is apparently a scarce species of lowland forest, overlapping in distribution with the Sooty-backed Hawk Owl. Some 300 to 330 mm long, it is 50 mm longer than the Sooty-backed Hawk Owl, but the long tail accounts for nearly half its length and it is, in fact, smaller in body size. The long tail and smallish, rounded head give the bird a hawk-like outline in flight. Upperparts, wings and tail are heavily barred in blackish and reddish-brown, the crown and nape streaked with similar colours, and the underparts buffish-white with dark longitudinal streaking. The brows are white, and the irides yellow. Almost nothing is known of its general behaviour, apart from the fact that it feeds on insects, small rodents and birds.

Also occurring in the Australasian region is the Fearful Owl (*Nesasio solomonensis*); it is an odd species of uncertain affinities which has some claim to being an ecological equivalent of the smaller forms of eagle owl, but its true relationships with other owls are unknown. It is confined to three of the larger of the Solomon Islands, Bougainville, Choiseul and Santa Isabel, and is said to be a bird of lowland and hill forest.

In body size it is considerably smaller than any of the eagle owls, being only 280 to 380 mm long, but it has a beak and talons as powerful as those of the Great Horned Owl (*Bubo virginianus*).

Though relatively small in body size, the Fearful Owl *Nesasio solomonensis* (280 to 380 mm) of the Solomon Islands has a large bill and extremely powerful talons; it occupies a niche which is filled by large wood owls or eagle owls in other parts of the world.

Nesasio solomonensis: lowland hill forest, Solomon Islands.

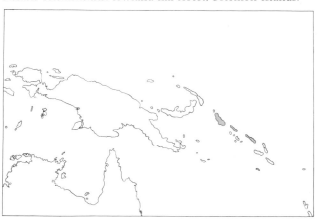

Its beak and talons certainly suggest that it is capable of killing relatively large prey, and it is known to take possums and birds, but nothing else is known of its ecology.

The Hawk Owl of the northern hemisphere, *Surnia ulula*, contrasts with the hawk owls of the southern regions in its bold plumage patterns and its deliberate diurnal hunting activity. Diurnal hunting is not really surprising, since the northern limits of its distribution reach the edge of the Arctic tundra: in these high latitudes there is almost continuous daylight during the summer months, and any owl of these regions must be adapted to some diurnal activity. The Northern Hawk Owl occurs along the broad zone of the northern coniferous forests and the sub-Arctic birch zone around the whole of the northern hemisphere. A bird of open places within this zone, it occurs in clearings, in open parts of forest where trees are widely spaced, or where deciduous trees give an extensive view through the forest. It is also found in low scrub, and in thinly scattered trees and shrubs along watercourses at the tundra's edge, and extends into lightly wooded areas at the southern edge of the forest zone.

This is a medium-sized owl, about 360 to 410 mm long, with a small facial disc which extends sideways and comes down in a brow low over the eyes, to give a low-crowned, rounded profile. Its wings are large and taper to a point; its tail is long and graduated towards the tip. In combination these feathers give an outline more like that of a hawk or a small, long-tailed falcon than like an owl. Though it may perch upright, its resemblance to a hawk is often enhanced by a tendency to lean forwards and raise its tail. The eyes are relatively small, and the ears lack the specialized asymmetrical development for locating sounds seen mainly in night hunters, though they do not differ from the situation found in the other hawk owls. The plumage is boldly marked. The facial disc is greyish-white with a bold black outer edge, and its eyes have a yellow iris. The crown of the head is finely chequered in black and white, and the whole of the back is mottled and barred in brownish-black and white; wings and tail are boldly barred. The underside is covered with fine transverse black barring on white, and is palest on the upper breast.

The bird's flight is swift and direct, the pointed wings and long tail again giving a hawk-like effect, more precisely, like a Sparrowhawk or even

Diurnal to a considerable extent, the Northern Hawk Owl *Surnia ulula* (360 to 410 mm) is rather shrike-like in its appearance and behaviour, generally perching in some prominent position from which it swoops down on to its prey. Map, page 158.

a Kestrel. In hunting it resembles a shrike, using a high vantage point as a look-out and swooping down on small prey. It flies fast and low near the ground, swooping up to perch at a new vantage point. Alternatively it may fly higher and more slowly, watching the ground below, hovering, and dropping when it sights a small creature.

The Hawk Owl's principal prey is rodents, the small mice, voles and lemmings typical of the regions in which it occurs. It will, however, take any prey that is available, including other small mammals such as squirrels or weasels, a variety of small birds, and even insects. Although a diurnal hunter, its main activity takes place at early morning or late evening and it can of course hunt during the long darkness of winter. Rodents living beneath the snow are difficult to catch and the owl may take more birds in winter. Its food supply is affected by the cycles of rodent abundance and scarcity: in years of abundance the owls lay large clutches and rear large broods of young, while in years of scarcity the broods are smaller or the birds do not nest at all. In bad years, Hawk Owls move southwards in large numbers at the end of summer or the beginning of winter, appearing in regions outside their normal range of distribution. Like many birds of Arctic and sub-Arctic regions, they are often unwary of man. In their southward irruptions they allow observers to get very close.

The main calls are a soft musical hoot, uttered at about two-second intervals and apparently used as a territorial call, and a trilling whistle heard at the beginning of the breeding season. The owls are very noisy when they have young. The nesting site is a natural hole or cavity. The irregular, broken top of a tall tree-stump, with a hollow in it, is a very typical site but a large woodpecker hole or the large old stick nests of crows, magpies and birds of prey may also be used. As in other owls the nest is normally unlined, unless this has already been done by the original builder of the nest. Breeding begins during late March and extends to early May. In poor food years clutches may be of 3 to 4 eggs, in good years of 10 to 12. Incubation, mainly by the female, begins with the first egg and lasts about 4 weeks. The eggs hatch over a period of several days so that the young are graded in size; the smallest is unlikely to survive if food is restricted. Downy and white, the young have a shrill, hissing call. Juvenile plumage is a grey-brown version of the adult plumage, less fluffy than that of other owls, and of a highly protective coloration. In most details of its life history the Northern Hawk Owl resembles the other owls of these regions. Its main difference is in its structural and behavioural adaptation to hunting by sight, in a more hawk-like fashion, in open habitats where there is scope for such behaviour and a vacant niche exists.

Though they share a number of hawk-like characteristics, the Northern Hawk Owl and the Oriental and Australasian Hawk Owls are quite different in appearance and probably not closely related. The Northern Hawk Owl nests in tree cavities, often taking over large woodpecker holes.

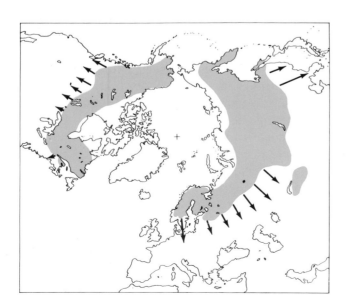

Map: *Surnia ulula*: northern coniferous forest clearings or where there are mixed deciduous patches; low scrub, scattered trees and shrubs near water; lightly wooded forest-edges. Arrows show direction of migration in irruption years.

CHAPTER NINE

Little, Pygmy and Elf Owls

*Athene, Speotyto, Micrathene, Aegolius, Glaucidium,
Xenoglaux, Pseudoscops*

Owls range in size from sparrow to eagle and hunt prey appropriate to their own dimensions. Among the smallest are seven genera, including about twenty-five species, which range across the world: the largest are pigeon-sized Little owls (*Athene*), the smallest Elf Owls (*Micrathene*), Pygmy owls (*Glaucidium*) and the recently discovered Long-whiskered Owlet (*Xenoglaux*). All feed on insects and other invertebrates and on a fairly wide variety of small mammals, birds and reptiles. Usually, they nest in holes, often in competition with starlings, flickers and other woodpeckers; some even nest underground in abandoned mammal burrows.

The genus *Athene* contains three closely related species of short, plump little birds known as Little owls, which together cover a wide geographical range and a variety of habitats in Europe, Asia and North Africa. Best known is the Little Owl (*Athene noctua*), a species widely distributed in the Palaearctic region from about 55°N in Europe to 30°N in North Africa, slightly further south in Ethiopia and Arabia. It extends from the Atlantic eastwards across central Russia and Siberia, to Mongolia and China and just reaches the Pacific coast of Asia, but is entirely absent from India and most of South-east Asia. Introduced into Britain after a number of unsuccessful attempts between 1874 and 1890, Little Owls were breeding in Northamptonshire, Kent and elsewhere by the end of the century. They soon spread rapidly throughout Wales and much of

In desert areas the Little Owl *Athene noctua* (190 to 230 mm) may nest in holes in cliffs or even in burrows in the ground (above). In woodland, it usually chooses a tree cavity (left).

England and have recently extended north, into southern Scotland.

Aptly named, this is a small, plump owl some 190 to 230 mm long with a compact, flat-headed appearance, no ear tufts of feathers, and a very short tail. The sexes are similar, mostly greyish-brown, mottled and barred with white on top, and pale with dark streaks underneath. The poorly developed facial disc and pale eyebrows, combined with the low forehead produce a frowning, disapproving expression. Perching on a tree or post, Little Owls often bob up and down in a comical fashion which may indicate anxiety and curiosity. The wings are broad and rounded, and the flight is silent and undulating, usually ending in a long upward glide to the perch.

Little Owls breed in cavities in trees (in Britain and Holland a favourite place being in pollarded trees), walls and cliffs, occasionally on the ground, in April and May. In western Europe most eggs appear in early May. Usually between 3 and 5 eggs are laid but clutches of only 2 or as many as 7 or 8 have been recorded. The eggs, matt white and elliptical, are incubated sometimes but not always from the first egg, usually by the female only. Incubation takes from 24 to 29 days and the nestlings emerge in a covering of dense, short white down. At first only the male feeds them, but later the female joins in and the chicks remain in the nest for about 24 to 26 days. Usually only one brood is attempted each year, but two have occasionally been recorded.

The food of this species is well documented in Britain. During the 1930s, when its range had spread widely, it was suspected to be a wholesale destroyer of game chicks, poultry and native songbirds and the British Trust for Ornithology sponsored an inquiry into its feeding habits. The conclusions were that throughout the year almost half the food of Little Owls consists of insects including flies (and craneflies), earwigs, moths, cock-chafers and other beetles. Hunting chiefly at night, they also take mammals up to the size of large rats and medium-sized rabbits. Few birds appeared in the diet, except during the breeding season when Starlings, House Sparrows, Blackbirds, Song Thrushes and other birds, and a very few game chicks were taken. Later it became evident that they take numerous earthworms. Little Owls often hunt by perching on a post or similar vantage point and watching for movement on the ground below.

Athene noctua: parklands, fields with hedges, rocky semi-desert regions and steppes.

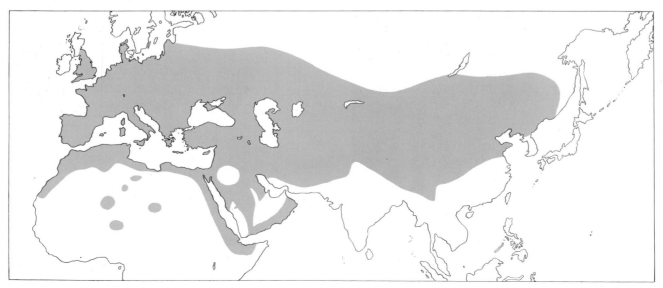

The Little Owl *Athene noctua* lives mainly in lightly wooded open country or rocky arid areas and typically hunts from a post or other perch, bobbing up and down if curious or alarmed. Its indistinct facial disks, pale 'eyebrows' and low forehead combine to give it a frowning, disapproving expression. Longer-legged and more terrestrial than all but the Burrowing Owl *Speotyto cunicularia*, it can run quite fast on the ground in pursuit of low-flying insects.

This species is found in a variety of habitats but chiefly open country with scattered trees such as parkland, orchards and fields with hedges or rocky, semi-desert regions and steppes; it generally shuns mountainous, hilly or densely wooded regions. Rather more terrestrial than most owls, Little Owls often settle on the ground and are able to run quite fast while chasing prey. The voice is varied. Two calls predominate—a beautiful, plaintive 'kiew', repeated at intervals of a few seconds, and a rapidly repeated loud, yelping 'wherrow'.

Throughout their broad range, Little Owls are sedentary and do not undergo regular migrations, although some individuals disperse and wander outside the breeding season. Taxonomists distinguish about fifteen subspecies or races, based mainly on differences of colour and size, although the characteristics of one race generally grade into those of neighbouring stocks so few of these subspecies are well defined. The darkest race, (*A. n. vidalii*), occurs in western Europe, including Britain; the palest, (*A. n. lilith*), inhabits the dry, sandy region at the eastern end of the Mediterranean in Syria and Israel.

In southern Iran, Pakistan, India, Bangladesh and parts of Indo-China, the Little Owl is replaced by the Spotted Little Owl, (*A. brama*). About 190 to 210 mm long, this species is about as big as the smallest Eurasian Little Owls, and of similar appearance and habits. It occurs as a common and widespread resident in gardens, sparsely wooded plains and open country with scattered trees, from dry desert regions to damp rainforest areas, reaching an altitude of about 1500 m in the Himalayan foothills. Like the Little Owl, it is not found in dense forest itself. As the common name suggests, it is more spotted than streaked, with underparts cross-barred. Rather more sociable than its near relative, it is often seen in pairs or family parties of three or four, and is largely active between dusk and dawn. Though sometimes out in broad daylight, it generally prefers to remain concealed in a tree-hole. Like other *Athene* owls, it bobs up and down when suspicious or alarmed, has an undulating flight and often hunts from posts or other vantage points. It feeds on large insects, earthworms, mice, lizards and birds, which are pounced upon and carried back to the perch to be eaten.

The breeding of Spotted Little Owls may occur any time from February to April; 3, 4 or 5 round, white eggs are laid in a sparsely lined hollow of a

The Spotted Little Owl *Athene brama* (190 to 210 mm) is ecologically similar to the Little Owl, replacing it in parts of the Middle East, India and Indo-China.

Map: *Athene brama*: gardens, open areas with trees, rainforest to 1500 m and desert.

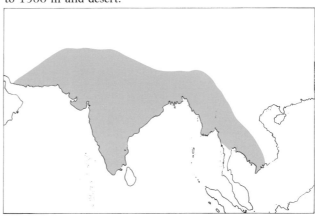

The Forest Little Owl *Athene blewitti* (210 to 230 mm) closely resembles the other Little Owls, differing mainly in being darker and shorter winged, a frequent feature of birds with a forest habitat. Though this bird was photographed in its appropriate range and habitat, and identified by its photographer as *Athene blewitti*, the species may be extinct.

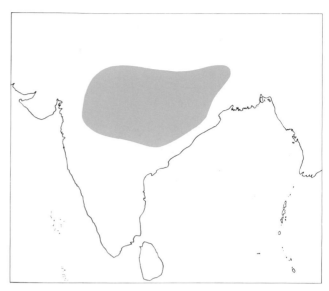

Athene blewitti: probable former range, dense deciduous forest.

tree, wall or ruin. Unlike the Little Owl, male and female apparently share incubation. The species is reported to be rather vociferous, uttering a variety of cackling, unmusical notes. The voice most frequently heard has been described as a loud, harsh, rapidly repeated 'chirurr-chirurr' interspersed with a discordant 'cheevak, cheevak' also described as 'zi-gwet'.

The Forest Little Owl (*A. blewitti*) may well be extinct and is at best very rare. Six specimen skins exist, all collected before the First World War, and a photograph purported to be of this species taken in 1968. It once occurred in the damp, dense tropical and sub-tropical deciduous forests and jungles in the foothills of the Satpura range of northern central India. Searches in parts of its presumed range in 1975 and 1976 were in vain. The species is similar to *A. brama*, but a little larger, with longer bill and legs but shorter wings. It generally lacks the speckling on crown and nape of the Spotted species, having more uniform, earth-brown upperparts and darker underparts, with a distinct bar across the throat.

The Burrowing Owl (*Speotyto cunicularia*), is superficially similar to Little owls but has very long legs for an owl. Like Little owls, it makes brief, undulating flights and shows the same comical bobbing behaviour when alarmed. It ranges from the plains of western North America

Speotyto cunicularia: terrestrial in open, treeless grassland.

As its name suggests, the Burrowing Owl roosts and breeds in burrows in the ground. Though capable of excavating them itself, it often takes over the abandoned burrows of such mammals as the highly gregarious Prairie Dogs in North America and the plains Viscacha in South America.

south in suitable areas through Central and South America as far as Cape Horn, with isolated populations in Florida, where it has recently extended its range, and parts of the Caribbean. This small, short-tailed owl varies in colour and size throughout its extensive range. In southern South America, Florida and Haiti it is almost chocolate-coloured, heavily spotted, streaked and barred with white; in semi-desert regions, such as parts of inland Brazil, it is light sandy-brown with white markings, and in elevated grasslands surrounded by tropical forested areas of South America the pale plumage may be spotted with dull orange. In length it varies from 180 to 260 mm, Andean populations being the largest.

Essentially a terrestrial species, the Burrowing Owl lives mainly on open, treeless grasslands,

The Burrowing Owl *Speotyto cunicularia* (180 to 260 mm) has longer legs and is much more thoroughly terrestrial than any other small owl. Like the Little Owl *Athene noctua*) it is largely crepuscular but also hunts by day and night. Map, page 163.

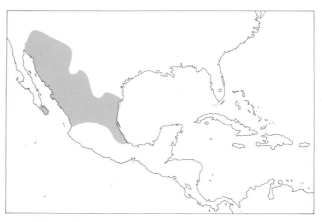

Micrathene whitneyi: dry grassy lowlands, wet savannahs, woodland, forest and cactus.

The tiny Elf Owl *Micrathene whitneyi* (130 to 140 mm) is one of the three smallest owls in the world. It is confined to the south-western United States and Mexico, where it is particularly associated with the giant Saguaro Cactus.

frequenting abandoned mammal burrows or tunnels which it digs for itself. It breeds in loose colonies formerly consisting of hundreds of pairs but now of up to a dozen or more, reputedly laying 2 to 11 eggs in a roughly lined chamber up to a metre below ground, possibly at the end of 3 m of meandering burrow. Both sexes incubate for a total of 4 weeks, and both help to feed the chicks.

Food of the Burrowing Owl ranges from much favoured large beetles and other insects to small rodents, occasionally frogs and birds. During the breeding season it gives cooing calls and a bird disturbed in its burrow gives repeated 'cack-cack' alarm calls, while the young make hissing and rasping sounds rather like those made by a rattle snake. Although mainly evening hunters, Burrowing Owls are also frequently active by day or night.

The Elf Owl (*Micrathene whitneyi*) sometimes called Whitney's Elf Owl, is one of the smallest owls, with a length of 130 to 140 mm, a rounded 'earless' head, rounded body and short tail. Its breeding range is confined entirely to the south-western United States, including Texas, eastern Mexico, and Socorro Island, where it is a

migratory summer bird. Its winter range has long been a mystery, but it has now been found immediately south of the Mexican central plateau. Perhaps best known for its association with the giant saguaro cactus, the Elf Owl commonly occurs also in a variety of woodlands and forests to an altitude of 2000 m, and on dry grassy lowlands and wet savannahs.

The preferred site for nesting is the abandoned hole of a flicker or other woodpecker, up to 10 m above ground in a giant cactus or tree, but any suitable sized cavity will suffice. The clutch consists of 2 to 5 (usually 3) pure white oval eggs, which are laid on alternate days some time during April or May. Both sexes incubate for about 2 weeks before the white, downy young hatch.

Unlike some of the other small owls described in this chapter, the Elf Owl is markedly nocturnal, remaining hidden during the day in some suitable hole or dense foliage, to emerge well after dusk and pursue the large insects which are its chief prey. This species has an extremely loud voice for its size; the calls most frequently heard are a series of about six rapidly repeated, high-pitched notes, descending in pitch towards the end.

The genus *Aegolius* contains four species of small owls, of which the best known is *A. funereus*—known as Tengmalm's Owl in Europe and the Boreal Owl or Richardson's Owl in North America. The Saw-whet Owl (*A. acadicus*) is a common species in North America mainly south of the Boreal Owl's range, and two other species occur more locally in the tropics and are little known at present. The Unspotted Saw-whet Owl (*A. ridgwayi*) occurs from parts of southern Mexico southwards to northern Costa Rica and the Buff-fronted Owl (*A. harrisii*) occurs in two widely spaced populations, one in extreme north-western South America and the other in south-eastern Brazil, Paraguay and northern Argentina.

Tengmalm's Owl (*A. funereus*) is a bird of northern coniferous forests. Found especially among spruce, it occurs also in mixed forests among pine, birch and poplar. In central Europe, it originally frequented pine forest on high ground, but it has now spread far into France. During the far northern summer it is obliged to feed in continuous daylight, but elsewhere it is chiefly a nocturnal species, spending the day in the tops of conifers or other dense trees. It feeds mainly on small mammals, less extensively on birds and occasionally also on frogs and other small animals.

Similar in size to the Little Owl (190 to 230 mm long) Tengmalm's Owl has a large round head with a yellow bill, spotted crown, short tail, long broad wings and well-defined facial disc without ear tufts: in many ways it resembles a kind of small Tawny Owl. The legs and feet are completely covered in soft white feathers.

Tengmalm's Owl lays its eggs in April or May, starting as early as mid-March in the south of its range or as late as June in the far north. The eggs, white and glossy, are laid at intervals of from 1 to 3 days in a hole in a tree, often in the disused nest-hole of a woodpecker. The usual clutch is 3 to 6 but up to 10 have been recorded. Unusually, only the female incubates, for a period approaching 4 weeks. The nestlings at first have a sparse covering of short down, but then develop a plumage which is buff-white above and plain earthen brown below, and leave the nest after about four and a half weeks.

Tengmalm's Owl is a sedentary bird, with a soft, liquid flute-like note, which it repeats at intervals of a few seconds, with regular alternate variations in stress.

Owlets often leave their nest some time before they are able to fly. Even after they have learned to fly, their parents feed them for several weeks or even months, giving them plenty of time to learn the skills involved in catching prey. These are young Tengmalm's Owls, *Aegolius funereus*.

Aegolius funereus: northern coniferous forest, also mixed forest of pine, birch and poplar.

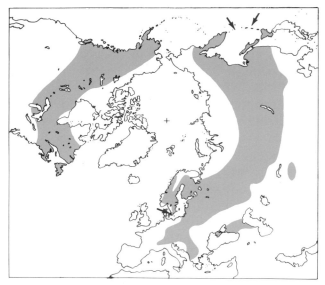

Tengmalm's Owl *Aegolius funereus* (190 to 230 mm), better known in North America as the Boreal or Richardson's Owl, is associated with conifers throughout its range, particularly with spruce in the north and various types of pine in the south. The characteristic shape of its facial disc gives it a permanently surprised expression. The song is a sequence of soft, staccato hoots, varying in speed from bird to bird. It has been described as sounding like water dripping or a tiny bell.

The northern Saw-whet Owl (*A. acadicus*) is widely distributed in damp, dense woodlands of North America, its range extending in a broad belt from south-eastern Alaska and California in the west to eastern Canada and the north-eastern United States. It extends south in mountain forest into central Mexico, but is generally absent from the lowland southern states. It overlaps with the Boreal (Tengmalm's) Owl along the Canadian border zone and locally in the Rocky Mountains, but the interaction of these species is not clear. In winter northern elements of the population move southward from their breeding grounds, and the population as a whole appears to shift slightly south, though the extent of this remains unknown and many owls seem to stay within the breeding range.

Saw-whet Owls closely resemble Boreal Owls, but are slightly smaller (about 170 to 190 mm long), with a black bill and streaked crown. Not active by day, they are largely crepuscular or nocturnal hunters, preying on small rodents and birds. Bats, frogs, even occasionally mammals and birds as large as the owls themselves, have been recorded.

These owls are most vociferous before and during the breeding season in March or April. One of their many varied calls is reminiscent of a grasshopper's stridulation. Other authors have described the song as a short, sweet whistle repeated endlessly, a hundred or more times per minute. The 'saw-sharpening' call which has given the bird its vernacular name is less often heard. (The noise of sharpening saws was well known in the days when the forests in the eastern states and provinces were being cut.) The owl nests in cavities, such as old woodpecker holes whose linings of moss, bark fragments, leaves, twigs and feathers are possibly left-overs from previous non-woodpecker occupants. The most frequent clutch-size is 5 or 6 eggs; 4 or 7 are sometimes recorded. The eggs are pure white, of the rather oval or almost spherical shape typical of the owl family. Incubation is reported to take from 21 to 28 days, starting soon after the first egg is laid so that the nest later contains young of widely different ages. The chicks are at first white, like those of the Boreal Owl, but dark, chocolate brown feathers of a distinctive juvenile plumage soon grow through.

The rare Unspotted Saw-whet Owl (*A. ridgwayi*) is a central American species of limited range, occurring in a narrow belt from the extreme south of Mexico south-east to Costa Rica and western Panama. Roughly the same size as the Saw-whet Owl, it is plain dark brown above and pale buff below, without barring or streaking. Little information is available on its ecology, behaviour or breeding biology; it is a southern descendant of the northern Saw-whet Owl. The call has been described as a series of rhythmic whistles on the same note but lower in pitch than the call of the Saw-whet Owl.

The two widely separated races of the Buff-fronted Owl (*A. harrisii*) of South America occur in south-east Brazil, Paraguay and northern Argentina (*A. h. iheringi*) and Colombia, Venezuela and Ecuador (*A. h. harrisii*). It is small, some 200 mm in length, chocolate brown above with a broad creamy bar across its upper back, and yellowish-buff below with a wide chocolate belt across its breast. Its forehead and face are buffish-yellow. Almost nothing is known of its behaviour and ecology but it has been found in cultivated areas and clearings at 3800 m. In part of its range, the vernacular name is 'Surrucucu', which may be a representation of its call.

The largest genus of small owls, *Glaucidium*, contains thirteen or fourteen tiny species collectively called the Pygmy Owls. Perhaps the best known and most widespread species is the Eurasian Pygmy Owl (*G. passerinum*). This lives in a broad belt 600 to 1000 km wide across Europe and Asia, from eastern Europe and central Scandinavia (excluding Denmark) through much of western and central Russia, across Siberia south of 58° to 60° N latitude, to north-eastern Mongolia, central Manchuria and the island of Sakhalin. Two subspecies or races are recognized, the eastern form of East Siberia, Manchuria and Sakhalin being on average slightly larger, rather paler and greyer with more distinct spotting than western stocks.

The Eurasian Pygmy Owl is found in open areas of mature coniferous and mixed forests, where it roosts throughout most of the day. Though widespread, it is nowhere abundant. Adult plumage is greyish-brown above, with light mottling and spotting and white with brown barring and streaking below. On the back of the neck is a prominent light half-collar. The head is rather small for an owl, rounded and lacking a well-defined facial disc, with no ear tufts. But, when the bird is frightened, it tightens its plumage so that small tufts appear on both sides of the head. The wings are short and rounded,

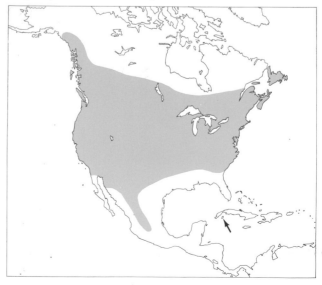

Map: *Aegolius acadicus*: damp, dense woodland.

**Unspotted
Saw-whet Owl**
Aegolius ridgwayi

Buff-fronted Owl
Aegolius harrisii

The Unspotted Saw-whet Owl *Aegolius ridgwayi* (170 to 190 mm) is a Central American descendant of the northern Saw-whet Owl and differs in appearance from it mainly in lacking prominent spots and streaks. The South American Buff-fronted Owl *A. harrisii* (200 mm) occurs in two widely separated populations; virtually nothing is known about the ecology of either.

Left: In its appearance and ecology the northern Saw-whet Owl *Aegolius acadicus* (170 to 190 mm) is very similar to the Boreal (Tengmalm's) Owl, but it is confined to North America and has a more southerly distribution. It earns its name from a very characteristic 'saw-sharpening' call which it utters mainly during the breeding season.

the tail is long for an owl, frequently flicked to the side when the bird is perching and on alighting cocked-up sharply like a European wren's tail. The legs and feet, which are fully feathered, are proportionally very large. The Eurasian Pygmy Owl flies like a shrike, often from look-out posts on the topmost twigs of small trees. It hunts most actively by day. Though only about 170 mm long, it is a pugnacious predator, occasionally taking prey much larger than itself. More usually it hunts small and medium-sized rodents, shrews, and birds, occasionally lizards and possibly a few insects. With its wide range of food species, it does

Map: *Aegolius ridgwayi*: S. Mexico to S.E. Costa Rica.
Aegolius harrisii: open humid forest at higher elevations, also woodland and drier areas.

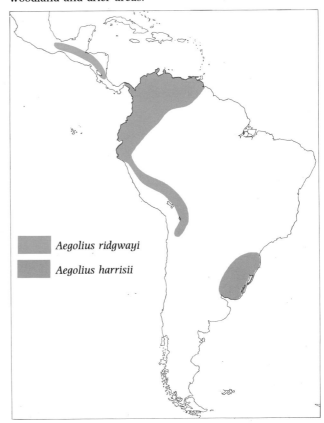

Aegolius ridgwayi

Aegolius harrisii

not depend on any one kind of prey, and is thus buffered against sudden dramatic fluctuations in its prey populations. Only when no terrestrial rodents are available does it take to titmice, goldcrests and other small birds in the tree crowns. Nevertheless, it is often seriously mobbed by a gang of arboreal birds.

Eurasian Pygmy Owls nest in holes and, like so many other small owls, often take over the disused holes of woodpeckers. The timing of the breeding season varies with the region; in Sweden for instance, egg-laying begins in April or May, occasionally as early as March. Three to 7 eggs, sometimes 8, are laid and incubated solely by the female; incubation usually begins when the third egg is laid and lasts for 28 days. Newly hatched chicks are clad in whitish down, graduating to dark brown plumage on fledging.

On late winter and spring evenings, as the breeding season approaches, the Pygmy Owl utters a musical piping 'hu' call, repeated regularly every few seconds and reminiscent of the call-note of a bullfinch. When the call is uttered from a perch, the sound is ventriloquial, seeming to come from different places as the bird turns its head. Occasionally members of a pair call alternately in duet.

The Eurasian Pygmy Owl *Glaucidium passerinum* (160 to 170 mm) often hunts by day, keeping watch from a vantage point in open woodland. In spite of its small size, it is a fierce predator and takes a wide variety of prey, from rodents to insects.

Map: *Glaucidium passerinum*: open areas of mature coniferous or mixed forest.

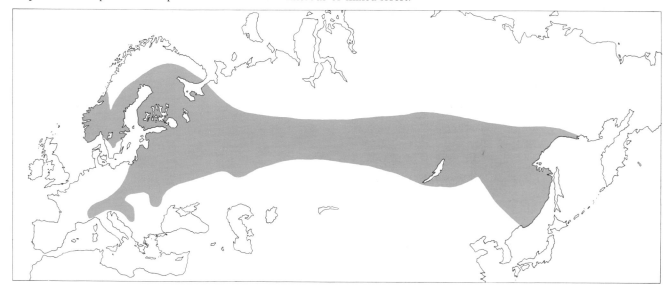

Cuban Pygmy Owl
Glaucidium siju

American
Pygmy Owl
Glaucidium gnoma

It is easily attracted by the imitation of its call, particularly the scale-call—a series of notes going up the scale. In winter some individuals move south or into lower mountain valleys, usually in response to bad weather.

The North American Pygmy Owl (*G. gnoma*) is very similar to that of Eurasia, and considered by some to be conspecific. A bird of the western Americas, it ranges from British Columbia and Vancouver Island in south-west Canada south through the Rocky Mountains, California, Arizona and New Mexico to Guatemala and perhaps further south. Within this range, a number of geographical races have been distinguished, which are virtually inseparable in the field but appear to have different voices. On this account they have been provisionally separated as the North American Pygmy Owl (*G. californicum*) and the Central American Pygmy Owl (*G. gnoma*) which ranges from Arizona and Central America south perhaps to north-west South America. The two sexes of both species are alike in plumage, the upperparts being greyish or reddish brown with buff-white speckling, particularly on the head, wings and shoulders; across the back of the neck is a half-collar of black and white. Underparts are white with dark brown streaks, and the tail is dark with light bars. The most usual habitat is open or mature coniferous and mixed woodland.

Like many other small owls, the North American Pygmy Owl nests in holes made by

The American Pygmy Owl *Glaucidium gnoma* (about 170 mm) ranges through open woodland from Alaska and Canada to Central America. Recent studies indicate that while northern forms seem more related to the Eurasian Pygmy Owl, those from Arizona and further south may be a separate species, more closely related to South American *Glaucidium*. The Cuban·Pygmy owl *G. siju* (about 170 mm) is confined to Cuba and the Isle of Pines.

Glaucidium gnoma and *G. californicum*: mature coniferous and mixed woodland. From Arizona northwards, *G. californicum*. *G. siju*: woodland.

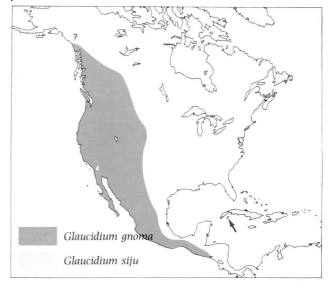

Glaucidium gnoma

Glaucidium siju

The Ferruginous Pygmy Owl *Glaucidium brasilianum* (130 to 140 mm) is a little known and patchily distributed species of Central and South America. It is as much a diurnal member of its genus as the other Pygmy Owls though its daylight activity is largely confined to the early morning and late afternoon. It forms a superspecies with closely related birds occurring in different parts of the region or in different habitats.

flickers and other woodpeckers, a clutch of 2 to 7, but usually 3 or 4 round, white eggs being laid. In most aspects of its breeding and feeding biology, including its tendency to remain sedentary, the North American Pygmy Owl closely resembles the Eurasian form, but it has bristled toes and a longer tail and its food contains a larger proportion of insects.

The pygmy owl of most limited range is undoubtedly the Cuban Pygmy Owl (*G. siju*), which is restricted to the Caribbean islands of Cuba and the nearby Isle of Pines. Like many other owls, this 170 mm long species occurs in two colour phases, one greyish-brown and the other reddish-brown. The upperparts are dark brown with pale mottlings, the underparts largely white with brownish markings on the throat and breast and the tail is barred with white. This is a

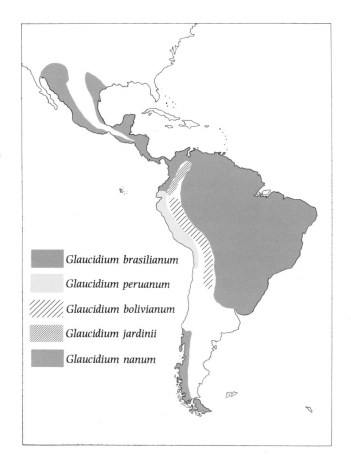

Glaucidium brasilianum

Glaucidium peruanum

Glaucidium bolivianum

Glaucidium jardinii

Glaucidium nanum

The Austral Owl (*Glaucidium nanum*) (130 to 140 mm) is closely related to both the Ferruginous Pygmy Owl and the newly described Peruvian Pygmy Owl (*G. peruanum*). The plumage patterns of all three birds are similar but they occupy different woodland or forest habitats and have different vocalizations.

Map: *Glaucidium brasilianum*: woodland and arid scrub.
G. peruanum: open woodland and arid scrub, western Peru to 3500 m.
G. jardinii: from Venezuela to the Maranon depression (Ecuador/Peru border).
G. bolivianum: from Peru to northern Argentina.
G. nanum: temperate and cold forest, southern Andes and Tierra del Fuego.

largely diurnal species inhabiting woodland. The most usual nest is a hole in a tree, where 3 or 4 white eggs are laid. Cuban Pygmy Owls produce piercing series of notes rising in pitch, and a slowly repeated hooting.

The Ferruginous Pygmy Owl (*G. brasilianum*) has a rather complex and discontinuous distribution from the extreme south-western United States in Arizona and Texas, through Central America south to southern Argentina and Chile. In this species were previously included the Andean Pygmy Owl (*G. jardinii*) from the

mountains of Costa Rica south to the Andes of Ecuador and Peru and the Austral Pygmy Owl (*G. nanum*) from the temperate and cold forests of the southern Andes and Tierra del Fuego. Most present authors, however, treat these owls as separate species, possibly to be united into a widespread superspecies, pending further study of these mysterious small owls in the field.

Already three species, forming a superspecies, have been recognized by Dr Claus König: the widespread Ferruginous Pygmy Owl (*G. brasilianum*) of woodland and arid scrub at lower altitudes, the Peruvian Pygmy Owl (*G. peruanum*) of arid scrub and open woodland on the Andean slopes of western Peru up to about 3500 m, and the Austral Pygmy Owl (*G. nanum*) restricted in general to the Patagonian forests of Argentina and Chile. For a long time the Andean Pygmy Owl (*G. jardinii*) was also thought to be a subspecies of the Ferruginous species, but it differs in its ecology and vocalizations. Beyond that, the pygmy owls of the montane forests of the Andes may also represent two species, distinguished by voice: *Glaucidium jardinii* from Venezuela and Colombia to Ecuador and the Yungas Pygmy Owl (*G. bolivianum*) from Peru to northern Argentina.

As the vernacular name suggests, the Ferruginous Pygmy Owl complex can be considered a rufous version of the North American Pygmy Owl. Its chief distinguishing features are rufous flanks, unspotted back, and a reddish-brown tail with dark-brown bars. However, Ferruginous Pygmy Owls are variable, if not realy dimorphic, some populations being decidedly greyish, others varying considerably in the degree of barring on the tail.

Very little is known about the ecology of these owls. Such accounts as there are suggest that in many essentials they resemble the North American Pygmy Owl but are prominently insectivorous. Like many of their near relatives they frequently hunt by day, sitting on a look-out post watching for some passing lizard or large insect such as a moth or grasshopper to pounce on. They tend to prefer woodland and dense rainforests but in the southern United States, frequent saguaro cactus desert and in South America also occur in open areas with scrub or scattered trees. The 3 to 5 white, almost spherical eggs are laid on the floor of the nest-hole which may be in a tree or termite nest. In the north of its range, eggs are laid between March and May, but there is considerable variation in latitude. The

The Least Pygmy Owl *Glaucidium minutissimum* (120 to 140 mm) is about the same size as the Elf Owl *Micrathene whitneyi* but much less well known. These two birds were being kept as pets by Karaja Indians in Brazil.

song is a regular series of short musical hoots on the same note, repeated in very rapid succession from 5 to 30 times. Another call is a louder double note repeated several times—'churrup-churrup-churrup'.

The Least Pygmy Owl (*G. minutissimum*) is probably, as its name suggests, the smallest of the pygmy owls, being a mere 120 to 140 mm long. It looks like the Ferruginous Pygmy Owls, but is smaller, with more uniform dark brown upperparts and fewer exposed white bars on the tail. It occurs from sea-level up to at least 1800 m in Mexico and Central America, Guyana, north-western Colombia, south-eastern Peru, Paraguay and the Amazon basin in Brazil. Its habitat varies from dense tropical forest to open bushy country. The call, in the best known part of its range, Central America, is a series of four low whistles: this, or the commotion of mobbing small song-birds may be the only indication of the Least Pygmy Owl's presence. On the whole the pygmy owls in South America are in a stage of active species diversification. Geographically defined ecological separation resulting partly from natural phenomena, partly from large-scale habitat

Glaucidium minutissimum: dense tropical forest to open bush country. Central American populations may be a separate species, *G. griseiceps*.
G. hardyi: forest, Central Brazil.
Xenoglaux loweryi: cloud forest, northern Peru.

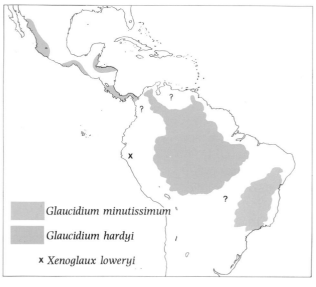

Glaucidium minutissimum

Glaucidium hardyi

× Xenoglaux loweryi

The Long-whiskered Owlet *Xenoglaux loweryi* (130 to 140 mm) was discovered in 1976 in Peru, 10 km north-east of Abra Patricia, 1890 m above sea level. It is so different from other owls that it is placed in a genus of its own.

Left: The Amazonian Pygmy Owl *Glaucidium hardyi* (120 to 140 mm) lives in the Amazonian forests, up to the foothills of the eastern Andes. Although similar in plumage to the Least Pygmy Owl, its voice is different and its exact relationship to other pygmy owls is still under investigation.

destruction caused by man, has strengthened local differences in voice. As voice, more than plumage characteristics plays a primary role in the recognition of breeding partners in owls, acoustical and other detailed studies recently undertaken in South America by Dr Claus König have already led to the recognition of more and other species units than are accepted today, e.g. a Mexican and Central American form, *Glaucidium griseiceps*, which is separated by the Amazonian forest from the East Brazilian Least Pygmy Owl (*G. minutissimum*), and an Amazonian Pygmy Owl (*G. hardyi*) in the canopy region, recently described by the French ornithologist J. Vieilliard and confirmed by König in 1991.

Recent years have seen the remarkable and exciting discovery of a completely new species of owl in remote parts of South America. One of these, discovered by John P. O'Neill and Gary R. Graves on 23 August 1976 in the cloud forests of northern Peru was so different as to warrant the creation of a new genus, *Xenoglaux*, meaning 'strange or foreign owl'. The species has some characteristics of *Microthene* and *Glaucidium* but is considered more closely related to the latter and was named the Long-whiskered Owlet, *Xenoglaux loweryi* after the ornithologist Professor George H. Lowery. This tiny owl, weighing in the region of 45 to 50 g, is remarkable in lacking ear tufts (like the other two genera) but in having unfeathered tarsi and feet (unlike both). It differs from *Microthene*, as does *Glaucidium*, in having twelve not ten tail feathers but, most remarkable, it differs from all other owls in the extraordinarily delicate feathers of the face which are very long and filamentous, projecting out from its face and forming a ruff. The bristles at the base of the bill are long and project upward between the eyes forming a fan-like 'crest'. The plumage is mainly dark brown but paler and barred on the lower belly and with blackish flight feathers. The pronounced whitish 'eyebrows' and intense amber-orange eyes give the little bird a staring expression, pronounced even for an owl. A call, believed to have been uttered by this owl, consisted of a series of short, mellow whistles at intervals of ten seconds or more. At a time of increasing extinctions, discoveries of new species are always welcome but when such exciting new forms as the Long-whiskered Owlet are involved, it is exceptionally so.

In the Old World there remains a series of seven poorly known *Glaucidium* species, three from Africa and four from India and the Far East. The Pearl-spotted Owlet (*G. perlatum*), 170 to 200 mm long, is probably the most widespread, occurring throughout large tracts of east and central Africa south of the Sahara, in the acacia woodlands, dry savannah and wooded valleys but not in the equatorial forest region of West and Central Africa or in the extreme south.

Both sexes are cinammon-brown above with copious speckles of black and white; like most of the pygmy owls it has a pale half-collar which is thought to suggest a pair of nuchal eyes and thus may confuse any attacking predator. Underparts are white with black streaking. Prey consists almost entirely of insects. The call is distinctive and far carrying, resembling a boy whistling; a

Above right: The Pearl-spotted Owlet *Glaucidium perlatum* (170 to 200 mm) is widely distributed in the savannah areas of Africa. Like other pygmy owls, it strongly resembles a very small sparrowhawk in flight, though it hunts in a shrike-like manner, preying by day on small rodents, birds, lizards and particularly insects. This individual is feeding on a red-billed quelea.

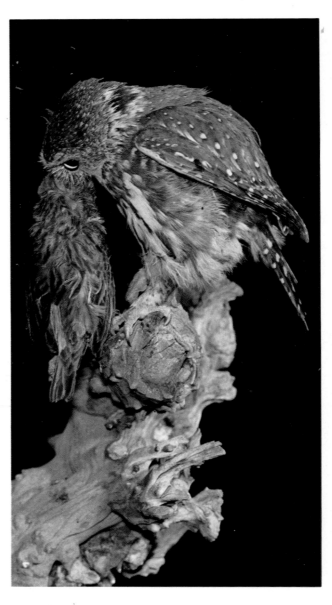

Map: *Glaucidium perlatum*: savannah and acacia woodland.

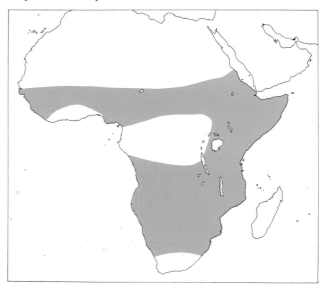

The Chestnut-backed (or Sjostedt's) Barred Owlet *Glaucidium sjostedti* (about 250 mm) is the largest of the pygmy owls. In its forest habitat it coexists with a more widely distributed and slightly smaller species (the Red-chested Owlet) but its ecological relationships are unknown.

The Red-chested Owlet *Glaucidium tephronotum* (170 to 180 mm) is a little known species from the African equatorial forest. It feeds largely on insects but, in common with other pygmy owls, it is very pugnacious for its size, readily tackling mammals and birds considerably bigger than itself.

Glaucidium sjostedti: tropical forest.

Map: *Glaucidium tephronotum*: dense forest.

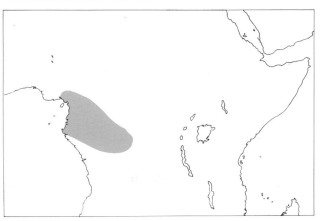

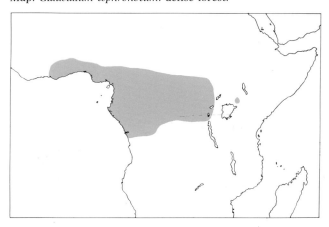

The Barred Owlet *Glaucidium capense* (210 to 220 mm) occurs in the same habitat as the smaller Pearl-spotted Owlet (*G. perlatum*). Little is known about its ecology but it may avoid competition by hunting at different times or having different prey preferences.

The Barred Jungle Owlet *Glaucidium radiatum* (about 170 mm) is widely distributed in forest and jungle on the Indian sub-continent.

Glaucidium capense: acacia bush.

Glaucidium radiatum: damp deciduous forest, secondary jungle.

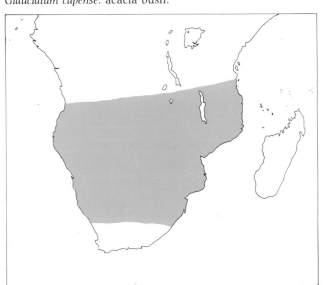

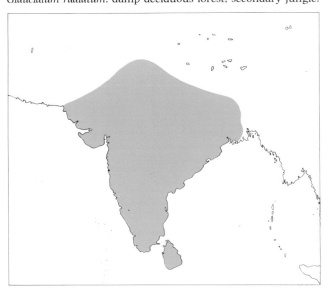

series of shrill notes ascending then descending the scale; also a 'wee-oo' or 'thi-oo' call.

The Red-chested or Yellow-legged Owlet (*G. tephronotum*), of tropical Africa, is around 200 mm long and is dark olive-brown or slate-grey above with a white spotted collar and a dark brown, white-spotted mantle and tail. The underparts are mainly white with dark brown spots and streaks, the sides uniform reddish-brown. This is a species of dense forest and nothing is known of its ecology or breeding biology.

The Barred Owlet (*G. capense*), 210 to 230 mm long, is large for a pygmy owl, with sepia upperparts, fine white barrings on the head and upper back, broad yellowish markings on the lower back, wings and tail. The white underparts are thickly marked with dark brown bars on the upper breast and triangular spots on the belly. This is a bird of the acacia bush and wooded river valleys, though of more limited distribution than the Pearl-spotted Owlet.

Even larger than the Barred Owlet is the Chestnut-backed or Sjöstedt's Barred Owlet (*G. sjostedti*), which is restricted to a relatively small area of western tropical Africa in Cameroon and Zaire. In many respects it resembles the Barred Owlet but differs in having yellowish orange underparts with dark yellow-brown barring on the flanks. The upperparts are mainly chestnut.

The Barred Jungle Owlet (*G. radiatum*) is a bird of the Indian sub-continent, ranging from 2000 m up in the Himalayan foothills south to Sri Lanka. It lives in damp, deciduous forest and secondary jungle, where suitable nest-holes are available.

The Collared Pygmy Owl (*G. brodiei*) ranges from the Himalayas and Assam hills (600 to 3000 m) to southern China, the lower Yangtze Valley, Taiwan, Hainan, the Malay Peninsula, Sumatra and Borneo. It usually lives in evergreen or mixed deciduous-evergreen forest, among oak, rhododendron and fir, but it also occurs in forest edges and more isolated groups of trees in cultivated country. This is one of the more diurnal species of the genus, and is often seen perching and hunting in broad daylight, though it is also active at twilight and at night. In this and many other aspects of its ecology, it resembles the Eurasian Pygmy Owl, which seems to be its closest relative. The call, usually consisting of four musical notes repeated at intervals and distinctively grouped has been described as 'hü hü-hü hü'. The diet includes insects and small birds.

The Collared Pygmy Owl *Glaucidium brodiei* (about 150 mm) is a bird of mountain forests throughout most of its range. Like the Eurasian Pygmy Owl (*G. passerinum*) it hunts both by day and night.

Glaucidium brodiei: evergreen or mixed deciduous forest; forest edges and groups of trees in cultivated land.

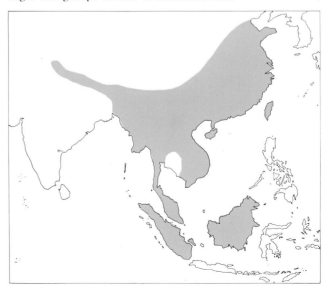

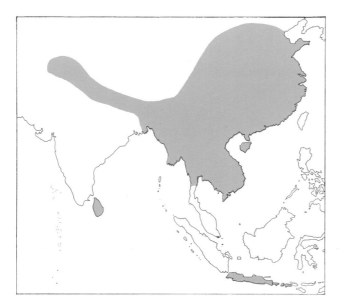

The Cuckoo Owlet *Glaucidium cuculoides* (230 to 250 mm), also known as the Barred Pygmy Owl, is another of the larger pygmy owls. It is mainly diurnal and sufficiently agile on the wing to catch quail in flight, though it normally pounces on its prey from a perch.

Far right: The Jamaican Owl *Pseudoscops grammicus* (about 310 mm) is almost exclusively nocturnal. Once considered to be closely related to the scops owl (*Otus*), it is now sometimes linked with the eared owls (*Asio*), sometimes with *Athene*, *Speotyto* and *Aegolius*.

Map: *Glaucidium cuculoides*: open forest of oak, rhododendron and pine; tropical/sub-tropical evergreen jungle. *G. c. castanonotum*: Sri Lanka. *G. c. castanopterum*: Java and Bali.

The Cuckoo Owlet (*G. castanopterum* or *cuculoides*) is another of the larger species, reaching 230 mm in length. In range very similar to the Collared Pygmy Owl, it extends further northward throughout most of China and is more restricted in south-eastern Asia, with isolated populations in Java and Bali. The island races, occurring in Sri Lanka, Java and Bali are sometimes regarded as separate species known as the Chestnut-backed Owlet (*G. castanonotum*) and Javan Owlet (*G. castanopterum*) respectively. Like a larger version of the Barred Jungle Owlet, the Cuckoo Owlet occurs in open forests of oak, rhododendron and pine at higher elevations and sub-tropical evergreen jungle at lower altitudes. Chiefly a diurnal owl, it is an agile predator, feeding on large insects, lizards, small birds and mice. Like other members of the family it is relentlessly mobbed by small and medium-sized birds and often flicks its tail from side to side—a habit of its genus. The calls are a trill and a series of harsh squawks, rising to a crescendo then ending abruptly. In the breeding season, which usually begins in April or May, a more musical and continuous bubbling whistle lasting for some seconds is uttered. Three to five eggs are laid in a disused hole; woodpeckers or barbets are sometimes forcibly evicted from their holes by Cuckoo Owlets.

Opinions differ widely as to the relationships of the Jamaican Owl (*Pseudoscops grammicus*) the only member of its genus. It is among the larger of the 'small' owls—310 mm in length, with rather short wings and tail. It is mainly dark tawny or yellowish-brown in colour, streaked and mottled with dark brown and black. The flight feathers of the tail and wings are barred irregularly with dark blackish-brown. It has a fairly well-developed facial disc, and short but conspicuous ear tufts. As its name suggests, it has been thought to be close to the scops owls (*Otus*)—but distinct enough to warrant being placed in a separate genus. In fact it is not now generally considered to be particularly close to *Otus*; some authorities put it close to the eared owls of the genus *Asio*, while others think it is linked with the *Athene*, *Speotyto* and *Aegolius* owls.

Its range is restricted to the island of Jamaica, which means that in terms of world population it is a very rare bird. It is found in both woodland and open country, nesting in cavities in trees, though sometimes the 2 eggs are laid in well concealed tree-forks.

Map: *Pseudoscops grammicus*: confined to Jamaica.

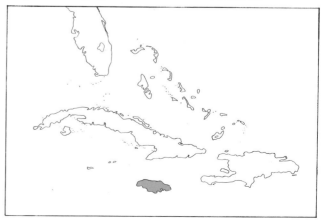

CHAPTER TEN

Conservation

Conservation is not synonymous with preservation, although it is concerned with taking measures to prevent extinction and minimize reductions in population size or variety of the plants and animals in any defined area. It is realistic to acknowledge that changes will result from the urban and agricultural expansion necessary to cope with human population growth. Equally, conservationists must deplore the inability of humans to limit their own numbers in relation to resources and support fundamental attempts to solve this basic problem. Conservation is based on ecological understanding and the planned use of land, water, air and other natural resources to prevent their destruction or waste. Sensible conservation recognizes the ecological interdependence of plants or animals on each other and it is within this broad context that the specific aspects involved in the conservation of owls must be seen. Conservation involves the management of plants and animals in both natural and man-altered environments: this management may involve rational exploitation, as in the case of game birds, attempts at control if species assume pest status, or strict protection, as when Snowy Owls (*Nyctea scandiaca*) nested for the first time in the Shetland Islands in 1967.

But while isolated or sensitive species may need rigorous protection from excessive disturbance, a modern understanding of bird population ecology has changed attitudes away from a negative 'leave well alone' approach. The prime objective is to ensure the provision of sufficient suitable natural habitat and given this ecological base most species can withstand considerable disturbance and will more or less look after themselves. Accordingly, two major approaches are adopted in conservation research. The first involves autecology, that is, the study of a single species as distinct from the community, in an attempt to define the habitat preferences and ecological needs of a species. Ideally such studies should reveal the factors affecting population size and the ability of the species to withstand interference.

The second aim of the conservationist is to provide a series of habitats in which as many species as possible can survive or to safeguard unique habitats even if they support relatively few species. The study of habitats involves an understanding of the physical factors (climate, hydrology and geology) as well as biotic factors (living component including the vegetation) which are responsible for the existence of a particular ecosystem. By ecosystem we mean the ecological system formed by the interaction of co-acting organisms and their environment. Again the keynote must be management because many habitats of special interest are not stable climax communities and would change with time; for example, certain types of grassland are prone to revert to scrub and then woodland. The safeguarding and management of habitats which have remained virtually unaffected by man since the dawn of civilization has considerable historical and aesthetic appeal, as well as scientific value. Thus, although some species can survive, even flourish, in man-altered habitats, the need remains to manage some natural habitat for it is only in this context that the true significance of the structural and functional adaptations exhibited by the species can be understood.

We need to know much more about the factors regulating the population size of different species in order to devise sensible management programmes. Unfortunately, the field studies involved become increasingly difficult with rare species so, although we can have a reasonable knowledge of the principles involved, our knowledge has come from relatively common species rather than endangered ones. In general, birds, like all other animals, produce more young each year than are needed to replace adult losses. The excess young are available for colonizing vacant habitats but if none exists this population surplus is doomed, for the carrying capacity of the habitat limits the number of animals. In the case of small Passerines, which have the potential for increasing their numbers up to eightfold in one breeding season, many of the surplus young birds provide food for predatory species. But in the absence of predators food stocks must eventually restrict numbers so that surplus individuals die of starvation and disease.

One owl that has been studied in this respect is the Tawny Owl (*Strix aluco*) at Wytham Wood, Oxford, by Southern (1970). In his study area of 541 hectares the owl population was remarkably stable with about 30 pairs. It appeared that for a given habitat and range of density of prey there was a maximum density at which the owl population was regulated by territorial behaviour. The chief prey animals were Woodmice (*Apodemus sylvaticus*), which varied in density from 4 to 7 per hectare, and Bank Voles (*Clethrionomys glareolus*) with a wide fluctuation in density of 6 to 40 per hectare. However, in some years at some seasons numbers fell below this level. The owl pairs had a territory of about 13 hectares in closed woodland and 20 hectares in mixed woodland and open ground once numbers had reached a stable level following the hard winter of 1946—7. It seems that territorial behaviour of this species living in natural climax woodland has evolved so that territories are on average of sufficient size to provide the adult with food. In Germany, where the food density averaged less, the mean territory size was 187 hectares per pair. Fluctuations in food resources at Oxford were first reflected in the ability of owls to lay eggs and then in their capacity to rear the chicks to fledging and in the subsequent post-fledging survival of the juveniles; in 1958, when rodents were particularly scarce, all the owls failed to breed. Fluctuations in food resources did not lead to changes in the number of adult owls in the woods. Failure to breed and the laying of fewer eggs than potentially possible were the important factors influencing changes in total numbers (adults plus young) from one year to the next. The final adjustment of population size involved mortality of young in autumn and winter in almost perfect proportion to the number of birds alive (mortality was density-dependent) which led to numbers remaining virtually constant at the beginning of each breeding season. An important lesson is that there is a limit to the owl density in a given habitat, this being determined by territorial behaviour. It would be worth improving food resources if the resultant young could disperse to colonize new areas, otherwise this expedience would not make much difference to the survival prospects of the adults.

Southern was able to make predictions about Tawny Owl densities in other habitats and gave indications that the rate of population turnover varied according to the density of rodent prey. The Tawny Owl needs to acquire experience and expertise in order to hunt prey successfully in woodland and its whole biology, including the stable territory habit, is geared to this end. Young birds remain with their parents from the time of fledging in late April/May until late July/early August during which time they learn about their surroundings and make no attempt to feed themselves. But quite the opposite applies to the moorland-dwelling Short-eared Owl (*Asio flammeus*) emphasizing the need to study different species on their own merit. This species alters the size of its territory from month to month according to the abundance of its main prey, the Short-tailed Vole (*Microtus agrestis*). If food is scarce the species becomes nomadic and seeks new hunting areas—posing quite different conservation requirements.

OWLS AND THEIR PREY

A particular habitat can support only a limited number of animals because the amount of energy available from soil nutrients and the sun determines how many simple plants and animals can exist to provide the base of the food chain. Since much energy is lost (80 to 90 per cent) at each trophic level in the food chain there are not usually more than five links before the top of the pyramid is reached and it is not surprising that these predators are vulnerable to any wastage in the exchange of energy in the ecosystem. Thus raptors and owls suffer first if the complexity of a food web becomes disturbed, for example, if the energy is channelled out of the system in the form of a game-bird crop. In this instance the problem is compounded by the activities of gamekeepers as discussed below. In general terms, natural habitats which support a complex web of life have predatory species occupying the top of the food chain, whereas man-exploited habitats do not because energy resources are deflected into other channels. The kinds of predator in any particular habitat are limited by the diversity of available prey in adequate numbers—major food items are either other birds or mammals though some birds of prey eat large invertebrates—and these food items are diversified according to size. The raptors occupy the feeding niches available by day and the owls by night. For example, in deciduous temperate woodland, foods for predators are mostly small or medium-sized birds or small mammals such as field mice, voles and shrews. By day the Sparrowhawk (*Accipiter nisus*) catches the small birds, while in suitable areas the Goshawk (*A. gentilis*) favours the medium-sized birds and mammals, such as rabbits caught at the woodland edge. In these hawks the female is larger than the male so the food supply can be effectively partitioned into four size categories; in the New World three *Accipiter* hawks occur sympatrically (have the same range) so there is a gradient of six sizes of predator. Female owls tend to be slightly bigger and heavier than the males, but the difference is by no means so great as with the *Accipiter* hawks. Perhaps the scope for partitioning prey by size is less in the case of owls which feed at night and rely to a greater extent on auditory rather than visual cues for locating prey. The food of the Tawny Owl at Oxford comprised 95 per cent small and medium-sized mammals and only 4 per cent of the prey units were birds. Similar results were noted at Bookham Common, Surrey. However, in large urban areas where *Accipiter* hawks are absent Tawny Owls feed to a much greater extent on birds than in woodland; at Holland Park, Kensington, in London, and in a Manchester suburb small birds contributed 93 and 89 per cent of the diet respectively. This implies an ability for flexibility which could help in the conservation of this species. In contrast, the Long-eared Owl does not appear to be flexible in this way. It normally feeds on a higher proportion of bird prey, about 10 to 20 per cent of all items, than the Tawny Owl and although a tree-haunting species which can feed in open or closed woodland it also feeds over open country: Woodmice and Short-tailed Field Voles usually make up around 80 per cent of the prey. It is possible that the Tawny Owl competes with the Long-eared Owl in disturbed deciduous woodland. Certainly from being a relatively thinly but widely distributed species at the turn of the century, the Long-eared Owl has suffered a marked decline during the present century, particularly in Wales and southern England, having become scarce by the 1930s in many counties where it was previously well distributed. This decline occurred before toxic chemicals, suspected to have affected some species (see below), could be implicated, but when clearance of marginal land for agriculture was proceeding. In fact, several authors have commented on the fact that in various places Long-eared Owls have become replaced by Tawny Owls: in Northumberland, the Lake District, and Wigtown, Scotland. The Long-eared Owl appears not to have changed its status in Ireland where agricultural development has been slower than in Britain and where, moreover, the Tawny Owl is absent. This kind of situation often confronts the conservationist who discovers that a dynamic species can capitalize on the feeding opportunities (make use of the feeding niche available) in a man-altered habitat at the expense of closely related forms which are more critical in their ecological requirements. Fortunately the Long-eared Owl appears to be more successful than the Tawny in coniferous woodland and it may prosper from the growth of coniferous forests, as has happened in Denmark. World-wide, the Long-eared Owl has a much wider distribution than the Tawny and it also occurs in North America.

PRESERVING THE HABITAT

With flexible species like the Tawny Owl, conservation involves guaranteeing a number of areas of mature woodland, and is backed by the knowledge that the species will also live in sub-optimal habitats such as the very open parkland of, for example, the English farm. But how much woodland should be kept? How many Tawny Owls do we want? It is in making decisions of this kind that conservationists are faced with the difficult task of making value judgements rather than scientific decisions. These judgements have to reflect other requirements for land use and public needs. Fragmentation of deciduous woodland in those areas of Europe which are intensively farmed poses the problem of defining the minimum areas which can support viable populations of the woodland owls. The hunting territories of owls are so large that even in favoured woodland considerable areas are needed to hold populations of a reasonable size. A reasonably sized population might be regarded as one which is self-sustaining and viable but we do not really know what is involved. It is not known over what distance sedentary species can communicate so that genetic interchange can continue. Special genetic conditions can apply in small isolated invertebrate populations but the topic is virtually unstudied so far as birds are concerned. Thus, instead of the gene frequency of the population remaining stable from one generation to the next, chance recombinations can occur which lead to local populations being formed which exhibit atypical genetic manifestations; this is known as genetic drift. So, while conservation policy must centre on safeguarding unique habitats, their size and distribution tend to reflect arbitrary factors such as what is available for sale, sympathetic land-owners, the activities of local and other conservation organizations, rather than scientific planning.

When a species becomes very specialized, conservation of course depends on protecting sufficient areas of the unique habitat. The Spotted Owl (*Strix occidentalis*) is a rare western counterpart of the widely distributed Barred Owl (*S. varia*) of North America. It inhabits heavy mature coniferous forest and wooded canyons. This habitat, particularly in Oregon, is being rapidly destroyed by modern clear-felling techniques and the species is becoming severely restricted in range, for it does not favour the new plantations which replace the old mature trees.

In the case of owls which have a cosmopolitan distribution, local scarcity can be balanced by protection in other regions. Special problems arise in the case of species formerly having a wide distribution which have become isolated in remote areas and speciated into new forms. The Seychelles Owl (*Otus rutilus insularis*) was thought to be extinct but was discovered in one place in the mountains of Mahé in 1959. Unfortunately

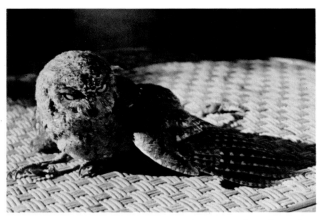

The Seychelles owl *Otus rutilus insularis* was thought to be extinct, but was rediscovered in 1959 in one place in the mountains of Mahé.

virtually nothing is known about its biology. Another owl which has significance for the study of evolution may already have disappeared. This is the New Zealand Laughing Owl, (*Sceloglaux albifacies*), representative of a monotypic genus. It is a relict species which may well have survived an early colonization of New Zealand by an owl line now extinct. Strict protection and positive conservation are helping to restore the Eagle Owl (*Bubo bubo*) to parts of Europe and Scandinavia, where it had been largely exterminated by man. It frequents wild rocky and forested country, remote from man, and shuns cultivation. Its bulk makes it dependent on large prey, up to the size of young roe deer and foxes, so that extensive areas need to be set aside to support this kind of fauna. The comments above regarding the capacity of birds to reproduce rapidly and replace themselves no longer apply when populations become fragmented and excessively disturbed. Breeding success declines and insufficient young are produced to make up for persecution, let alone colonize the places from which adults have disappeared.

Provision of reserves would in many situations be inadequate unless rigid legal protection was also afforded. In Britain, the first act for the protection of seabirds was passed in 1869, although before this time there had been a bill in 1822 protecting animals from cruelty. In 1872 an Act was passed protecting certain birds in the breeding season followed by the 'Wild Birds Protection Act 1880', which then remained the main legislation for over 75 years. This Act was spoiled by numerous orders which modified the close season locally and introduced confusion and it was only in 1954 that the 'Wild Birds Protection Act' rationalized the situation and gave full protection to owls and their eggs. This Act was modified in minor ways by the 'Protection of Birds Act 1967'. In 1981 the U.K. introduced the Wildlife and Countryside Act, which consolidated many of its wildlife protection measures, including those for birds, bringing its legislation in line with international conventions. It is under this legislation that the U.K. enforces the Convention on International Trade in Endangered Species of Wild Fauna and Flora (CITES) which came into force in 1975. Other international conventions which can afford protective measures for owls are the Convention on the Conservation of European Wildlife and Natural Habitats (Berne Convention 1982), the African Convention on the Conservation of Nature and Natural Resources (African Convention 1969) and the Convention on the Nature Protection and Wildlife Preservation in the Western Hemisphere (Western Hemisphere Convention 1942). In addition the European Commission has issued Directives and Regulations that affect many aspects of owl conservation. Other countries have schemes giving legal protection and have faced in various ways the problem of enacting legislation which can be effectively enforced. In many countries, bird protection is the responsibility of government departments concerned with agriculture and tends to favour game-preservation interests and the farmer. The International Council (previously International Committee) for Bird Preservation was founded in 1922 by ornithological representatives from the U.S.A., Britain, France and Holland. It now covers nearly 80 countries, co-ordinates the needs of bird protection throughout the world and reviews the status of endangered species. It is an effective lobby in persuading governments to take remedial action when avifaunas are threatened.

Sometimes a new habitat can be created intentionally or otherwise which favours a particular species. The Little Owl (*Athene noctua*) was artificially introduced to Britain, particularly Kent and Northampton, late in the nineteenth century and spread to almost all England and Wales by 1925. It has now been reported in southern Scotland. It is a species well suited to farmland for its habits are more terrestrial than the other owls and it preys extensively on beetles

and other large insects and earthworms. However, widespread destruction of hedgerows and their trees, which provide nest-sites, coupled with the intensification of farming, have probably led to major decreases in some areas. Numerous plantings of coniferous forest by the Forestry Commission have provided extensive new habitats throughout Britain, particularly on marginal hill land in the north and Scotland. Although extensive blocks of exotic conifer, e.g. Sitka spruce (*Picea sitkensis*) and Norway spruce (*P. abies*) have roused the wrath of many naturalists and conservationists there is no doubt that several species have profited. During the early stages of growth when the trees are less than 2 metres high an extensive grass cover develops which harbours numerous voles. Such sites are much favoured by the Short-eared Owl and Hen Harrier (*Circus cyaneus*) and both species have expanded their range and become more numerous for this reason. As the trees develop these species will be replaced by the Tawny and Long-eared Owls; it is evident why a dynamic attitude to conservation is necessary.

Provision of artificial nest-boxes in areas lacking natural breeding sites but which are otherwise suitable can be effective. Many of the Tawny Owls studied by Southern at Oxford use such boxes and this has facilitated scientific study. Since foresters aim at healthy stands of trees and in many cases deplore old and rotting wood this expediency may be very important in some woodland. Indeed the maintenance of large Ural Owl populations in commercial forests in southern Finland is dependent primarily on the provision of nest-boxes.

THE EFFECTS OF PESTICIDES

The position of raptors and owls at the top of the food chain has made them particularly vulnerable to poisoning by various toxic chemicals which can be accumulated in sub-lethal doses by prey species and other animals lower in the chain. This major conservation problem has resulted from an enormous post-war expansion of industry, with resultant increase in toxic waste and an intensification of agricultural dependence on insecticides and herbicides. The agents causing most damage are stable fat soluble chemicals which are not readily broken down by decay processes in the environment. In consequence, they can be stored in the fatty tissue of animals with little or no immediate detrimental effect but they become concentrated in predatory species which eat these animals and cause death or serious sub-lethal consequences. The synthetic organochlorine compounds used as insecticides, of which D.D.T., dieldrin and heptachlor are important examples, have been a major source of environmental contamination, these having been applied directly to crops. Indirect but serious contamination has also resulted from the industrial waste of compounds such as polychlorinated biphenyls (P.C.B.s).

In Britain an unexpected and synchronous decline occurred of the Peregrine Falcon (*Falco peregrinus*), Sparrowhawk (*Accipiter nisus*), Kestrel (*F. tinnunculus*) and Barn Owls (*Tyto alba*), coincident in time and space with introduction of the highly toxic organochlorine seed dressings. The Barn Owl had suffered a widespread decrease in the nineteenth century due to human persecution but subsequently partly recovered. Numbers probably fell slightly until the late 1940s but there was a marked and widespread drop after 1955, coinciding temporarily with the loss of the Peregrine and other raptors and also a decline of the Little Owl. A national census of Barn Owls was held in 1963 under the auspices of the British Trust for Ornithology and it was discovered that the decline was most widespread and sudden in eastern England, where arable farming was most intense. Many bodies of birds of prey were recovered containing high residues (over 16 parts of residue per million equivalent parts of tissue) of dieldrin which appeared to be the direct cause of their death. But argument and dissention greeted the early evidence for a decline of these predatory species and the situation was complicated by sub-lethal effects. For instance, Peregrines, Sparrowhawks and Golden Eagles began breaking their eggs with unprecedented frequency about 1950, the main reason having been a decrease in egg-shell thickness. Much research has been concentrated on establishing the temporal coincidence of egg-shell thinning with the increasing use of synthetic organochlorine compounds and in showing that agents like D.D.T. and its metabolite D.D.E. cause detrimental physiological changes, for example, by affecting the hormonal mechanisms involved in calcium metabolism, which become manifested in egg-shell thinning and egg infertility.

The population crash of Peregrine Falcons noted in Europe between 1950 and 1965 also occurred

Poisoned Tawny Owl *Strix aluco*. The position of owls and other raptors at the top of the food chain makes them especially vulnerable to poisoning by various toxic chemicals, which can be accumulated in sub-lethal doses by prey species lower in the chain.

in North America and stimulated an important international conference sponsored by the University of Wisconsin. Experts reviewed current knowledge about the Peregrine and other raptorial birds and presented their evidence that one of the most remarkable declines to be recorded in a wild animal population in recent years resulted from the widespread use of chlorinated hydrocarbon insecticides. The proceedings of the meeting, *Peregrine Falcons, their biology and decline*, were published by the University of Wisconsin Press in 1969.

In Britain in 1964 a voluntary ban was agreed between government, industry and the farmer on most uses of aldrin, dieldrin and heptachlor and the populations of some of the raptors such as the Kestrel and Peregrine are well on the road to complete recovery from the toxic contamination prevalent in the 1950s and early 1960s. Coincident with agreement for a voluntary ban, studies of predatory birds were initiated at the Monks Wood Experimental Station of the Nature Conservancy, ready to provide further data for the Advisory Committee on Pesticides and other Toxic Chemicals when they re-examined the problem in 1967. Requests were made for dead predators to be sent to Monks Wood for post-mortem examination and, in order of occurrence, Kestrel, Barn Owl, Tawny Owl and Sparrowhawk headed the list. But whereas 18 per cent of the Kestrels and Sparrowhawks examined contained tissue residues of either dieldrin or heptachlor in excess of 10 ppm or pp'-DDE in excess of 30 ppm (these are arbitrary levels at which it is highly likely that they caused the death of the subject) only 8 per cent of Barn Owls were so affected. Virtually all birds examined contained some residue but this need not have caused death; indeed in many cases the subject clearly died of injury, for instance through flying into telegraph wires.

In some cases it is known that particularly toxic chemicals will have detrimental side-effects. When endrin was used to control voles throughout 3459 acres of south German forests in 1957, 11 Barn Owls, 3 Long-eared Owls and 1 Little Owl were subsequently recovered dead.

In the 1980s a new potential problem of chemical poisoning arose for some species of owls, stemming from the use of new second generation rodenticides. These chemicals were developed as replacements for Warfarin, to which rats and mice in many regions had become resistant. But they are more toxic than Warfarin, and liable to cause secondary poisoning of rodent predators. One such compound, brodifacoum, is known to have killed screech owls in an American orchard area where the chemical was applied against voles, and the same chemical is thought to have contributed to the collapse of Barn Owl populations in some Malayan oil palm plantations. Both problems arose where the chemical was used in the open against a major prey species. For this reason, second-generation rodenticides would be best restricted to use around buildings against commensal rats and mice, which usually form minor prey. Even then, however, Barn Owls living around the buildings can become contaminated, and occasionally die, as shown by recent work in Britain. Of 143 Barn Owl carcasses examined in 1985—89, 15 per cent contained rodenticide residues, including three at lethal level.

Recently population statistics for sixteen bird species in the United States, including several owls and raptors, have been analysed to test whether any differences, possibly attributable to the use of pesticides, could be detected during the periods of 1925—45 and 1946—65. First, the mortality rate for each during the two periods was calculated from the recoveries of ringed birds. Second, productivity was measured in terms of the clutch-size and mean proportion of young fledged per nest, while a third parameter, the age of sexual maturity of the species, was usually already known. From these data the recruitment rate necessary for a stable population, with the birth rate equalling the death rate, could be calculated and compared with the actual situation.

In the case of the Great Horned Owl (*Bubo virginianus*) it was estimated that 1.47 young must be fledged per nesting attempt, including unsuccessful attempts, to maintain a stable population. The observed production in different areas of the United States was in close agreement with an average of 1.44 young per successful nest. In fact, both the recruitment and mortality rate appear to have remained relatively stable for the last forty years, with about 33 per cent of the adults dying each year.

In the case of the Barn Owl (*Tyto alba*) it was estimated that only 43—53 per cent of the population need nest successfully each year in the north-eastern United States to maintain a stable population and even fewer in the southern states (26 to 27 per cent). The differences depend on the fact that the reproductive rate and mortality rate are correlated with latitude. Thus in the north-eastern United States 4.16 young are produced per nest (4.43 in Switzerland) and 3.92 in the southern states, corresponding mortality rates being 50 per cent and 35 per cent (56 per cent in Switzerland). Again no changes in recruitment or mortality rates were detectable between the periods 1926—47 and 1948—67. Indeed, for none of the species studied was there any increase in mortality rate over the years. Nor was there any change in the recruitment rate, except for declines in the case of the Brown Pelican (*Pelecanus occidentalis*), Osprey (*Pandion haliaetus*), Cooper's Hawk (*Accipiter cooperii*), Red-shouldered Hawk (*Buteo lineatus*), and the American Sparrowhawk (*Falco sparverius*). These species have all suffered population declines which other studies have attributed to pesticide use and they feed on fish, reptiles, amphibians or birds. But, a survey in 1972 found that no change in recruitment rate was detectable in any of the species which feed primarily on mammals and this included the owls. The indications are that, compared with certain of the raptors, the feeding habits of owls have fortunately not made them particularly vulnerable to pesticide contamination.

CHAPTER ELEVEN

Owl Pellets

Bird pellets, or castings, are accumulations of the undigested portions of food items consumed by birds which are not excreted in the normal manner as faeces, but are regurgitated through the mouth in compact masses. They are usually composed of hard, not easily digested, materials of comparatively little nutritional value to birds—the bones, claws, beaks or teeth of mammals, birds, reptiles, amphibians and fishes; the headparts, thorax or wing-cases of insects; the jaws and chaetae of earthworms; seed husks and other coarse vegetable materials. These hard parts of food items are usually enclosed by softer, but indigestible, substances such as the fur of mammals, bird feathers and vegetable fibres. Thus the bird's pellet is often characteristic and provides valuable clues about the type of prey.

Pellets are often associated exclusively with the nocturnal and diurnal birds of prey but, according to a survey by the International Bird Pellet Study Group in 1969, 330 species of over 60 families produce pellets. These include common Old World birds like the Robin (*Erithacus rubecula*) and Starling (*Sturnus vulgaris*), waterside feeders such as the Kingfisher (*Alcedo atthis*) and Heron (*Ardea cinerea*), and farmland species like the Rook (*Corvus frugilegus*) and Tree Sparrow (*Passer montanus*).

All members of the four raptor families which have been studied in detail are known to produce pellets regularly—the Tytonidae and Strigidae (owls), Accipitridae (kites, hawks, eagles, harriers) and Falconidae (falcons). The pellets form in response to a mechanical barrier posed by the small pyloric opening—an extension of the stomach—and in the absence of free acidity in the stomach, digestion cannot take place and resistant materials are periodically regurgitated. These can prove extremely valuable in a study of the food habits of a species. This is particularly so in the case of the owls because their ability to digest bone is poor and consequently any pellets produced contain a good skeletal record of the prey eaten. Furthermore, unlike the diurnal raptors which have very stout beaks and strong neck muscles which enable them to tear and partially consume prey, owls generally bolt entire, suitably sized food items. As a result a careful examination of their pellets can provide an accurate record of the diet.

The identification of food traces is often a difficult and time-consuming job. Certain species produce pellets that are both easy to collect and analyse, but all material is worth examining. Apart from providing valuable information about various aspects of the diet of owls—individual tastes, seasonal, regional and habitat differences etc—they have important secondary uses. Owl pellets of many species provide rapid field indicators of the presence and often relative abundance of mammals and other animals in an area—data of value to local and national surveys. Some owls are effective samplers of small mammals, producing skeletal material in quantities that would take many hours of trapping to accumulate, and owl pellets often also include bird rings. Finally, as an educational tool, they can be used effectively to demonstrate the role of avian predators in the ecosystem, and the nature of food chains.

Pellets are found at day-time roosts and night-time feeding stations—but their accumulation varies from species to species. The habits of two of the more widely studied owls, the open country Barn Owl and woodland dwelling Tawny Owl illustrate this point. The Barn Owl frequents a wide variety of open habitats—pastoral, arable and mixed farmland, upland pasture, water-meadows, saltmarsh, open parkland and deciduous woodland, waste ground and the rough grassland associated with young forestry plantations, open downland and disused quarries. Small pellets are formed and regurgitated at night while the bird is hunting and larger second pellets are later deposited at the day-time roost or nesting site, which is often in a farm barn, disused or derelict building, haystack or hedgerow tree. Such sites quickly become littered with pellets, and sizeable samples can be collected at regular intervals. If the owls are not disturbed excessively, such sites may be frequented for months, even years. The pellets of other open country hunters such as the Snowy Owl, Little Owl, Elf Owl and Short-eared Owl can also be most profitably collected at the day-time roost or at obvious vantage points on the bird's hunting range.

In contrast, collecting Tawny Owl pellets (and those of other woodland owls) in quantity can prove to be a very time-consuming business. The Tawny Owl frequents woodland, copses, well-timbered gardens, parkland, farmland and even urban areas and, though it is a strongly territorial and sedentary species, the nocturnal roosts and feeding stations at which it deposits pellets are usually well scattered. During the winter, when it roosts high up in trees, the falling pellets quickly become scattered and fragmented. In the summer months Tawny Owl pellets quickly break down among the moist ground vegetation. However, it is a species that will take fairly readily to nest-boxes and, by regularly visiting the nest and locating surrounding tree roosts, useful collections of pellets and prey remains can be made.

It is often possible to identify the origin of a pellet without seeing the owl, but generally a view of the predator at the nest or roost is desirable. In general terms, the larger the owl, the larger the pellet. Those of the Eagle Owl are normally 70 to 110 mm long and 30 to 40 mm in width, the Long-eared Owl normally 35 to 65 mm by 15 to 25 mm and the Little Owl's pellets 30 to 40 mm by 10 to 15 mm. Such sizes are

dependent to a degree on the hunting success of the owl, which has been shown to be affected by weather conditions in several species. Strong winds and rain affect the hunting success of open country species like the Barn Owl, which may produce a small pellet as a result, while wet conditions often result in Tawny Owls casting up fibre pellets containing the remains of earthworms, beetles, slugs, or other invertebrates, which are often easy prey in wet weather.

Methods of dissecting the pellets vary with the size of the sample and type of information required. Each sample collected should be dried and stored. In the case of small samples, each

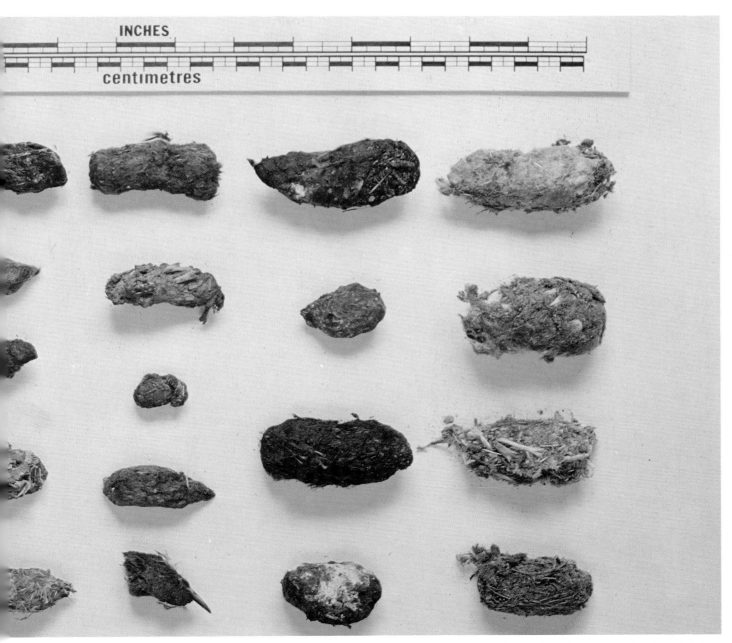

Owl pellets. Vertical rows from left to right: Little Owl *Athene noctua*, Long-eared Owl *Asio otus*, Short-eared Owl *Asio flammeus*, Tawny Owl *Strix aluco*, Barn Owl *Tyto alba* and Snowy Owl *Nyctea scandiaca*.

pellet can be placed in a separate polythene envelope containing naphthalene, and analysed separately. The insecticide is necessary because pellets form suitable repositories for insect eggs and, if these are allowed to hatch, the emerging fly, moth or beetle larvae, combined with fungal attack, will quickly reduce the pellet to a disintegrated mass of bone fragments.

After recording the dry weight and size of the pellet, it can be broken down in a dry state with dissecting needles or forceps. Where large samples are involved the pellets can be soaked in a dish of warm water and the contents separated with forceps or by a mechanical rotating paddle. The aim is to separate the hard parts (bones and chitinous fragments) from the softer substances (fur, feathers and fibre), so that individual prey items can be examined under a good pocket lens or low power microscope. In well-studied areas, regional handbooks are sometimes available to help in identifying fragments of prey. Where problems arise, local or national museums may help. The shape, size and particularly dentition of

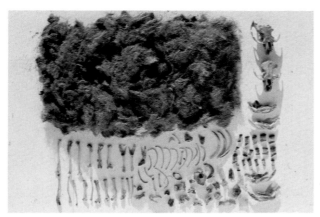

Contents of Short-eared Owl pellet.

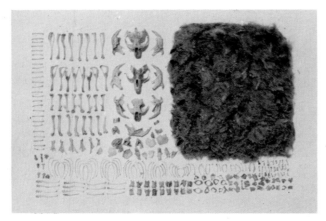

Contents of Long-eared Owl pellet.

Contents of Snowy Owl pellet.

vertebrate skulls are important in identification, as are the head-parts, wing-cases and appendages of invertebrates. It is often possible to accumulate a reference collection of prey traces quickly by storing named items in glass tubes or plastic pill boxes, or by mounting them washed and varnished on stiff board.

After analysis and identification of prey species, care is needed in drawing conclusions about diet. The pellets of some birds contain a very biased record of the birds' diet. Those of the heron, for instance, are composed of little more than a mass of clumped hair. Its digestive powers are good and only the most resistant hard parts remain—the ear-bones of fish and cheek teeth of mammals for example. Although the digestive powers of owls are poorer, the same principle applies. Soft-bodied foods, such as nestling birds and certain invertebrates, may be overlooked or not properly identified. Small mammals or birds may be decapitated or larger food items may be partially consumed (often when parent owls are feeding their young), so complicating any analysis. Similarly, the skulls of small insectivorous birds, amphibians and reptiles will frequently disintegrate, placing an emphasis on the correct identification of bones such as the pelvic girdle, sternum and synsacrum.

Batches of 20 pellets or 40 or more prey items are normally required to provide a basic indication of an owl's diet at any one time—indeed, the larger the sample the better. Invertebrate prey such as earthworms and beetles can rarely be quantified and should be expressed on a presence or absence basis. Larger food items can be added together and expressed as a percentage of the prey total, in tabular form or as pie diagrams. Listing foods in this way can, however, give a false impression of the relative nutritional value of a food item to the owl. Clearly, small animals such as Pygmy Shrews (*Sorex minutus*) or House Sparrows (*Passer domesticus*) are of much less importance to the owl, than, for example, Brown Rats (*Rattus norvegicus*) or Blackbirds (*Turdus merula*). Conversion factors based on the weight of prey items must be applied if nutritional values are required.

Pellets, therefore, are a useful source of data: careful searching in the field, patient analysis in the laboratory and careful interpretation of findings can provide a wealth of information about the feeding habits of the world's owls.

CHAPTER TWELVE

Owl voices

Communication is as important to owls as it is to any other group of animals. Those which are largely or even partly diurnal can rely to some extent on purely visual signals and very often these owls do not have particularly well developed vocal repertoires. Their nocturnal cousins, on the other hand, have obvious problems with visual communication. Like most birds, owls appear to have a poorly developed sense of smell, so the use of this sense—so vital to many nocturnal animals—is not an option. Instead, those owls which are most active between dusk and dawn must rely on their voices.

Most owls which have been closely studied have a wide and often very varied repertoire of utterances which are used as contact-notes, alarm calls and so on, or during the most intimate moments of their courtship rituals. Some of these calls are familiar to ornithologists, whether or not they are working on owls, but many are not. The best known calls are usually those by which territorial rights are advertised, for whatever reason, and which are 'songs' with the same function as those of any songbird. These songs may be both loud and far-carrying in species with large territories, or rather quiet in others. They may be simple in form, or fairly complex. Some owls sing duets: in some species, these involve the male and the female using similar versions of the same song, while in others the components of the duet are different. Some owl songs are so well known that they give the bird its popular name: the Saw-whet Owl *Aegolius acadicus* has a song which is said to resemble the sound of a saw being sharpened, for example, while the name Boobook Owl *Ninox novaeseelandiae* is simply onomatopoeic.

It is difficult to do justice to bird calls and songs in books because they can be extraordinarily difficult to express phonetically and even in syllables. Most owls, fortunately, have relatively simple calls and songs and these can be described reasonably well in words. The most accurate record of a bird's vocal utterances, however, is given by sonograms (sound spectrograms)—although experience shows that many people find these difficult to interpret and to translate into an impression of sound and rhythm. The picture given by a sonogram is basically a graph which shows the distribution of sound energy against frequency (pitch, measured in kiloHertz) on the vertical scale and time (duration, in seconds) on the horizontal scale. The third parameter used is that of amplitude (loudness), which is shown by the depth of shading (ranging from pale grey to dense black) of the trace across the graph.

A fully detailed account of all the vocalizations of all the owls is beyond the scope of this book; in any case, these are incompletely known or only partially interpreted for many species and completely unknown for many others. New information is still coming forward, some of which has important implications in the field of owl taxonomy. Vocalizations can provide important clues in understanding speciation in certain groups of closely-related owls, such as those in the genus *Otus*, or a particularly difficult group such as the *Glaucidium* owls in the Andes of South America. Another interesting feature of owl songs is that widely separated species may sound remarkably similar: a good example is provided by the south-east Asiatic *Glaucidium cuculoides*, whose beautiful 9-second trill sounds very like that of *Otus guatemalae* from Central and South America.

Owls also share with many other birds a pattern of vocal variation within a species—local or regional dialects, in fact. Any owl with a very wide geographical range is likely to show this sort of variation and studies of voice characteristics linked to distribution should be treated just as seriously as the often better known variations in plumage and size.

Some examples from well-studied species will illustrate the range of calls and songs and some of their functions. Although they are basically similar in structure, and all essentially fairly simple, the songs of the large group of scops and screech owls are very varied and in some cases surprisingly pleasant to the human ear. Their common factor is the regular repetition of short, often musical notes. Differences between species mainly pertain to tempo, arrangement and pitch of notes; these may also vary between males of the same species, or between the sexes. The mainly New World screech owls usually have fairly rapid songs consisting of many notes, typified for example by the Eastern Screech Owl *Otus asio* which utters a fairly quiet, fast trill. Old World scops owls, in contrast, have slower, more measured songs consisting of one or only a few notes. One of the best known is the pure, single whistle of the European Scops Owl *Otus scops*, which is repeated with almost metronomic regularity, sometimes for up to half-an-hour without interruption. A continuous 40-minute performance containing 900 consecutive calls has been heard! Owl enthusiasts can often produce very creditable imitations of owl songs, which is sometimes useful as a general birdwatching aid and can be helpful in more serious studies of owls, too. The song of the European Scops Owl is fairly easy to imitate, but human efforts will not necessarily disturb the rhythm of a singing bird.

Well-known songs can lend themselves to a different sort of interpretation to that put forward by ornithologists. A classic example of this is provided by *Otus sunia* in the Far East. The basic song of this bird is a repetition of three notes, but sometimes only the second and third notes are given—without any change in the time of the song. In Korea, it appears that two-note and three-note songs have long been recognized by local people, who ascribe different meanings to them. Three syllables mean a rich harvest, but only two indicate a poor crop!

Various owl calls and songs have been used to conjure up images of night and an after-dark 'atmosphere', none more so perhaps than the famous hooting song of the Tawny *Strix aluco*, so beloved of film and programme makers in the Old World. The wood owls of the genera *Strix* and *Ciccaba* have particularly loud and bold songs, in keeping with their life-styles in mainly closed habitats and often large territories. A splendid example of duetting is provided by the Barred Owl *Strix varia* of the New World, where a loud series of hoots delivered by the male may be answered by an amazing cackling and wailing laugh from his mate. The effect on an unsuspecting listener can be decidedly frightening.

Most of the eagle owls of the genus *Bubo* produce a few, or a short series of, deep, almost mournful hoots which carry over considerable distances. The rich basso utterances of the Great Horned Owl *B. virginianus* are as well known in the New World as are the distinctive notes of the Eurasian Eagle Owl *B. bubo* in parts of the Old. The German name of the latter, incidentally, is *Uhu*—which describes the two-note song in perfect phonetics. The calls of the big fish and fishing owls *Ketupa* and *Scotopelia* are not all known or adequately described, but Pel's Fishing Owl *S. peli* has a screeching howl and a purring sound resembling that of a leopard or other large cat, as well as a loud hoot rising to a screech and terminating in an eerie wail—which must be every bit as terrifying in the darkness of an African forest as any other owl sound on earth. In contrast to these other large species, the Snowy Owl *Nyctea scandiaca* is a relatively silent bird. It is of course a diurnal owl during the breeding season and as such can use visual signals to communicate: the striking white plumage of the male and his wing-waving displays make him very visible over long distances.

Short-eared Owls *Asio flammeus* are often abroad in full daylight and they too have a fairly limited vocal repertoire. They also have a display flight which involves wing-clapping, but this may be as important audibly as it is visually: similar wing-clapping displays are performed by the closely related but much more thoroughly nocturnal Long-eared Owl *A. otus*.

Among the smaller species, the Little Owl *Athene noctua* has a monotonous song of rather quiet, almost tooting notes, but also several loud, ringing calls, such as a repeated and very distinctive 'kiew...kiew...'. The Burrowing Owl *A. cunicularia* sings a mellow, dove-like 'coo-c-hoo' at night and has a better known chattering or cackling call; when alarmed, or disturbed in its burrow, it produces a repeated 'cack...cack...' and also a hiss like that of a rattlesnake. The song of Tengmalm's (or Boreal) Owl *Aegolius funereus* is a repeated 'po...po...po...' which, surprisingly, can be heard up to two kilometres away in still conditions. Pygmy owl songs also consist of repetitions of short musical or metallic notes. That of the Eurasian Pygmy Owl *Glaucidium passerinum* has been likened to the calls of a Bullfinch and, like the vocalizations of a number of smaller owls,

can be confusingly ventriloquial.

A great deal remains to be learned about owl songs and calls. Learning how to recognize at least the songs and the commoner calls of some of the least known of the world's owls would be a great step forward in finding out more about their distribution and numbers; learning what these sounds mean will help us to understand more about their way of life. It is no exaggeration to say that future studies of these fascinating birds will involve as much listening as looking.

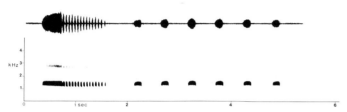

Sonogram of the song of the South American Pygmy Owl, *Glaucidium bolivianum*, consisting of a long trill followed by a series of single calls. From a recording made in Salta, Argentina in September 1987.

To prepare a sonogram, a sound recording of the bird's call is read into a sonograph machine, which translates sound into an image that can be seen on screen and printed out on a special printer. The vertical scale shows sound energy (pitch), the horizontal shows frequency and duration. The lowest line represents the main song with, above, harmonic overtones. The image at the top is an oscillogram, prepared in the same way but representing only strength of sound.

Below: Sonograms are useful for comparing the songs of different species. However, care must be taken to ensure that calls compared were made in the same circumstances so that, for example, the alarm call of one species is not compared with the normal song or the mating call of another.

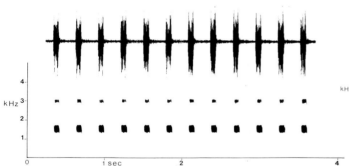

Song of the Austral Pygmy Owl, *Glaucidium nanum*.

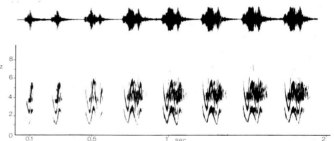

Alarm call of the Austral Pygmy Owl.

O. sunia: SE Asia
ku ku ku-ku,....ku ku ku-ku,....ku ku ku-ku,....ku ku ku-ku,....ku ku ku-ku,....ku ku ku-ku, etc

O. sunia: Japan and Korea
*yü kyü hü,....yü kyü hü,....yü kyü hü,........kyü hü,....yü kyü hü,....yü kyü hü,....*etc

O. sunia: India
hu kyu hu,.........................hu kyu hu,.........................hu kyu hu,...........

Songs transcribed from recordings may be easier to read than sonograms but are less accurate, depending more on individual interpretation. These three transcriptions, made

from recordings of the Oriental Common Scops Owl, *Otus sunia*, show how the song of a single species may vary over its range.

S. varia:
1. *hu hu hu-hu.....hu hu hu-hu-aw,...*

Purely verbal descriptions seem fanciful without the help of sound. The song of the Barred Owl, *Strix varia*, transcribed

here from a sound recording, is traditionally written as 'Who cooks for you, who cooks for you all'.

Sonograms reproduced by kind permission of Dr Claus König, from *Ökologie der Vögel* (Ecology of Birds) 13, Vol 1, 1991.

PART III

CHECK LIST OF SPECIES

GLOSSARY

BOOKS FOR FURTHER READING

INDEX

Check list of species   Arrangement of the species is alphabetical.

This check list is based on the information in individual chapters. The sequence follows Sibley and Monroe: *The Distribution and Taxonomy of Birds of the World*, Yale, 1990, and differences between the lists are noted.

CLASS: Aves
ORDER: STRIGIFORMES
FAMILY: *TYTONIDAE* (Barn and grass owls)
SUBFAMILY: *TYTONINAE*
GENUS: *TYTO*

Tyto alba	Barn Owl
T. aurantia	Golden (or New Britain Barn) Owl
T. capensis	African Grass Owl
T. glaucops	Ashy-faced Owl
T. inexpectata	Minahassa (Barn) Owl
T. longimembris	Eastern Grass Owl
T. multipunctata	Lesser Sooty Owl
T. nigrobrunnea	Taliabu (or Sula's Barn) Owl
T. novaehollandiae	Masked Owl
including *castanops* and *manusi*	
T. rosenbergii	Sulawesi (or Celebes Barn) Owl
T. sororcula	Lesser Masked Owl
T. soumagnei	Madagascar Red Owl
T. tenebricosa	Sooty Owl

SUBFAMILY: *PHODILINAE*
GENUS: *PHODILUS*

Phodilus badius	Bay Owl
P. prigoginei	Itombwe Owl

FAMILY: *STRIGIDAE* (Typical owls)
GENUS: *OTUS*

Otus albogularis	White-throated Screech Owl
O. alfredi	Flores Spotted Scops Owl
O. angelinae	Greater Sunda Spotted Scops Owl
including *vandewateri*	
O. asio	Eastern Common Screech Owl
O. atricapillus	Black-capped Screech Owl
including *lophotes=watsonii* and *sanctaecatarinae*	
O. bakkamoena	Collared Scops Owl
including *whiteheadi=megalotis*	
O. barbarus	Santa Barbara Spotted Screech Owl
O. brookii	Rajah's Scops Owl
O. choliba	Choliba Screech Owl
including *roboratus* and *koepckeae*	
O. clarkii	Bare-shanked Screech Owl
O. cooperi	Cooper's Screech Owl
O. flammeolus	Flammulated Scops Owl
O. guatemalae	Vermiculated Screech Owl
inc. *cassini, hastatus, roraimae, pacificus, vermiculatus*	
O. (Mimizuku) gurneyi	Giant Scops Owl
O. hartlaubi	São Tomé Scops Owl
O. hoyi	Hoy's Screech Owl
O. icterorhynchus	Sandy Scops Owl
O. ingens	Rufescent Screech Owl
O. ireneae	Sokoke Scops Owl
O. kennicotti	Western Common Screech Owl

O. lambi	Lamb's Common Screech Owl
O. lawrencii	Bare-legged or Cuban Screech Owl
O. longicornis	Philippine Spotted Scops Owl
O. manadensis	Magic Scops Owl
including *magicus, elegans, beccari, mentawi*	
O. marshalli	Cloudforest Spotted Owl
O. nudipes	Puerto Rican Vermiculated Screech Owl
O. podarginus	Palau Spotted Scops Owl
O. rufescens	Rufescent Scops Owl
O. rutilus	Ruddy Scops Owl
including *insularis, capnodes, pembaensis*	
O. scops	European Common Scops Owl
including *senegalensis*	
Otus sagittatus	White-fronted Scops Owl
O. seductus	Balsas Screech Owl
O. silvicolus	Lesser Sunda Scops Owl
O. spilocephalus	Spotted Scops Owl
including *balli, hambroeki*	
O. sunia	Oriental Common Scops Owl
including *brucei*	
O. trichopsis	Spotted Screech Owl
O. umbra	Mentaur Scops Owl

Sibley includes *guatemalae, sanctaecatarinae* and *hoyi* in *atricapillus* but separates *vermiculatus* as a full species. He separates *koepckeae* as a full species. His arrangement of the *bakkamoena* and *manadensis* complexes differs and he includes *O. mindorensis* as a full species. He does not list *O. lambi* and includes *Ptilopsis* with *Otus*.

GENUS: *PTILOPSIS*

Ptilopsis leucotis	African White-faced Screech Owl

GENUS: *LOPHOSTRIX*

Lophostrix cristata	Crested Owl
L. (Jubula) lettii	Maned Owl

GENUS: *BUBO*

Bubo africanus	Spotted Eagle Owl
B. bubo	Eurasian Eagle Owl
including *benegalensis, ascalaphus*	
B. capensis	Cape Eagle Owl
B. coromandus	Dusky Eagle Owl
B. lacteus	Milky Eagle Owl
B. leucostictus	Akun Eagle Owl
B. nipalensis	Forest Eagle Owl
B. philippensis	Philippine Eagle Owl
B. poensis	Fraser's Eagle Owl
B. shelleyi	Shelley's Eagle Owl
B. sumatranus	Malaysian Eagle Owl
B. virginianus	Great Horned Owl

GENUS: *KETUPA*

Ketupa blakistoni	Blakiston's Fish Owl
K. flavipes	Tawny Fish Owl
K. ketupa	Malaysian Fish Owl
K. zeylonensis	Brown Fish Owl

GENUS: *SCOTOPELIA*
Scotopelia bouvieri	Vermiculated Fishing Owl
S. peli	Pel's Fishing Owl
S. ussheri	Rufous Fishing Owl

GENUS: *NYCTEA*
Nyctea scandiaca	Snowy Owl

GENUS: *SURNIA*
Surnia ulula	(Northern) Hawk Owl

GENUS: *CICCABA*
Ciccaba albitarsus	Rufous-banded Owl
C. huhula	Black-banded Owl
C. nigrolineata	Black and white Owl
C. virgata	Mottled Owl

Sibley places all *Ciccaba* species in the *Strix* genus.

GENUS: *STRIX*
Strix aluco	Tawny Owl
S. butleri	Hume's Wood Owl
S. hylophila	Rusty-barred Owl
S. leptogrammica	Brown Wood Owl
S. nebulosa	Great Grey Owl
S. occidentalis	Spotted Owl
S. ocellata	Mottled Wood Owl
S. rufipes	Rufous-legged Owl
S. seloputo	Spotted Wood Owl
S. uralensis	Ural Owl
including *davidi*	
S. varia	Barred Owl
S. woodfordii	African Wood Owl

GENUS: *PULSATRIX*
Pulsatrix koeniswaldiana	White-chinned Owl
P. melanota	Rusty-barred Owl
P. perspicillata	Spectacled Owl

GENUS: *GLAUCIDIUM*
Glaucidium brasilianum	Ferruginous Pygmy Owl
including *bolivianum, jardinii, nanum, peruanum*	
G. brodiei	Collared Pygmy Owl
G. capense	Barred Owlet
including *castaneum*	
G. cuculoides	Cuckoo Owlet
including *castanopterum* and *castanonotum*	
G. gnoma	North American Pygmy Owl
including *californicum*	
G. hardyi	Central Brazilian Least Pygmy Owl
including *griseiceps*	
G. minutissimum	Least Pygmy Owl
G. passerinum	Eurasian Pygmy Owl
G. perlatum	Pearl-spotted Owlet
G. radiatum	Barred Jungle Owlet
G. siju	Cuban Pygmy Owl
G. sjostedti	Chestnut-backed Owlet
G. tephronotum	Red-chested Owlet

Sibley has *castanopterum* and *castaneum* as separate species. He lists G. *albertinum* as a separate species.

GENUS: *XENOGLAUX*
Xenoglaux loweryi	Long-whiskered Owlet

GENUS: *MICRATHENE*
Micrathene whitneyi	Elf Owl

GENUS: *ATHENE*
Athene blewitti	Forest Little Owl
A. brama	Spotted Little Owl
A. noctua	Little Owl

GENUS: *SPEOTYTO*
Speotyto cunicularia	Burrowing Owl

GENUS: *AEGOLIUS*
Aegolius acadicus	Saw-whet Owl
A. funereus	Tengmalm's (Boreal) Owl
A. harrisi	Buff-fronted Owl
A. ridgwayi	Unspotted Saw-whet Owl

GENUS: *NINOX*
Ninox affinis	Andaman Hawk Owl
N. connivens	Barking Owl
N. jacquinoti	Solomon Island Hawk Owl
N. meeki	Admiralty Islands Hawk Owl
N. novaeseelandiae	Boobook Owl
N. odiosa	New Britain Hawk Owl
N. perversa (ochracea)	Ochre-bellied Hawk Owl
N. punctulata	Speckled Hawk Owl
N. rufa	Rufous Owl
N. scutulata	Oriental Hawk Owl
N. solomonis (variegata)	New Ireland Hawk Owl
N. squamipila	Moluccan Hawk Owl
N. strenua	Powerful Owl
N. superciliaris	Philippine Hawk Owl
including *spilonota, spilocephala*	
N. theomacha	Sooty-backed Hawk Owl

Sibley separates from *novaeseelandiae, rudolphi* and *boobook*.

GENUS: *UROGLAUX*
Uroglaux dimorpha	Papuan Hawk Owl

GENUS: *SCELOGLAUX*
Sceloglaux albifacies	Laughing Owl

GENUS: *PSEUDOSCOPS*
Pseudoscops grammicus	Jamaican Owl

GENUS: *ASIO*
Asio capensis	African Marsh Owl
A. clamator	Striped Owl
A. flammeus	Short-eared Owl
A. madagascariensis	Madagascar Long-eared Owl
A. otus	Long-eared Owl
including *abyssinicus*	
A. stygius	Stygian Owl

GENUS: *NESASIO*
Nesasio solomonensis	Fearful Owl

Glossary

allopatric Having non-overlapping ranges.

asynchronous hatching 'Staggered' hatching of eggs. Eggs are laid over a period of days; owls, hawks, eagles and some other species begin to incubate when the first egg is laid, so eggs hatch at different times, in order of laying. The earliest hatchlings stand the best chance of survival when food supplies are limited.

binocular vision Vision in which both eyes view the same scene from slightly different aspects: an aid to judging distance.

clinal Gradually varying in form over a particular area.

colour phase Many owls have two main colour forms, rufous and grey, known as colour phases.

conspecific Of the same species.

ear tufts Erectile tufts of feathers above the eyes of many species. They have nothing to do with ears. Controlled by scalp muscles, they probably play a part in social communication.

facial disc Saucer-shaped disc of feathers surrounding the eyes, which acts as a sound reflector. It varies in extent and definition from species to species, being most fully developed in those that are most nocturnal.

facial tufts Ear tufts.

horns Ear tufts.

intergradation The way in which categories sometimes merge imperceptibly without clearly defined limits.

irruption The movement outside their normal range which excess individuals of some species are forced to undergo in years when food supplies become limited.

isolating mechanisms Any mechanisms that keep related species reproductively distinct (e.g. geographical isolation, variation in breeding seasons, lack of sexual attraction between different species, sterility or lack of viability of hybrids, etc.) or ecologically distinct (e.g. geographical isolation, preferences for different habitats, feeding methods and foods etc.).

lores The sides of the head between the eyes and the bill.

mantle The back and folded wings.

monotypic genus A genus with only one species.

montane forest Mountain forest.

nominate race The race from which a species takes its name.

orbit Eye socket.

pellet Accumulation of undigested parts of food, regurgitated through the mouth in a compact mass.

relict form A race or species that has become geographically isolated in a small part of its former range.

sedentary Not migratory.

tapetum Reflecting layer behind the retina of the eye possessed by many nocturnal animals, which enables dim light to be utilized more efficiently.

wing load Relationship of body weight to wing area.

Books for further reading

AMADON, D. and BULL, J. (1988) *Hawks and Owls of the World*. Proc. West. Found. Vert. Zool., Vol 3; 4:295-357

BENT, A. C. (1958) *Life Histories of North American Birds of Prey*. Dover Publications Inc., New York

BLAKERS, M., DAVIES, S. J. J. F. and REILLY, P. N. (1984) *The Atlas of Australian Birds*. Melbourne University Press, Melbourne

BUNN, D. S., WARBURTON, A. B. and WILSON, R. D. S. (1982) *The Barn Owl*. T & A.D. Poyser, Calton, Staffordshire

CLARK, R. J., and MIKKOLA, H. (1989) 'A preliminary revision of threatened and near threatened nocturnal birds of prey of the world.' pp. 371-388 in *Raptors in the Modern World* (eds. Meyburg, B.-U. and Chancellor, R. D.). World working group on birds of prey and owls, Berlin

CLARK, R. J., SMITH, D. G., and KELSO, L. H. (1978) *Working Bibliography on Owls of the World*. National Wildlife Federation Raptor Information Center, Tech. Ser.1, Washington, D.C.

COATES, B. J. (1985) *The Birds of Papua New Guinea. Vol I Non-Passerines*. Dove Publications, Alderley, Queensland

CRAMP, S. et al. (1985) *Handbook of the Birds of Europe and the Middle East and North Africa. Vol IV Terns to Woodpeckers*. Oxford University Press, Oxford

DEMENT'EV et al. (1966-68) *Birds of the Soviet Union*. National Science Foundation, Washington, D.C.

DE SCHAUENSEE, R. M. (1970) *Guide to the Birds of South America*. Oliver and Boyd, London; Livingston, New York

FLEAY, D. (1968) *Nightwatchmen of Bush and Plain*. Jacaranda Press, Brisbane; Cowman, Tri-Ocean, New York

FISHER, J., SIMON, N. and VINCENT, J. (1969) *The Red Book: wildlife in danger*. Collins, London; Harper and Row, New York

FJELDSA, J. and KRABBE, N. (1990) *Birds of the High Andes*. Apollo Books

GROSSMAN, M. L. and HAMLET, J. (1964) *Birds of Prey of the World*. Clarkson Potter Inc., New York

HARRISON, C. (1982) *An Atlas of Birds of the Western Palaearctic*. Collins, London

HOLMGREN, V. C. (1988) *Owls in Folklore and Natural History*. Capra Press, Santa Barbara, Ca.

HOSKING, E. and NEWBERRY, C. W. (1945) *Birds of the Night*. Collins, London

JOHNSGARD, P.A. (1989) *North American Owls, Biology and Natural History*. Smithsonian, Washington, D.C.

KEMP, A. and CALBURN, S. (1987) *The Owls of Southern Africa*. Struik Winchester, Capetown

LLOYD, G and D. (1972) *Birds of Prey*. Paul Hamlyn, Feltham; Bantam Books, New York

MACWORTH-PRAED, C. W. and GRANT, C. H. B. (1952-73) *Handbook of African Birds*. Longmans, London

MIKKOLA, H. (1982) *Ecological Relationships in European Owls*. Publ. of the University of Kuopio, Nat. Sci. Ser. Orig. reports 6

MIKKOLA, H. (1983) *Owls of Europe*. T. & A.D. Poyser, Calton, Staffordshire

NERO, R. W. (1980) *The Great Gray Owl. Phantom of the Northern Forest*. Smithsonian Institution Press, Washington, D.C.

NERO, R. W., CLARK, R. J., KNAPTON, R. J. and HAMRE R. H. eds (1987) *Biology and Conservation of Northern Forest Owls*: Symposium proceedings, USDA Forest Service Gen. Tech. Rep. RM-142

RIPLEY, S. D. and SALIM ALI (1968) *Handbook of the Birds of India and Pakistan*. Oxford University Press, London; Smithsonian Institution, Washington, D.C.

SPARKS, J. and SOPER, T. (1970) *Owls: their Natural and Unnatural History*. David and Charles, Devon; Taplinger, New York

STEYN, P. (1982) *Birds of Prey of Southern Africa. Their identification and life histories*. Croom Helm, Bromley, Kent

STEYN, P. (1984) *A Delight of Owls. African owls observed*. Tanager Books, Dover

STUART, J. (1977) *The Magic of Owls*. Walker & Co, New York

SURESH KUMAR, T. (1985) *The Life History of the Spotted Owlet (Athene brama brama Temminck) in Andhra Pradesh*. Raptor Research Centre, Hyderabad

VOOUS, K. H. (1960) *Atlas of European Birds*. Nelson, London

VOOUS, K. H. and CAMERON, A. (1988) *Owls of the Northern Hemisphere*. Collins, London; MIT Press, Cambridge, Mass.

WEINSTEIN, K. (1985) *The Owl in Art, Myth and Legend*. Crescent Books, New York

The Authors: biographical notes

John A. Burton started his natural history career in the Exhibitions Section of the British Museum Natural History, before becoming a freelance natural history writer and consultant. For many years he was Executive Secretary of the Fauna and Flora Preservation Society, and he is currently the European Representative of the Programme for Belize. He has written and edited over 20 books, mostly field guides or books dealing with conservation of threatened species.

Dr Philip Burton read zoology at University College London, and received his Ph.D degree for work on the feeding behaviour and anatomy of waders. His main research subject is the anatomy of birds.

Dr Michael Fogden trained as a zoologist at the University of Oxford and has specialized in the ecology and physiology of birds in the tropics. He spent several years working in the rainforest of Borneo, and has worked as a Ford Foundation Research Fellow on tropical animal ecology and for the Centre for Overseas Pest Research. He is well known for his outstanding natural history photographs.

Howard Ginn read zoology, botany and physiology at Cambridge. He has worked as a research officer for the British Trust for Ornithology, at the Wildlife Advisory Branch of the Nature Conservancy Council and at the Huntingdon Research Centre where he was involved in evaluating the toxicity of various compounds.

David Glue trained as a zoologist at London University and later joined the British Trust for Ornithology as a Research Officer in the Population section. He has been concerned with the organization and results of bird surveys and censuses and has published papers on many aspects of bird biology.

Michael Everett has worked for the Royal Society for the Protection of Birds since 1964, mainly in reserves management and rare bird protection but most recently as a press officer. Owls are among his particular interests: he is author of A Natural History of Owls, a regular contributor to magazines and journals and senior author of 'News and Comment' in the monthly magazine *British Birds*.

Dr Colin Harrison is a biologist, formerly working in the sub-department of Ornithology of the British Museum Natural History. He has studied wild birds in many countries and worked on bird behaviour under aviary conditions. In the museum he worked on the structure of systematics of birds and on their nests and eggs. Among his publications is An Atlas of Birds of the Western Palaearctic.

Dr Gerrit P. Hekstra graduated in biology from the Free University, Amsterdam. After teaching for several years, he became Secretary of the Biological Council of the Royal Netherlands Academy of Sciences and the national committee on Man and the Biosphere. Since 1982 he has been co-ordinator of ecological planning at the Ministry of Housing, Physical Planning and Environment. He has done extensive work on American Screech owls (Otus).

Dr Heimo Mikkola worked on owls and other birds of prey from 1965-72 in the University of Oulu, and has made a special study of the Great Grey owl (Strix nebulosa). He completed his doctoral thesis on ecological relationships in European owls at the Department of Applied Zoology, University of Kuopio, Finland, in 1982. His major work on owls, Owls of Europe, was published in 1983. He is now the representative for the Food and Agriculture Organization (FAO) of the United Nations in Mozambique and Swaziland.

The late Dr R. K. Murton read zoology at University College London and after graduating joined the Ministry of Agriculture, Fisheries and Food as an ornithologist employed to study the biology of species harmful to agriculture and food production. He moved to the Nature Conservancy in 1970.

Ian Prestt is a Fellow of the Institute of Biology and has B.Sc and M.Sc degrees from the University of Liverpool. He has held various posts in the Nature Conservancy. In 1991 he retired as Director of the Royal Society for the Protection of Birds and was appointed its President.

Dr John Sparks is a zoologist who has undertaken extensive post-doctoral research into bird behaviour at London University and The Zoological Society of London. He has written a number of books on various aspects of animal life.

Dr Bernard Stonehouse trained as a biologist at the Universities of London and Oxford. Working on animal ecology for most of his career, he has held appointments at the University of Canterbury, New Zealand, Yale University, the University of British Columbia and the University of Bradford, England. He recently retired from his post as Director of the Scott Polar Research Institute, Cambridge.

C. A. Walker is a member of the Department of Palaeontology at the British Museum Natural History, studying fossil birds and reptiles. He has written articles and papers for scientific journals and conferences on both fossil and recent birds.

The late Reginald Wagstaffe studied ornithology at the University of Cincinatti, Ohio. He worked as a professional zoologist and botanist in a number of museum posts, specializing in the taxonomy of birds.

Wouter van der Weijden studied biology at the Free University of Amsterdam, and has made an extensive study of the songs of the Scops and Screech Owls. He is now at the Centre for Agriculture and Environment in Utrecht, working on ways to improve the relationships between agriculture, environment and wildlife.

Index

NOTE: Page references in italics refer to illustrations

A

Aegolius,
  acadicus, 28, 166, 167, *168,* 169, 199
  funereus, 12, 28, *30,* 128, *166, 167,* 199
  harrisii, 166, 168, *169,* 199
  ridgwayi, 167-8, *169,* 199
Aegothelidae, 34
Agathokles, 17
Agrippa, death of, 20
Archaeopteryx lithographica, 24
art and owls, *2,* 14, *15, 21, 24*
Ashy-faced Owl *see Tyto glaucops*
Asio, 12, 27, 34, 108, 132-3, 199
  abyssinicus, 134, *135*
  brevipes, 27
  capensis, 108, *140,* 140, 199
  clamator, 108, *133,* 133-4, *134,* 199
  flammeus, 28, 34, 108, 134, *137,* 137-9, *138, 139,* 183, 190, *191, 192,* 199
  madagascariensis, 108, *136,* 137, 199
  otus, 28, 34, 108, 109, 133, *134, 135,* 190, *191, 192,* 199
  pigmaeus, 27
  priscus, 28
  stygius, 108, *136,* 137, 199
Athene, 159-61, 199
  blewitti, 163, 163, 199
  brama, 161-3, *162,* 199
  cretensis, 28
  cunicularia, 28
  murivora, 28
  noctua, 16, 16-17, 28, *159,* 159-61, *160, 161,* 186, 190, *191,* 199
Athene, *see* deities, association with
Athens, sacred owl of, 16-17
attitude of public to owls, 14-18
Australian Aborigines, 'owl man' of, 14, *15*

autecology, 182

B

Barking Owl, *see Ninox connivens*
Barn Owl
  Common, *see Tyto alba*
  Minahassa, *see T. inexpectata*
  New Britain, *see T. aurantia*
  Sulawesi, *see T. rosenbergii*
  see also Tytonidae
Barred Owl, *see Strix varia*
Bay Owl *see* Phodilinae; *Phodilus badius*
behaviour
  Asio, 134
  Athene, 160-1, 163
  attacking, 45, 93, 115, 119, 124, 147
  Bubo, 66. 68. 72. 74. 76. 79
  defensive, 40, 93, 115, 119, 122, 124, 181
  Glaucidium, 169-70, 173
  Ketupa, 51, 52-4
  Nyctea, 80-2
  Otus, 87, 92, 101, 104
  Phodilus badius, 50
  predatory, 9, 10, 34, 38-9, 54, 59, 62, 126, 129, 130, 169, 170
  Scotopelia, 58, 59
  Strix, 115, 121, 122
  Surnia, 157-8
  territorial, 40, 53-4, 66, 92, 183
  Tyto alba, 38-40
bill, 31, 34, 62, 145, 147, 156-7
Black and white Owl, *see Ciccaba nigrolineata*
Black-banded Owl, *see C. huhula*
Boobook Owl, *see Ninox novaeseelandiae*
Brazilian Owl, *see Strix hylophila*
breeding, 11
  Aegolius, 166, 167
  Asio, 133, 134, 138-9, 140
  Athene, 159, 160, 161-3, 165
  Bubo, 65, 66-7, 68, 70, 73, 76
  Ciccaba, 13

experiments, 115
  Glaucidium, 170, 172, 173-4
  Ketupa, 56-7
  Micrathene, 165
  Ninox, 142, 145, 147
  Nyctea, 82-3
  Otus, 92-3, 98-9, 101, 103, 104
  Phodilus, 50
  Pulsatrix, 110
  Scotopelia, 59
  Strix, 115, 116, 117, 119, 120-1, 126, 128, 130, 133, 134, 140
  Surnia, 158
  Tyto alba, 40
Brodkorb, *Catalogue of Fossil Birds,* 24
Bubo, 17, 22, 27, 62, 79, 198
  africanus, 28, *32, 33,* 69, *70,* 70-3, *71,* 198
    africanus, 69, *72*
    cinerascens, 72
    milesi, 72
  binagadensis, 28, 198
  bubo, 25, 28, 33, 62, *63,* 64-5, *64-7,* 198
    ascalaphus, 64-6, 72, 198
    bengalensis, 66, 198
    nikolskii, 62
  capensis, 68, 69, 198
    mackinderi, 69
  coromandus, 76, *76-9, 77,* 198
  florianae, 27
  insularis, 28
  lacteus, 69, *73,* 73-6, 198
  leguati, 28
  leucostictus, 74, *75,* 76, 198
  nipalensis, 78, 79, 198
  philippensis, 79, 79, 198
  poensis, 74, 76, 198
    vosseleri, 74, 76
  poirreiri, 26
  shelleyi, 74, *75,* 76, 198
  sinclairi, 28
  sumatrana, 79, 80, 198
  virginianus, 2, 22, 23, 28, 67, *67-8, 68,* 198
Buff-fronted Owl, *see Aegolius harrisii*
Burrowing Owl, *see Speotyto cunicularia*

C

cactus, Saguaro, 165
caeca, intestinal, 34
Caprimulgiformes, 9, 11, 12, 24, 34
carving, Palaeolithic, 14
Ciccaba,
    albitarsus, 108, 112, *114*, 115,
        199
    huhula, *114*, 115, 199
    nigrolineata, *113*, 113, 199
    virgata, 28, *112*, 112-13, 199
Circus cyaneus, 186
claws, 34, 54, 62, 156-7
competition, 50, 70, 74, 76, 87, 112,
        126-8, 139, 141, 142, 159, 184
conservation research, 182-3
Crescens, Petrus von, *Opus ruralium*,
        20
Crested Owl, *see Lophostrix cristata*

D

death, association with, 18-20
decoys, 20-2
deities, association with, 16-17
diet, *passim*
distribution
    geographical, *passim*
    geological, 24-8

E

Eagle Owl, 12, 20, 25, *33*, 34
    Akun, *see Bubo leucostictus*
    Cape, *see B. capensis*
    Dusky, *see B. coromandus*
    Eurasian, *see B. bubo*
    Forest, *see B. nipalensis*
    Fraser's, *see B. poensis*
    Mackinder's, *see B. c. mackinderi*
    Malaysian, *see B. sumatrana*
    Milky, *see B. lacteus*
    Nduk, *see B. p. vosseleri*
    Pharaoh, *see B. b. ascalaphus*
    Philippine, *see B. philippensis*
    Shelley's *see B. shelleyi*
    Spotted, *see B. africanus*
    Verreaux's, *see B. lacteus*
    see also *Bubo*
ear, structure of, 10, 12, *30*, 32-4
earliest owls, 11, 24
eating of owls, 20

ecosystem, 182, 184, 189
egg-shell, thinning of, 187
egg-white protein, 11-12
eggs *see* breeding
Elf Owl, *see Micrathene whitneyi*
Eostrix,
    marinelli, 25
    mimica, 24, 25
evil, counteraction of, 17, 19, 20
evolution, 22-8, 94, 148-50, 185
eyes, structure of, 9-10, 29-32, *30*

F

farming,
    effect of intensive, 12, 22, 40, 184,
        186, 187
    and *Tyto alba*, 22
Fearful Owl, *see Nesasio solomonensis*
Fish Owl,
    Blakiston's, *see Ketupa blakistoni*
    Brown, *see K. zeylonensis*
    Malaysian, *see K. ketupa*
    Tawny, *see K. flavipes*
Fishing Owl
    Pel's, *see Scotopelia peli*
    Rufous, *see S. ussheri*
    Vermiculated, *see S. bouvieri*
Fishing Owls,
    African, *see Scotopelia*
    Asian, *see Ketupa*
Flammulated Owl, *see Otus flammeolus*
Fleay, David, 142
flight, 34, 38, 51, 134, 138, 160,
        163
food chain, 183-4, 189
fossil record, 11, 23, 24-8, 37

G

genetic drift, 185
Glaucidium, 168-81, 199
    bolivianum, *172*, 173
    brasilianum, 28, *172*, 173-4, 199
    brodiei, *179*, 179, 199
    californicum, 171-2
    capense, *178*, 179, 199
    castanonotum, *180*, 181, 199
    castanopterum, *180*, 181, 199
    cuculoides, *180*, 181, 199
    gnoma, 218, *171*, 171-2, 199
    griseiceps, *174*, 175
    hardyi, *175*, 175, 199

jardinii, *172*, 173, 199
    minutissimum, 34, *174*, 174-5
    nanum, *172*, 173, *173*, 199
    passerinum, 28, 168-71, *170*, 199
    perlatum, *176*, 176-9, 199
    peruanum, *172*, 173
    radiatum, *178*, 179, 199
    siju, 28, *171*, 172-3, 199
    sjostedti, *177*, 179, 199
    tephronotum, *177*, 179, 199
Gloger and Bergmann (rules), 108-9
Golden Owl, *see Tyto aurantia*
Grass owl
    African, *see Tyto capensis*
    Eastern *see Tyto longimembris*
Graves, Gary R., 175
Great Grey Owl, *see Strix nebulosa*
Great Horned Owl, *see Bubo
        virginianus*
Gymnoglaux, *see Otus lawrencii*

H

habitat, 10-11
    preservation of, 40, 117-18, 184-6
    provision of, 182, 186
Hawk owl, 34, 62
    Admiralty Islands, *see Ninox meeki*
    Andaman, *see N. affinis*
    Great, *see N. strenua*
    Madagascar, *see N. superciliaris*
    Moluccan, *see N. squamipila*
    New Britain, *see N. odiosa*
    New Ireland, *see N. solomonis*
    Northern, *see Surnia ulula*
    Ochre-bellied, *see N. perversa*
    Oriental, *see N. scutulata*
    Papuan, *see Uroglaux dimorpha*
    Philippine, *see Ninox philippensis*
    Solomon Islands, *see N. jacquinoti*
    Sooty-backed, *see N. theomacha*
    Speckled, *see N. punctulata*
Hawk Owl, *see also; Ninox; Sceloglaux;
        Surnia ulula; Uroglaux*
head, rotation of, 10, 30, 32
hearing, 10, *30*, 32-4, 141, 142
hunting *see* behaviour, predatory
hybridization, 66, 88, 92, 101, 115-
        16

I

International Council for Bird
        Preservation, 37, 51, 118

irruptions, 80-2, 122, 157-8
isolation of species, 58, 67, 84, 88,
    95, 99, 104, 116, 124, 148,
    150, 174, 185
Itombwe Owl *see Phodilus prigoginei*

J

Jamaican owl, *see Pseudoscops
    grammicus*
Julius Caesar, 18

K

Ketupa, 51-8, 198
    blakistoni, 51-8, *52-3*, 198
    flavipes, 51-8, *54*, 198
    ketupa, 51-8, *55*, 198
    zeylonensis, 28, *33*, 51-8, 56, *57*,
        198
Knocking Owl, *see Pulsatrix
    perspicillata*
Konig, Dr. Claus, 173, 175

L

Laughing Owl, *see Sceloglaux albifacies*
Lechusa stirtoni, 27
legislation, 185-6
literature and owls, 17
Little Owl, *see Athene noctua*
Little Owl
    Forest, *see Athene blewitti*
    Spotted, *see Athene brama*
    see also Athene
Long-eared Owl, *see Asio abyssinicus;
    A. otus*
Long-eared Owl, Madagascar, *see A.
    madagascariensis*
Lophostrix,
    cristata, 106, *107*, 198
    lettii, 84, 106, *107*, 198

M

Macbeth, 18, 20
Madagascar Red Owl, *see Tyto
    soumagnei*
magic and owls, 16, 17, 18, *19*
Maned Owl, *see Lophostrix lettii*
Marsh Owl, African, *see Asio capensis*

Masked Owl, *see Tyto novaehollandiae*
Masked Owl, Lesser, *see Tyto sororcula*
Micrathene whitneyi, 34, *165*, 165,
    199
migration, 101, 103, 104, 116, 122,
    142, 157, 161, 167
Milne, A. A., 17
Minahassa Owl, *see Tyto inexpectata*
Minerva,
    antiqua, 25
    californiensis, 25
    leposteus, 25
    saurodosis, 25
mobbing attacks, 9, 10, 20, 22, 38,
    93, 142, 170, 174, 181
Morepork Owl, *see Ninox
    novaeseelandiae*
Mottled Owl, *see Ciccaba virgata*
Mourer-Chauviré, 26

N

Necrobyas, 27
    arvernensis, 26
    edwardsi, 25
    harpax, 25
    minimus, 25
    modius, 25
    rossignoli, 25
    viconti, 25
Nesasio solomonensis, 147, *156*, 156-
    7, 199
nesting, *see* breeding
nightjars, *see* Caprimulgiformes
Ninox
    affinis, 152, *152*, *153*, 199
    connivens, 142-5. *144*, 199
    jacquinoti, 90, 148, *149*, 150, *150*,
        199
    meeki, 105, 148, *149*, 150, *150*
    novaeseelandiae, 28, 142, *143*, 148,
        199
    odiosa, 148, *149*, *150*, 199
    perversa, *150*, *151*, 152, 199
    philippensis, 152, *152*, *153*
    punctulata, *150*, *151*, 152, 199
    rufa, 142, *147*, 199
    scutulata, 141-2, 152, *154*, 199
    solomonis, 148, *149*, 150, *150*, 199
    squamipila, *150*, 150-2, *151*, 199
    strenua, 142, 145-7, *146*, 199
    superciliaris, *152*, 153, *153*, 199
    theomacha, 142, 148, *148*, 154,
        199

Nocturnavis incerta, 25
Nyctea scandiaca, 14, 28, *33*, 62, 80-
    3, *81*, *82*, *83*, 182, 190, *191*,
    192, 199

O

Ogygoptynx wetmorei, 25
Oligostrix rupelensis, 25
omen, owls as, 14
O'Neill, John P., 175
Ornigmegalonyx
    acevedoi, 28
    gigas, 28
    minor, 28
    oteroi, 28
Otus, 27, 84, 198
    albogularis, 84, 89, *90*, 90, 94,
        198
    alfredi, 98, 99, *100*, 198
    angelinae, 98, 99, 198
    asio, 84, 90, 92, *92*, 198
    atricapillus, 88, 88-9, *89*, 90, 198
    bakkamoena, 95, 95-6, 198
    barbarus, 86, 87, 88, 198
    brookii, 96, *97*, 198
    brucei, 101
    choliba, 90-1, *91*, 198
    clarkii, 89, 198
    cooperi, 90-1, *91*, 198
    flammeolus, 28, 101, *102*, *103*,
        103, 198
    guatemalae, 84, 85, 85-7, *87*, 198
        cassini, 86, 198
        guatemalae, 86, 198
        hastatus, 86, 198
        pacificus, 86, 198
        roraimae, 86, 88, 198
        vermiculatus, 86, 198
    gurneyi, 94, *94*, 198
    hartlaubi, 104, 104, *105*, 198
    hoyi, 89, *89*, 198
    icterorhynchus, 104, 104, *105*, 198
    ingens, 88, 89, *89*, 198
    (ingens) clarkii, 87, 87-8, 198
    ireneae, 104, 104, *105*, 198
    kennicotti, 84, 90, 92, *92*, *93*, 198
    lambii, 90, 92, 91-2, 198
    lawrencii, 28, 85, *85*, 198
    longicornis, 98, 99, 198
    manadensis, 99, *100*, *101*, 198
    marshalli, 86, 87, *87*, 88, 89, 198
    megalotis, 96

mentawi, 100, 101, 198
nudipes, 28, *85,* 86, 86, 88, 198
podarginus, 84, *98, 99, 100,* 198
roboratus, 90, 91, 198
rufescens, 96, 96, 99, 198
rutilus, 99, *100, 101,* 198
  insularis, 185, 198
sagittatus, 94, 94, 198
sanctaecatarinae, 89, 198
scops, 28, 84, *103,* 104, 198
seductus, 90, *91,* 91-2, 198
senegalensis, 26, 101-3, 104, 198
silvicolus, 94, 96, *97,* 198
spilocephalus, 96, *98,* 98-9, *99,* 198
sunia, 84, 101, *102,* 103, 198
trichopsis, 28, *87,* 87, 88, 198
watsonii, 88, 89, 198
whiteheadi, 96, 198
wintershofensis, 26
Owl and the Nightingale, The, 17
Owl and the Pussy-cat, The, 17
Owlet
  Barred, *see Glaucidium capense*
  Barred, Jungle, *see Glaucidium radiatum*
  Chestnut-backed, *see Glaucidium sjostedti,*
  Cuckoo, *see Glaucidium cuculoides*
  Long-whiskered, *see Xenoglaux loweryi*
  Nightjars, *see Aegothelidae*
  Pearl-spotted, *see Glaucidium perlatum*
  Red-chested, *see Glaucidium tephronotum*

P

Palaeobyas
  cadurcensis, 25
  cracrafti, 25
Palaeoglaux perrierensis, 25
Paratyto arvernensis, 27
pellets, 27, 38, 39, 40, 189-2
pesticides, effect of, 12, 22, 40, 104, 184, 186-8
Phodilinae, 36, 198
Phodilus
  badius, 49, 49, 198
    arixuthus, 49-50
    assimilis, 50
    parvus, 49
    prigoginei, 50, 50, 198
photography, decoy for, 22

Pliny the Elder, 18
plumage, 10, 33, 34, 37, 38, 84, 90, 108-9, 141, 160
  see also under individual owls
population
  density, 183
  statistics, 187, 188
  studies, 183, 188
Powerful Owl, *see Ninox strenua*
pre-avis, 23
prey
  effect of availability of, 66, 68, 80-2, 104, 122, 126, 134, 138, 157, 183
  studies of food taken, 66, 127-8, 139
  see also behaviour, predatory
Prosybris antiqua, 26
Protostrigidae, 24, 25, 26
Pseudoscops grammicus, 180, 181, 181, 199
Ptilopis leucotis, 84, *105,* 105-6, *106,* 198
Pulsatrix, 108, 109-10, 199
  arrendoi, 28
  koeniswaldiana, 110-11, *111,* 199
  melanota, 110-11, *111,* 199
  perspicillata, 108, *109,* 110, 199
Pygmy Owl
  Collared, *see Glaucidium brodiei*
  Cuban, *see G. siju*
  Eurasian, *see G. passerinum*
  Ferruginous, *see G. brasilianum; G. jardinii*
  Least, *see G. minutissimum*
  Northern, *see G. gnoma*
Pygmy Owls, *see Glaucidium*

R

retina, 29-32
roosting, 20, 38, 54, 84, 142
Rufous Owl, *see Ninox rufa*
Rufous-banded Owl, *see Ciccaba albitarsus*
Rufous-legged Owl, *see Strix rufipes*
Rusty-barred Owl, *see Pulsatrix melanota*

S

Saw-whet Owl, *see Aegolius acadicus*
Saw-whet Owl, Unspotted, *see Aegolius ridgwayi*

Sceloglaux albifacies, 142, 154-6, 185, 199
Scops Owl, 12, 18, 33
  Andaman, *see Otus balli*
  Celebes, *see O. manadensis*
  Collared, *see O. bakkamoena*
  Common, *see O. scops*
  Common African, *see O. capensis*
  Flores, *see O. alfredi*
  Giant, *see O. gurneyi*
  Madagascar, *see O. rutilus*
  Mentaur, *see O.umbra*
  Oriental, *see O. sunia*
  Palau, *see O. podarginus*
  Rajah's *see O. brookii*
  Reddish, *see O. rufescens*
  Sandy, *see O. icterorhynchus*
  Sao Tomé, *see O. hartlaubi*
  Sokoke, *see O. irenae*
  Spotted, *see O. spilocephalus*
  Sunda, *see O. silvicolus*
  White-faced, *see O. leucotis*
  White-fronted, *see O. sagittatus*
Scotopelia, 58-61, 199
  bouvieri, 58-61, *60, 61,* 199
  peli, 58-61, *60-1,* 199
  ussheri, 58, 58-9, *59,* 199
Screech owl, 12
  African White-faced, *see Ptilopis leucotis*
  Bare-shanked, *see Otus clarkii*
  Bearded, *see O. barbarus*
  Black-capped, *see O. atricapillus*
  Choliba, *see O. choliba*
  Clark's, *see O. clarkii*
  Cooper's, *see O. cooperi*
  Cuban, *see O. lawrencii*
  Eastern, *see O. asio*
  Pacific, *see O. cooperi*
  Puerto Rican, *see O. nudipes*
  Roborate, *see O. roboratus*
  Rufescent, *see O. ingens*
  Santa Barbara, *see O. barbarus*
  Spotted, *see O. trichopsis*
  Tawny-bellied, *see O. watsonii*
  Vermiculated, *see O. guatemalae*
  Watson's, *see O. watsonii*
  Western, *see O. kennicotti*
  White-throated, *see O. albogularis*
Selenornis henrici, 25
Seychelles Owl, *see Otus rutilus insularis*
Short-eared Owl, *see Asio flammeus*
Short-eared strigid Owls, 12
skull, *30, 31, 32,* 33

slang, 20
Snowy Owl, *see Nyctea scandiaca*
Sooty Owl, *see Tyto tenebricosa*
Sooty Owl, Lesser, *see Tyto multipunctata*
Sophiornis quercynus, 25
Sophiornithidae, 25
Spectacled Owl, *see Pulsatrix perspicillata*
Speotyto
    cunicularia, 11, 27, 33, 34, 85, 161, *163*, 163-5, *164*, 199
    megalopeza, 27
Spotted Eagle Owl, *see Strix occidentalis*
Strigidae, 12, 24, 26-7, 27, 34, 36, 198
Strigiformes, 11, 12, 24
Strigogyps dubius, 25
Striped Owl, *see Asio clamator*
Strix, 27, 34, 108-9, 199
    aluco, 10, 12, 18, 22, 28, *30*, 33, 40, 109, 115, 124-8, *125*, *127*, 183, *191*, 199
    brea, 28
    brevis, 26
    butleri, 108, 109, 128-9, *129*, 199
    dakota, 26
    hylophila, 118-19, *119*, *120*, 199
    leptogrammica, 130, *132*, 147, 199
    nebulosa, 28, 108, 109, 115, 120-2, *121*, 199
    occidentalis, 32, 115, 116-18, *118*, 185, 199
    ocellata, 28, 105, 130, *131*, 199
    rufipes, 118, *119*, 119, *120*, 199
    seloputo, 130-2, *131*, 147, 199
    uralensis, 28, 108-9, 115, 122-4, *123*, *124*, 199
    varia, 28, 115, 116, *117*, 199
    woodfordii, 108, 129-30, *130*, 199
Stygian Owl, *see Asio stygius*
Sulawesi Owl, *see Tyto rosenbergii*
superstitions and myths, 14, 17, 18, 22
Surnia ulula, 28, 34, 141, *157*, 157-8, *158*, 199
symbolism of owls, 17

T

Taliabu Owl, *see Tyto nigrobrunnea*
Tawny Owl, *see Strix aluco*
television programmes, 14-15

Tengmalm's (Boreal) owl, *see Aegolius funereus*
territories, *see* behaviour, territorial
traps, 20-2
Tyto, 12, 27, 36, 198
    alba, 10, 12, 18, 19, 22, 26, 28, 31, *32*, *34*, 36-9, *37*, 39, *188*, 191, *198*
    alba, 38
    aurantia, 37, *48*, 48, 198
    capensis, 40, *41*, 42-4, 198
    cavatica, 28
    edwardsi, 26
    gigantea, 26
    glaucops, 40, 198
    ignota, 26
    inexpectata, 37, 46, *47*, 198
    letocarti, 28
    longimembris, 40, *41*, *42*, 42-4, 198
    melitensis, 28
    multipunctata, *42*, *43*, 44-5, 198
    nigrobrunnea, 37, 45, 46, *47*, 198
    noeli, 28
    novaehollandiae, 28, 45, 45-6, 198
        castanops, 46, 198
        manusi, 46, 198
    ostologa, 28
    pollens, 28
    punctactissima, 28
    riveroi, 28
    robusta, 26
    rosenbergii, 46, *47*, 198
    sanctialbani, 26
    sauzieri, 28
    sororcula, 45, *45*, 198
    soumagnei, *48*, 49
    tenebricosa, 44, 44-5, *45*, 198
Tytonidae, 12, 24, 25-6, 27, 36, 198

U

Ural Owl, *see Strix uralensis*
Uroglaux dimorpha, 142, *154*, 154, *155*, 199

V

variation, geographical, 62-3, 68-70, 76-9, 80, 84, 86-7, 90-2, 99, 101, 106, 108-9, 116, 141-2, 159
Vieillard, J., 175

vision,
    binocular, 9, 30, 32
    field of, 30, 32
vocalizations, *passim*

W

White-chinned Owl, *see Pulsatrix koeniswaldiana*
wings, 10, 34, 38, 160
Winking Owl, *see Ninox connivens*
witchcraft and owls, 20
Wood Owl
    African, *see Strix woodfordii*
    Brown, *see Strix leptogrammica*
    Hume's, *see S. butleri*
    Mottled, *see S. ocellata*
    Spotted, *see S. seloputo*

X

Xenoglaux loweryi, 175-6, 199

Acknowledgements

Austing/Lane 117, 168, 172
Beste/Ardea 143 (top),
Bevan/Ardea 159 (left)
Blomgren/N 83
Rick Bowers 93
Breeze-Jones/Coleman 19 (bottom)
Burgess/Ardea 164 (bottom)
G. Chaloupka 15
Christiansen 159 (right)
Curth/Ardea 127
De Zylva/Okapia 132
Erize/Coleman 164 (top)
Fink/Ardea 33 (bottom left), 62, 81,
92, 112, 133, 165
M. Fogden 72, 96, 109, 177
Colin Fountain 33 (top left)
Free University Amsterdam 154
Freeman/NSP 110
Frithphoto/Coleman 43
Gillsater/Coleman 139 (bottom)
Michael Gore 59
Grandjean 163
Haagner/Ardea 71
Hautala 166
Hedvall 121, 123, 158

David Hollands 42, 44, 144, 146, 147
Eric Hosking 32, 91, 103, 161, 176
Johnson/Ardea 73 (right)
Kemp/NSP 130
Claus König 173
Lankinen/Coleman 118
Laubscher/Coleman 106
Lawton Roberts/Aquila 65
Lee Rue/Coleman 68
Lenton/Aquila 80
Lindblad/Coleman 124, 167
Lindgren/Ardea 45, 49, 148, 155
The Mansell Collection 16, 17, 19 (top)
Markham/Coleman 39
Newman/NHPA 140
Norström/N 187
J. P. O'Neill 86, 87, 89, 90, 175
Ott/Coleman 67, 157
Plage/Coleman 55
Paton 139 (top)
Pizzey/Coleman 41
Reinhard/Coleman 37, 63, 95, 125,
135, 162, 170, 180
Reinhard/Okapia 180
Richards/Aquila 70
Sager 185
Schultz/Coleman 174
Serventy/Coleman 143 (bottom)
Societé Royale de Zoologie d'Anvers 74
Stagsden Bird Gardens 33 (top right),
56, 57
Steyn/Ardea 73 (left)
Taylor 69
Victoria and Albert Museum 21
Willcock/Ardea 137

Reference for the illustration of *Tyto nigrobrunnea* on p.46 was kindly provided by Dr Siegfried Eck and Herr Quintscher of the Staatliches Museum fur Tierkunde, Dresden.

Index by Susan St Clair-Thompson